$161

DATE DUE			

DEMCO 38-297

3 1215 00093 9121

THE
IMPERIAL
CONGRESS

THE IMPERIAL CONGRESS

Crisis in the Separation of Powers

Edited by

Gordon S. Jones and John A. Marini

Foreword by

Representative Newt Gingrich

The Heritage Foundation

The Claremont Institute

PHAROS BOOKS
A SCRIPPS HOWARD COMPANY
NEW YORK

Pharos Books are available at special discounts on bulk purchases for sales promotions, premiums, fundraising or educational use. For details, contact the Special Sales Department,
Pharos Books, 200 Park Avenue, New York, NY 10166.

Cover design by Eve Sandler
Text design by Nancy Eato

First published in 1988.

Library of Congress Cataloging-in-Publication Data

The Imperial Congress.

1. Separation of powers—United States. 2. United
States. Congress. I. Jones, Gordon S. II. Marini, John.
JK305.I47   1988   320.473   88-25371
ISBN 0-88687-408-4

Printed in the United States of America

Pharos Books
A Scripps Howard Company
200 Park Avenue
New York, N.Y. 10166

10 9 8 7 6 5 4 3 2 1

The American Founders knew only too well that all previous democracies had been woefully short-lived. One sign of their genius is that we are now entering our third century under the democratic Constitution which they crafted. And one key to understanding their success, is understanding how and why they took such pains to make practicable what those who came before had only theorized about—the separation of powers.

Today, such understanding has eroded, as has the separation of powers itself. As a result, not only does our government perform badly, but our liberties, and the future of our free institutions, are endangered. Yet they are not endangered by a zealous executive, as many liberals would have us believe, nor even primarily by an activist judiciary, as many conservatives understandably feel, but rather by an Imperial Congress.

The essays in this book recall the original purposes of the separation of powers, show how it has been undermined, and suggest ways to its restoration. They are offered in the spirit of James Madison, the father our Constitution, who wrote in Federalist *48 that in America, "it is against the enterprising ambition of [the legislative branch] that the people ought to indulge all their jealousy and exhaust all their precautions."*

Larry P. Arnn
President
The Claremont Institute

Edwin J. Feulner, Jr.
President
The Heritage Foundation

CONTENTS

FOREWORD

Our founding fathers knew how fragile self-government could be. They struggled for a generation to create a self-governing republic dedicated to the principles of freedom and representative democracy; a republic carefully balanced and strong enough to ensure that government of the people, by the people, and for the people would endure.

The genius of the Founding Fathers is the separation of powers found in the United States Constitution. No other constitutional tenet was considered more essential to the preservation of liberty. As James Madison wrote in *Federalist* 47:

> No political truth is certainly of greater intrinsic value, or is stamped with the authority of more enlightened patrons of liberty.... The accumulation of all powers, legislative, executive, and judiciary, in the same hands, whether of one, a few, or many, and whether hereditary, self-appointed, or elective, may justly be pronounced the very definition of tyranny.

Thomas Jefferson shared Madison's fear of one branch dominating the others. In 1781, he warned:

> The concentrating of [power] in the same hands is precisely the definition of despotic government. It will be no alleviation that these powers will be exercised by a plurality of hands, and not by a single one.

The 100th Congress is a far different institution from that envisioned by the Founders. Indeed, the 100th Congress approaches the despotic institution about which James Madison and Thomas Jefferson wrote. It is an imperial Congress reigned over by an imperial Speaker enacting special-interest legislation. Writing in *Federalist* 71, Alexander Hamilton warned of such arrogant legislative power:

> The representatives of the people, in a popular assembly, seem sometimes to fancy that they are the people themselves, and betray strong symptoms of impatience and disgust at the

least sign of opposition from any other quarter; as if the exercise of its rights, by either executive or judiciary, were a breach of their privilege and an outrage to their dignity.

Hamilton clearly saw that people who are elected to power come to think that they are the power itself. He and his contemporaries understood the dangers inherent to democracy when one branch of government encroaches upon the authority of another.

Madison, Jefferson and Hamilton tried to insure against the rise of an imperial Congress. Yet, as the separation of powers continues to erode, the present-day Congress has become the most unrepresentative and corrupt of the modern era. It is a Congress that lusts for power but evades responsibility for its actions. Increasingly dominated by a corrupt machine that deceives the American public, it exempts itself from the standards of conduct it imposes on the executive branch and the American people.

Such an imperial Congress mocks the American precept of self-government that was so carefully crafted by the Founding Fathers. Every citizen should be concerned about the arrogance and corruption of the present-day Congress. At stake is the liberty of the American public. We must reform Congress to make it truly representative once again.

NEWT GINGRICH, M.C.

---

* Karen Van Brocklin contributed to this foreword.

ACKNOWLEDGEMENTS

The editors wish to express their deep appreciation to the Philip M. McKenna Foundation and the Katherine Mabis McKenna Foundation, who provided the bulk of the support for this project, and without whom it could not have been undertaken. We are also grateful to F. Evans Farwell and Richard Gilder for their significant support. The balance of the funding has come from The Heritage Foundation's President's Club and other dedicated Heritage members, and friends and supporters of The Claremont Institute, to all of whom we owe much thanks.

We also wish to give full credit to Mark Liedl, whose editorial assistance went far beyond the modest role of contributing editor. It is not too much to say that in many ways he, not we, should be listed as editor of this volume.

We also acknowledge our debt to Miss Teresa Guza and others at The Heritage Foundation for their patience in typing, copying computer disks, mastering the details of harmonizing various word processors, and entering corrections, again and again. Modern technology may make these tasks easier, but it cannot make them fun, and we appreciate those who put up with them.

Despite all this assistance, we know that imperfections may remain. We only hope that our results measure up to the importance of the subject.

GORDON S. JONES
JOHN A. MARINI
October, 1988

THE
IMPERIAL
CONGRESS

GENERAL INTRODUCTION

Our thesis is that America faces a constitutional crisis stemming from two causes: the congressional failure to observe traditional limits on its power, and the acquiescence of the other two branches of government in the resulting arrogation of power.

We will demonstrate that Congress has evolved into a different kind of institution from the legislative body established by the Constitution. Its members now enjoy a security in office, a level of staff support, a close and routine influence over executive agencies, and an ability to deploy the resources of government that far surpass their constitutional mandate. Members of Congress now spend little time debating—they seldom even vote in any open way upon—the fundamental questions that face the country. The most important legislation is drafted by unelected congressional staff, supported by a network of lobbyists representing special interests. Such legislation is often hundreds or thousands of pages long, and covers a variety of subjects that have no discernible connection. In these vast tangles of legislation, the political views of individual congressmen are increasingly obscure, but their power to administer the minutia of executive branch operations is ever more apparent.

Congress is becoming an administrative rather than a legislative body. In short, it is increasingly engaged in the executive function of administering laws as it delegates more and more of its traditional law-making responsibilities to the federal courts and to "independent agencies."

Congressional control over the permanent bureaucracy, from micromanaging programs to hiring and firing executive branch personnel, constitutes a threat to the separation of powers and ultimately to democratic rule. This fact has been inadequately understood by conservatives, due to a preoccupation with the battle for control of the White House and a historic skepticism about the powers of the executive branch. The dangers from an Imperial Congress deserve a careful and reasoned examination.

Our examination will be presented in three main parts. Part I

1

traces the origins of the bureaucratic state from the Progressive era to the present, and the replacement of the "governing" function with "administration." It examines how that shift alters the whole nature of government, leading to a present order that is vastly different from the one established by the Constitution.

Part II describes the current operations of Congress. It shows how Congress has moved away from its constitutional role of representative lawmaker, and how its behavior encroaches on the prerogatives of the executive branch.

Part III argues that the problem is essentially political, to be solved by forthright political action, largely by the executive branch reasserting its prerogatives, and through electoral politics. It proposes specific recommendations for restoring the separation of powers.

THE CONSTITUTIONAL FRAMEWORK

Americans are widely regarded as a practical people, dedicated to getting things done. That dedication is certainly an important part of the national character, but it is by no means all of it. When it comes to government, Americans have always tolerated a great deal of inefficiency, perhaps even demanded it, believing that strict efficiency in government is not always conducive to freedom.

The American political system, committed to parchment in Philadelphia in 1787, but hammered out over the 150 preceding years, embodies a number of innovations peculiarly suited to the American people. Among these are the Electoral College, the federal system, and the subject of this book, the separation of powers. To be sure, the words "separation of powers" do not appear in the Constitution. Rather, the doctrine describes the operation of government—the relationships among the three branches of government working within the powers assigned to each by the Constitution.

In 1787, the Founding Fathers found themselves in a dilemma. Faced with an obvious need for a more powerful central government, and yet mistrustful of the centralized power that had been the proximate cause of the Revolutionary War, they sought mechanisms for balancing and diffusing power. One of the most important of those mechanisms, as explained in *The Federalist Papers*, was the separation of powers: the allocation of specific powers among three distinct branches of government, each peculiarly suited to carrying out those limited powers, and each ill-equipped to exercise efficiently or justly the powers assigned to the other branches.

A System of Diffused Powers

The Constitution diffuses power throughout the system both horizontally and vertically. The vertical diffusion is most apparent. It is what we call the federal system. The scope of the federal, or central, power is limited to those areas explicitly detailed in the Constitution, and all other powers are reserved to the states and the people. This vertical check on autocratic power has clearly weakened over time, as power has flowed to Washington. That fact makes it all the more imperative that horizontal diffusion, achieved through the separation of powers, remains in good repair.

The Separation of Powers

Our concern is the *separation* of power, but the system of checks and balances incorporated in the Constitution does *mix* powers horizontally among the three branches of government. The president has a role to play in legislation, the legislative branch participates in a limited way in the selection of executive and judicial branch officials, and the judiciary is given some power to check both the legislative and executive branches.

Thus, there is a mixing of powers, but this mixing is strictly limited. The Constitution sets distinct boundaries. All of the legislative power granted by the Constitution is delegated only to the legislative branch. Presidents can veto and courts can declare unconstitutional, but neither can write laws. At the same time, Congress, whose powers are carefully enumerated, is given absolutely no power to execute law. The executive power is assigned to the president and the executive branch that he directs.

It is important to emphasize how clear are the limits on legislative power. The Constitution explicitly limits Congress's powers to those enumerated: "All legislative powers *herein granted* shall be vested in a Congress of the United States" (Article I, emphasis added). By contrast, the Constitution uses much broader language to describe the executive power: "The executive power shall be vested in a President of the United States" (Article II). To many scholars, this plenary grant of executive power, juxtaposed to the limited grant of legislative power is the heart of the current crisis in the separation of powers.

The Progressive Assault on the Separation of Powers

The American system of divided power has always been troubling to some observers and activists in America. And it remains contrary to the norm of government in other countries. Most modern democracies (and emerging nations) lean to a more unified executive and legislative system, the so-called parliamentary model. Indeed, dissatisfaction with the inefficiency of the American system arose almost immediately after adoption of the Constitution and the first sessions of the federal government. The argument was then, as it is now, that too much division of responsibility, too much separation of power, made quick, decisive action impossible.

These criticisms were stated most directly during the Progressive era, when they were forcefully argued by Woodrow Wilson and others. The Progressives explicitly rejected the constitutional framework as unsuited to the demands of the modern administrative state. The quick pace of activity in "modern" America, they believed, could not tolerate the sluggish response virtually assured by the provisions of the Constitution. They argued for some form of integration between executive and legislative branch, under which the president would be able to move swiftly his program through Congress and into law. They also believed that the details of executive administration could be safely and efficiently entrusted to a legislative branch possessing new executive powers.

In one form or another, these arguments remain today, although the explicit attack on the Constitution is now muted. The Constitution has become an untouchable icon to a degree it had not in the days of the Progressives. Rhetorically, the idea now is simply to update the Constitution, make it a bit more flexible, but not to reject it entirely.

CHARACTERISTICS OF AN IMPERIAL CONGRESS

Despite the rejection of the Progressives' argument, in practice the American system seems to be trending in that direction. This fact is amply demonstrated by the chapters in Part II of this book, which describe the mechanisms that the legislative branch has developed to enable it to reach beyond its constitutional limits and into the realm of the executive. Some of the more salient characteristics of this modern Congress are outlined below.

Micromanagement of Executive Agencies

One of the clearest examples of Congress exercising traditional executive functions is its growing tendency to micromanage details of defense and foreign policy.

What does it mean, for Congress to "micromanage" executive branch agencies? As Chapter 4 shows, it means an infinite complexity of rules and regulations imposed piecemeal by a multiplicity of congressional committees and subcommittees, leading to the eventual overload of the administrative circuits. The sheer number of reports required by Congress has a sclerotic effect, as do the political pressures for defense contracts and military installations.

This kind of micromanagement has its effect on procurement policy, where political pressures lead to inefficiencies and even to fraud. It also leads to confusion and uncertainty in foreign policy. Congressional involvement in foreign policy now includes negotiations between the Speaker of the House and the heads of foreign governments, interpretation of treaties, interference in trade matters, and legislation dictating specific actions the president must take in foreign policy. Under the circumstances, it is hard to devine what U.S foreign policy is, or what a defense policy to support it might look like. Our allies and enemies alike are uncertain as to American intentions and commitments.

Pork Barrel Budgeting

There is only one person elected on a national scale, whose campaign is dominated by the kinds of foreign and domestic issues which may properly be called matters of national concern. Only the president has the broad national perspective and constituency to order federal budget priorities that best serve the national interest. As any state governor knows, responsible budget decisions can only be made if the chief executive has the power to make them. A budget process dominated by a state legislature, or by Congress, yields programs designed to placate narrow special interests, and appropriations bills whose adornments make Christmas trees look dowdy. The result: massive deficits, tax hikes, or both.

Throughout American history, Congress and the president have skirmished over control of the budget. As Chapter 6 demonstrates, the periods of congressional dominance have been marked by free-wheeling spending and mounting deficits. But never has the U.S. budget been more dominated by Congress than since passage of the Budget Control and Impoundment Act in 1974. And never before has America faced such massive federal deficits and such an utter inability of government to deal with them.

Congress now uses the mechanism of the budget process to affect, if not to determine, the national agenda. By rolling all of the appropriations bills into a single piece of legislation which is practically veto-proof, Congress can assert its will on everything from foreign policy to personnel matters. In practice, the majority in Congress all but ignores the budget proposed by the president.

That is exactly what happened under Presidents Ford and Carter, and except for the first year of the Reagan Administration, congressional leaders regularly pronounced the president's budget "dead on arrival" at Capitol Hill. That is true even though Ronald Reagan was elected with an overwhelming mandate to reorder priorities and reduce spending.

In place of the president's budget, Congress passes a single massive appropriations bill, called a Continuing Resolution. This bill, passed months late, contains the entire federal budget in one mountainous volume. It is thousands of pages long, with an accompanying explanatory report that is even longer. Congress passes it just before going home for the year. No member has read it, and only a few can claim any familiarity with more than a very small portion of it. As the Fiscal Year 1988 Continuing Resolution demonstrated most clearly, wholly extraneous matters may have been added to these bills in the dead of night, even matters which have never been considered by either of the two houses individually. Since the entire federal budget is wrapped into this monstrosity, and Congress has adjourned, the president has little choice but to sign it.

The dominance of Congress in budget matters has reached the point where budget decisions are now being made almost without regard to the wishes of the public. A number of techniques have been developed to exclude the public and to relieve elected officials of budgetary responsibilities. The increasing use of such bipartisan, blueribbon commissions as the National Economic Commission is one example. Another is the November 1987 "budget summit" of congressional leaders and administration negotiators, which produced the outlines of the final budget compromise. That negotiated settlement allowed both elected branches to escape responsibility for budgeting in 1988.

Because the policy-makers in Congress are unable, or unwilling, to make their policy openly, and suffer the electoral consequences of making that policy, they resort to such extraconstitutional methods of making policy, avoiding the accountability that should accompany representative government.

Entrenched Incumbency

The success rate of incumbents running for reelection is profoundly threatening to the doctrine of the separation of powers. When individual congressmen are effectively freed from concern about reelection, they are encouraged to extend their influence into other areas. In 1792, the First Congress was elected. Two years later, 60 percent of those first representatives who ran for reelection were returned. Members spent the ensuing 200 years improving their chances for reelection. In 1986, they approached perfection, as more than 98 percent of incumbents who ran for reelection were returned to office.

In order to achieve that level of success, Congress has taken steps to insulate itself from public pressure, and to provide itself with tools which can be used to generate political capital useful for reelection. There is a serious question as to the degree the House can be said to be representative at all. To a substantial extent, it is now an entrenched oligarchy, whose members have only a tenuous relationship to the voters who send them to Washington.

One evidence of this tenuous connection is the disparity between election returns and the actual partisan composition of the House. In 1986, for example, Republican candidates received 45 percent of the votes cast for members of Congress, but elected only 41 percent of the members. At times the disparity has been as much as 10 percentage points. Another evidence is the number of very liberal members elected from districts which give percentages of 60 percent or more to such conservative presidential candidates as Ronald Reagan. This result has been achieved by use of techniques for hiding congressional voting records from the voting public, and by confusing the voters with other actions.

Voter ignorance of policy positions is most effectively assured by preventing troublesome policy differences from being presented to the members of the House and Senate for votes. That can be accomplished by limits on debate, restrictions on amendments, and use of leadership agreements to avoid controversy. The leadership can also short-change the minority party in terms of staff and other resources, and can use its discretionary powers to reward and punish individual members. The use of these and other techniques is, at this time, most advanced in the House of Representatives, as discussed in Chapters 7 and 8, but as Chapter 9 shows, the Senate is moving rapidly in the same direction.

By now, members of Congress have achieved almost total deracination from their constituencies. Given the benefits which they enjoy, and the edge provided by friendly State legislators who gerrymander safe legislative districts (and who hope perhaps some day to benefit from them), the House of Representatives dangerously exceeds its constitutional limits.

Control of the Civil Service

With their reelection almost assured, individual congressmen enjoy a longevity in office that far exceeds the president's. Chapter 5 presents a graphic description of the impact of this longevity on the career civil servant. His loyalties will never lie with the comparatively transitory political appointee. They will belong to the person who was there before this president came into office, and who will be there when this one (and probably the next one) is gone.

It is axiomatic that executive branch bureaucrats will respond to those who can most directly influence their long-term career advancement and prospects. In that sense, it is clear that the professional bureaucracy of the federal government regards Congress as its true employer.

Consider, for example, the matter of civil service salaries. Typically, the president proposes pay increases for the civil service, a proposal which, as often as not, is rejected by Congress as too low. Even when it cannot muster the votes to overturn the president's parsimonious proposal, Congress rhetorically supports the civil service. That is particularly true of the members of the committees with jurisdiction over the civil service.

Criminalization of Policy Differences

One of the most troubling characteristics of the administrative Congress is its resort to the criminal justice system to settle questions which ought properly to be the subject of political debate. The specific mechanism used by Congress is the so-called "independent counsel." Chapter 10 provides a short history of this Watergate-born institution, and an analysis of the specific cases dealt with by independent counsel, or, more properly, "special prosecutors". The conclusion: the institution of the special prosecutor is inconsistent with the American system of justice.

To begin with, there is no presumption of innocence. In fact, the usual standard of investigation is stood on its head: the prosecutor does not investigate a specific crime, but a specific individual, to see if somewhere, sometime, he or she may have broken a law. Nor do normal budgetary constraints operate on these prosecutors. They have the checkbook of the American taxpayer to draw upon.

Even when no crime is ever found or prosecuted, the damage to a targeted individual's reputation is considerable, and the monetary costs incurred (on both sides) are astronomical. Most importantly, as with other independent agencies, there is a total absence of responsibility. Voters have no one to hold accountable. Congress merely asks for a probe; its connection to prosecutorial excess (or malfeasance) is tenuous at best. For his part, the president cannot discipline a misguided prosecutor, and thus he cannot be held responsible.

Unaccountability

This characteristic is at the heart of legislative violation of the separation of powers because it insulates Congress from the checks that the electorate would otherwise impose. Some of the techniques that Congress uses have already been discussed, but a particularly powerful one is the use of "independent regulatory agencies."

Close observers of the American political system have often been uncertain as to the exact nature of the "independent agencies." They have been called the Fourth Branch of Government, and described as "quasi-legislative", "quasi-judicial", and "quasi-executive." In fact, as the analysis in Chapter 11 shows, the independent agencies are unconstitutional institutions, profoundly destructive of representative, responsible government. Through them congressmen can avoid responsibility for their own legislative failings, while creating for themselves opportunities to intervene on behalf of constituents for favorable treatment by those agencies.

The worst aspect of the independent agencies is their lack of accountability to the voters. Congress creates the agencies, endows them with vague but broad mandates for action, confirms their members, and sets their budgets (often specifying detailed operations). But members of Congress can honestly say they are not responsible when these agencies displease the voters.

For its part, the executive branch devotes little time or attention to such agencies, since its responsibility for them is limited to nominating the commissioners or board members. The executive has no mechanism of control over the commissions, and their actions are often unpopular with the constituencies most closely affected.

SOLUTIONS

Part III of this book suggests what can be done to restore the separation of powers, and with it, a responsive and truly representative form of government.

Some who have examined this problem have concluded that there are mechanical answers, that it is a matter of making the proper adjustments to the rules and procedures by which government is conducted in America. Thus there are those who look for changes in the length of term of representatives, restrictions on political contributions, or such drastic constitutional changes as the adoption of a parliamentary system.

The authors of this book are of a different opinion. While some of them do propose specific institutional changes, by and large they conclude that the problems are political, not mechanical. America is in the midst of a constitutional crisis not because its institutions have failed, but because its politicians have failed to present clear policy differences to the electorate.

Reviving Politics

American politics has been reduced to a question of which candidate can best guide constituents through the vast bureaucratic maze in Washington. Elected officials play the role of managers, each striving to carve out a managerial niche, with little thought for (much less debate over) the broad implications of the programs being managed.This is strongly borne out in the campaigns for the House and Senate. Congressional candidates rarely debate meaningful policy differences.

Instead, these policy differences are hidden behind such "issues" as competence, compassion, and sensitivity. In Congress the camouflage takes the form of procedures that limit debate and amendments to legislation. Policy is obscured by a proliferation of constituent services, often responding to problems created by the failure of Congress to deal with policy questions directly and honestly.

While individual constituents are mollified, the cynicism of the larger public grows, threatening serious delegitimization of American political institutions.

Presidential Leadership

Because Congress is unlikely to limit itself, the authors of this book conclude that the change has to come through executive branch action. They advocate forceful action by the executive branch, in the person of a recently-elected popular president, to bring these issues before the public, where they can be settled through the mechanisms of a representative democracy. As party leader, national figure, and occupant of the "bully pulpit," the president is the only person with the resources to draw the policy differences clearly. He can do so by informing the electorate and mobilizing it against an entrenched Congress, much as Franklin Delano Roosevelt mobilized the country against an unresponsive Supreme Court in the 1930s.

To accomplish this task, the president will need to use all the resources at his command. He will have to gain control over his own executive branch by insisting on political appointees who recognize the stakes involved; he will have to use the nomination and confirmation process to advance his policy platform; he will have to marshal his prestige behind advocates of his position within and without his administration. He will have to change the whole political climate, using the moral authority accorded him by virtue of his national election.

The idea is not to increase the power of the presidency because of a preference for executive action. It is a recognition that only the president commands the public relations resources in modern America to insist on that debate. Only a figure elected nationally, with the popular mandate that comes with that election, can force the forthright political discussion of the basic issues confronting this polity as every other polity: the nature of mankind, personal responsibility, autonomy, liberty. These are questions so foreign to recent political debate that they are often not recognized, even when they do surface in presidential campaigns.

This prescription implies confrontation. It involves making enemies, in the press, among the intelligentsia, in Congress, even in certain quarters of the president's own party. It means that the president cannot worry about his "place in history." Churchill wrote his own history, and such a president might try that. In general, however, the victors write the history, and if the president is successful, his place in history will be assured. He simply must conclude that it is worth the risk of opprobrium, calumny, and even impeachment to lay these issues before the public for their decision.

CONCLUSION

In the last six presidential elections Americans have gone to the polls to elect the candidate who promised most explicitly to reduce the size and impact of the federal establishment. Nevertheless, to date, that establishment has proven remarkably resistent to change. The promised reform has been thwarted by resistance in Congress and in executive agencies allied with Congress. Only when Americans understand that alliance and the fundamental danger it poses to constitutional government can they recreate a truly representative government in Washington.

The message of *The Imperial Congress* is that the American people can understand it, when it is presented to them clearly and understandably, and that an informed, courageous president can so present it. By thoughtful, bold, and immediate action, beginning with the executive, the separation of powers can be restored, allowing the two popularly-elected branches to check each other as the Framers intended. That done, the American people will once again govern themselves.

GORDON S. JONES
JOHN A. MARINI

PART

I

The Constitutional Framework of Separated Powers

Introduction by

JOHN A. MARINI

*T*he separation of powers is the central institutional feature of the American constitutional order. For nearly two centuries, it has served as a primary means of ensuring the protection of individual liberties, as well the maintenance of the rule of law, within the large, diverse American republic. As a practical matter, the success of the separation of powers hinges upon preventing legislative branch domination—because of its supremacy as the ongoing lawmaking body—of the constitutional system. Consequently, the great political problem of constitutional government is to uphold the predominance of the legislative authority, while preventing the legislative body from dominating government. In other words, the constitutional order is a means of institutionalizing the rule of law, and not legislative will, as fundamental to good government.

The Constitution, through the separation of powers, attempted to balance the executive and legislative branches, as institutions with specific virtues, against each other. The virtue of the legislative body lay in its capacity to *deliberate*, represent constituencies, and reconcile diverse interests. The virtues of the executive were largely administrative virtues: the capacity to *act* with energy, secrecy, and dispatch. In devising a governmental framework in which the legislature was to operate primarily as a deliberative body, it was reason, not will, that was to be the characteristic feature of the body. The executive power, on the other hand, was lodged in a single individual, to ensure prudent and energetic administration of the law. And the courts were made independent of the ordinary process of democratic politics—elections—to ensure sound judgment of the laws.

The separation of powers no longer operates as it was intended. The transformation of the institutions of American government has accompanied a gradual change in opinion concerning the meaning and the ends of constitutional government, which began in the Progressive era. Such Progressives as Woodrow Wilson insisted that the real source of power in the modern state lies in the administrative realm; in the practical operation of the bureaucracy. The distinction between politics and administration was to replace the fundamental distinction between the powers of government. The administrative realm, unlike executive or legislative power, lies outside the proper sphere of the separation of powers.

Throughout most of our history, the American nation was centrally governed but administratively decentralized. Congress concerned itself primarily with the general interests of the nation, and it functioned as a deliberative and representative lawmaking body. Private or specialized interests were brokered in the economic marketplace, or administered at the state and local level of government. In the period between 1965 and 1975, Congress created a bureaucracy capable of centrally administering nearly all the details of American life. It attempted to solve not only the political problems of the nation, but the social and economic problems of all Americans as well. Prior to the growth of the administrative state, the general interests of government could be articulated and partisan compromises could be accommodated within the political branches. This was so because the administrative functions of the national government, not to mention the organized constituencies allied to those functions, were few. After the centralization of administration, the interests of the executive and the legislative branches diverged, regardless of party. More specifically, administrative centralization has undermined the capacity of political institutions, as well as the political incentives of individuals in the political branches, not to mention the courts, to perform their duties and functions in a constitutional manner.

Individual members of Congress have become quite good at representing organized interests and constituencies, but Congress as an institution has become almost incapable of pursuing a public interest. Furthermore, the increased congressional role in the administra tive process has threatened to undermine the energy of the executive.

It was almost inevitable that once Congress ceased performing the deliberative and lawmaking functions envisioned by the Constitution, the role of the executive would likewise be transformed. As a result, the national government is deprived of the energy characteristic of a single executive. As government's role has expanded and its functions have increased, it has become more intrusive and bigger, but not stronger. Legislative/bureaucratic government poses a threat to the vitality or the energy associated with executive power. In *The Public Philosophy,* Walter Lippmann writes that democratic states are susceptible to this derangement "because congenitally the executive is weaker than the elected representatives. ... And the normal tendency of elections is to reduce elected officers to the role of agents of organized pluralities." Such governments are, to be sure, big governments, but they are not strong governments. "They are," Lippmann suggested, "swollen rather than strong, being too weak to resist the pressure of special interests and of the departmental bureaucracies."

It seems that modern democratic governments are faced with the paradox of being less able to govern effectively the more they try to administer the social and economic details of life in society. This is particularly so when members of the legislature can, at crucial junctures, direct and administer bureaucracies, in a manner compatible with their own interests. This may serve organized interests well, but the national interest is left without powerful representation. The energy of the executive, lodged in the single hands of the president, is dissipated when members of the legislature become the critical actors in the administrative process.

It is difficult to retain a Constitution with a genuine separation of powers when the principal branches no longer perform their constitutional functions. When Congress does not deliberate, no consensus on political or social issues can be created. And it is not a question of whether controversial issues are decided in a manner suitable

18

to Republicans or Democrats, or even that they be decided in a liberal or conservative way. Rather, it is important, in a democracy, that vital issues be deliberated in a public forum by those charged to do so.

It is clear, after several decades of experience, that one political party's control of the presidency has not resulted in the transformation of American government. Nor will such change occur through the judiciary. In the final analysis, fundamental change in American politics requires the transformation of the legislature. There is little doubt, however, that the president remains the critical catalyst who can create the kind of partisan consensus that will be necessary to once again, re-establish constitutional government.

1. Separation of Powers and the Administrative State

CHARLES R. KESLER

The first necessity is to understand the implications of the doctrine of the separation of powers as it was historically understood. In this opening essay, Professor Charles Kesler explains the origins of the separation, a truly remarkable innovation of the American constitutional system.

Designed to keep power diffused, the separation was useful as a governing system. However, as the nation grew, and the pace of life picked up, the separation of powers came under attack as inadequate to the administrative role of government. The attack on the separation was led by the Progressives, beginning as early as the mid-19th century, but it was not consummated until the last half of the 20th century.

Judging from their conduct in recent years, the branches of our national government seem to be suffering a prolonged identity crisis. It used to be expected, roughly speaking, that the Congress would pass laws, the president would execute them, and the Supreme Court would interpret them in individual cases. This was the political framework established by the Constitution and adhered to for the greater part of our political history. Increasingly, however, it is not the way the federal government operates. And as departures from the Constitution's plan grow more common, a permanent derangement of the American political system becomes more probable.

While the formal separation of powers promulgated in the

Constitution and explained in the *Federalist* remains, and in some respects continues to function well, the actual distribution of powers has changed dramatically. Like squaredancers who miss a call and end the dance with the wrong partners, the branches of the federal government find themselves in strange company making awkward excuses. Congress has become increasingly energetic and administrative, the judiciary willful and legislative, and the executive (in its institutional, not electoral, connection) tentative and judicial. Under these conditions, it is the Congress's and the Supreme Court's power that have grown at the net expense of the president's. But more important than the balance of power between the branches is the *maldistribution of powers,* the mixing and confusing of governmental functions, which has resulted.

THE CURRENT STATE OF AFFAIRS

The problem can be easily illustrated. When President Reagan signed the long-term Continuing Resolution and the fiscal year 1988 Budget Reconciliation Act, he hefted the multi-thousand-page bill before the television cameras and vowed never to sign such a monstrosity again. Then he signed it and everyone promptly left Washington on vacation. That spectacle was a sign that the Congress is losing the capacity, or the desire, to legislate responsibly, and that the presidency (or at least this president) is resigned to the legislature's abdication of constitutional authority.

Increasingly, the bills that Congress passes are ill-digested, little more than vague charges to the executive agencies to accomplish some general and ill-defined purpose. But the statutes' very vagueness is the license with which committee and, more significantly, subcommittee chairmen are armed to threaten and cajole the executive departments. In one sense,this is nothing new. Congress has always looked over the executive's shoulder, sometimes more, sometimes less gloweringly; and imprecise grants of power to regulatory agencies have been common since the late nineteenth century. What is new is the extent to which Congress's role as legislator is being subordinated to its role as overseer of the executive branch. With a vast array of federal programs to be overseen and a multiplicity of subcommittees to do the overseeing, congressional intervention in administrative affairs has increased substantially. As a result, Congress today invests more energy and exerts more influence in playing ombudsman, investigator, and regulator, than in discharging its duty as lawmaker.

This newfound emphasis on administering the executive branch, combined with the Congress's old-fashioned delight at delivering benefits and services to home districts and states, leaves congressmen little time or appetite for public stands on highly partisan issues. House members, in particular, find it advantageous when running for reelection to emphasize not their partisan affiliation, but their ability to deliver goods and services to their districts. And their districts, in gratitude for their good offices, have reelected House incumbents at astonishing rates—98 percent were returned in 1986.

Serious lawmaking, the kind involving divisive moral and constitutional questions, is more and more left to the judiciary. It is the Supreme Court that has in effect legislated on abortion, obscenity, school prayer, the death penalty, and countless other issues touching the welfare and morals of society; even as the Court has arrogated to itself the right to have final say on the most important constitutional questions determining how Americans govern themselves—for example, the one-man, one-vote standard of representation. But in truth, Congress has been eager to foist the responsibility for making difficult political choices upon the Court, if for no better reason than that it allows incumbents to have their cake and eat it too.

With the contemporary executive the case is different. Beset by both Congress and the Court, the president and his appointees have found it difficult to defend their institutional prerogatives. Partly this is their own fault, the result of an unwillingness to risk serious partisan and constitutional confrontations. Partly it is a confession of the enormous political power now wielded by the other branches, Congress in particular. President Reagan's success in winning passage of his tax and defense policies in his first term might seem to refute this contention. But after the 1982 elections, his zeal for political combat waned rapidly, and in his second term the initiative soon passed to Congress. In this struggle, the investigative and prosecutorial powers of Congress figured importantly, as executive branch officials were held up to ethical and legal standards not usually associated with politicians (certainly not with congressmen) and germane, if at all, perhaps only to judges, for whom even the appearance of a conflict of interest is automatically disqualifying. On the whole, the executive branch is torn between the search for a national electoral mandate to legitimize and empower it against the Congress and Court, and the knowledge that the means to capitalize on such a mandate are ultimately elusive, given the executive agencies' dependence on congressional subcommittees and their various clients.

This quick sketch of the politics of American national government is not meant to be exhaustive, of course, but it does convey the salient facts about the current situation in Washington. Those facts point to the following conclusion: the chief constitutional basis of our politics, the separation of powers, is under severe pressure from the institutions and practices of the administrative state. Paradoxically, the principal beneficiary of the growth of the executive bureaucracy has been Congress, not the president, who sees his responsibilities (as head of the executive branch) continually enlarged but his power steadily diminished. Even so, it is not all congressmen equally who have seen and approved of the growth in the federal government's authority, or who have cheered Congress on in its own superintendence of the executive. There has existed for almost a century a faction within the national legislature in favor of the administrative state as the emblem and vehicle of national progress. This faction has included both Democrats and Republicans but, since 1912, predominantly Democrats. Indeed, since the New Deal, allegiance to the administrative or welfare state has been the first tenet of the liberal Democratic creed. Given their dominance of the national legislature in those years, the responsibility for congressional actions must lie primarily with that party.

THE FRAMERS' CASE FOR SEPARATED POWERS

Separation of powers was an idea accepted by all sides in the American founding, though its precise meaning remained unclear—at least until its famous exposition in the *Federalist*, the defense of the Constitution written by "Publius" the pen name of Alexander Hamilton, James Madison, and John Jay. The confusion over the meaning of separation of powers arose mainly from the status of the executive power: If the executive were subordinate to the legislature, as its name implies it should be, would not the legislature quickly overpower the executive? And in that event, how could the powers long remain separated? The initial context of this problem was the English Civil War, when the idea of separated powers first appeared in the pamphlets and essays of parliamentary writers who distinguished between legislative and executive powers in order to subordinate the executive to the legislative. The aim of such republicans as John Milton and Philip Hunton was to establish the rule of law by guaranteeing that those who made the law could not execute it, and that those who executed it could not make it, for the sake of their private advantage. In effect, of course, the doctrine was anti-monarchical, inasmuch as it reduced the King to the status of an "executive" (that is, someone who carries out the will of another).[1]

Balancing Executive and Legislative Power

Such a weak executive could hardly balance the power of the legislature, however. John Locke, addressing himself to this difficulty in his *Second Treatise* (c. 1688), added a third power to the balance to strengthen the executive. The "federative" power, as he called it, concerned foreign relations (the ability to federate or ally with other countries). While this federative power was theoretically distinguishable from the executive, in practice it was inseparable from the executive, because it, like the executive, presupposed the united power of society. Circumstances would frequently demand that these two powers be exercised for the common good, but in the absence of a standing law and sometimes even against the law. Locke's justification for this extra-legal but prudent action was described as the "prerogative" power, which was necessarily executive. In this fashion, Locke acknowledged what was reasonable in the claims of each side in the English Civil War—the rule of law for the

Whigs and of prerogative for the Tories. But he combined them in the idea of a liberal regime freed of both excessive jealousy of the executive power and the pretensions of divine right.[2]

His doctrines lived on in the thought of the so-called "Commonwealthmen," a circle of eighteenth-century republican radicals who resisted the "corruption" of the House of Commons by the King and his ministers. Through their patronage power, the ministers could confer pensions and sinecures on complacent members of Parliament, compromising the legislature's independence. The practice was denounced on this side of the Atlantic as well, and figured prominently in the Americans' criticisms of the British in the 1770s and in their distrust of the colonial governors appointed by the crown. This distrust was later embodied in the weak executives formulated by the new state constitutions after the Revolution. Thus the separation of powers as Americans thought of it in the early 1780s harked back to the Commonwealthmen's fear of corruption and the seventeenth-century republicans' preference for a weak executive.

The Framers of the Constitution of 1787 solved the problem of reconciling a strong, durable separation of powers with republican government by means of a new doctrine of constitutionalism. The most authoritative account of their achievement may be found in the *Federalist*, which provides two justifications for the separation of powers—liberty and good government.

Preserving Liberty

The argument from liberty holds that separation is needed in order to prevent tyranny. According to Publius's famous definition, "The accumulation of all powers legislative, executive, and judiciary, in the same hands, whether of one, a few, or many, and whether hereditary, self-appointed, or elective, may justly be pronounced the very definition of tyranny."[3] Tyranny is a danger because man's passions and reason are not perfectly harmonious; his reason may be distorted by desire. Although each man has by nature the rights to life, liberty, and the pursuit of happiness, he cannot secure these rights without joining together with other men to form a civil society, a people. Despite the legal unity of this people, it is composed of individuals whose impassioned opinions and interests divide them into majorities and minorities. As a precaution against injustice, therefore, the powers of government must be so divided that no man or group of men may wield all of them at once. This precaution would not be necessary if reason and passion *were* utterly harmonious, and if the whole comprising such reason and passion were *a priori* unitary rather than synthetic. These conditions, however, are unique to God, who alone justly unites the legislative, judicial, and executive powers in the same hands. The Declaration of Independence affirms this by appealing at once to "the laws of Nature and of Nature's God," "the Supreme Judge of the world," and "the Protection of Divine Providence."[4]

But men are prone to seek power, which has an "encroaching" nature, and the *Federalist* insists that if the people's liberty is to be secure, they must take precautions against the oppressions of their governors. The republican form of government, the elective principle itself, is the main defense. But Publius also proposes "auxiliary precautions," chief among which is the separation of powers. This separation will be enforced not by "parchment barriers" but by reciprocal checks—the president's veto, for example, and the Senate's confirmation power—requiring that the powers be partially mixed in order to be kept independent. "Ambition must be made to counteract ambition," in the words of *Federalist* 51. This "policy of supplying, by opposite and rival interests, the defect of better motives," is designed to reinforce the people's distrust of their representatives, but, simultaneously and ironically, to increase the people's confidence in the Constitution.[5]

The last step is crucial, inasmuch as the people's jealousy for their liberty must be directed more against the legislature, the branch ostensibly closest to them, than against any other. In every form of government, the *Federalist* cautions, the most powerful branch is always the most dangerous to the people's freedom. In a monarchy, it is the executive that ought to be feared. But in a republic, it is the legislative. In the state governments, for example, with their weak executives, it is the legislative department that is "everywhere extending the sphere of its activity and drawing all power into its impetuous vortex." Therefore, Publius admonishes, "it is against the enterprising ambition of this department that the people ought to indulge all their jealousy and exhaust all their precautions." To protect their rights and liberties the people must insist on limited national government, but that means the people must limit Congress more effectually than they had the state legislatures; and the *Federalist* argues that the Constitution's improved separation of powers (along with bicameralism) will do just that.[6]

Promoting Good Government

The people should feel, then, not that the Congress is peculiarly theirs, as if the other branches belonged to someone else or to another class; but that what is theirs is the Constitution. In the course of the *Federalist*'s argument, this opinion that the Constitution is good because it is theirs is gradually transformed into the opinion that it is theirs because it is good. Publius' second, positive argument for the separation of powers is responsible for this transformation. For in addition to the negative function of preventing tyranny, the separation of powers actively promotes good government. That is to say, it allows the branches of the federal government to perform their respective functions well or at least better than they otherwise could. In the first argument, "power" is treated as a generic thing, abstracted from any ends for which it might be used, regarded as a dangerous end in itself (hence its "encroaching" nature). But in the second, "power" is divided into "powers," acknowledging that each has a "nature" that aims at the excellent performance of certain definite functions.[7]

Contrary to Woodrow Wilson and more recent critics of the separation of powers such as James MacGregor Burns and Robert Dahl, the purpose of separation was not to produce governmental "deadlock" but to produce good government, which is not the same thing as simply popular or majoritarian government. These critics reduce the separation of powers to its negative role, equating separation with "checks and balances." While insisting that each department must have a will of its own to preserve its independence, the *Federalist* considers "the regular distribution of power into distinct departments" to be something quite different from "legislative balances and checks." In fact, the term "balances and checks" is used only with reference to the relation between the House and Senate.[8] The separation of powers, though it does help to check governmental tyranny and to balance the Constitution, is primarily designed to elicit sound and deliberate legislation, a firm and energetic executive, and an independent judiciary faithful to the Constitution.

These qualities are treated by the *Federalist* as the consequences of certain carefully ordered quantities. The ability of the national legislature to deliberate well is traced to the relatively small size and two-year term of the House of Representatives (allowing congressmen to learn their job and to discover the common interests that make general legislation possible) and to the smaller size and longer term of the Senate (making it a force for stability, moderation, and wisdom). The executive will be energetic because it is one rather than plural, and will have a "moral certainty" or at least a "constant probability" of being occupied by "characters preeminent for ability and virtue" because of the president's mode of appointment (the electoral college), his four-year term of office, and his indefinite eligibility for reelection.[9] The independence and fidelity of the judiciary (the critical third power of government first hailed by Montesquieu) are guaranteed by the judiciary's indirect mode of appointment and good behavior tenure.

In each case, "fit characters" are summoned to the office by virtue of its formal characteristics—its job description, if you will—and the task of the people or their representatives is to select the best man for the job. If the negative function of the separation of powers depends on connecting "the interest of the man" with "the constitutional rights of the place," as Publius argues in *Federalist* 51, then the positive function requires that the virtue of the man be linked to the constitutional duties of the place. As the *Federalist* discusses each of the branches, it gradually brings the positive function of separated powers to the fore, describing the special contribution that each can make to good government. From this viewpoint, even the negative or checking function of separation is reinterpreted as something positive: for example, the president's veto is shown to be not

merely a defensive tool but a means of improving the deliberations of the legislature by slowing, moderating, and correcting
them.[10]

The Constitution as Supreme Authority

Although "parchment barriers" are unreliable, the Constitution can be relied on because the people's—and in a different
way, their representatives'—passions and interests will be tied
to their opinion of the Constitution's importance for good government. As such, the Constitution underlies both the positive
and negative functions of the separation of powers. For without
some idea of what the branches' duties are, it is impossible to
know when and how to defend their rights and their
independence.

This argument is not disproven by subsequent developments
in American politics, in particular the rise of political parties. It
is true that the Constitution of 1787 had to be amended to accommodate the practice of presidential and vice-presidential
candidates running for office on the same party ticket. The
Twelfth Amendment, ratified in 1804, changed the method of
voting in the Electoral College by requiring the electors to cast
separate ballots for president and vice-president. (Originally,
the electors voted for two candidates for president, with the
runner-up becoming vice-president.) But the point of the
amendment was to make party competition compatible with the
separation of powers by securing the president's independence
from Congress. Without that change in the Constitution, the
power of electing the president effectively would have devolved
from the people (represented indirectly in the Electoral College) to the House of Representatives, where ties between presidential and vice-presidential candidates would be decided (as in
1800), and where all sorts of electoral mischief was possible.

Present-day political and constitutional reformers, again following the lead of Wilson and other Progressive political scientists, argue that political parties evolved in America in order to
overcome the separation of powers, to bring the executive and
legislative together in a party program. Undoubtedly, political
parties did foster some cooperation between the branches on
questions of public policy. But the overriding consideration for

Jefferson and his contemporaries was to ensure that parties and their public policies were shaped by and kept subordinate to the general principles of the Constitution. This was the purpose of the Twelfth Amendment. With that subordination firmly established, the system of party government could operate safely and benignly. So rather than the party system being designed to overcome the "deadlock" resulting from separated powers, it quickly became an additional safeguard of separation, with the parties' own vitality and respectability depending on their integration within the constitutional system.

The existence of parties did show, however, that the constitutionality (not to mention the wisdom) of specific policies was disputable. But the condition of their civil disputation was, of course, that the comprehensive goodness of the Constitution was considered indisputable. Here, too, the party system was dependent on the constitutionalism most clearly articulated in the *Federalist*. The doctrine of constitutionalism holds not only that the people's rights are best secured in a written constitution structured around the separation of powers, but that the people have correlative duties to (and under) that constitution. In the final analysis, indeed, those duties become the ground of the people's rights—that the people are able to live up to their rights, to vindicate them, reveals that the people are worthy of being free.

The supreme achievement of the Framers' constitutionalism was to elicit what Publius in *Federalist* 49 calls "veneration" or "reverence" for the Constitution. By identifying the people's sovereign will not with its latest but its oldest expression, the Framers succeeded in identifying the people's authority with the Constitution, not with the statutory law made by their representatives. In this manner, republicanism in America came to be constitutionalized, and the people whose choice had authorized the Constitution in the first place came to regard *it* as the lofty authority that should guide their own choices and those of their posterity.[11]

It was the separation of powers that made possible this identification of the Constitution with the awesome stature of the moral law, for separation helped to keep the Constitution inviolate by elevating it above momentary popular whims. That is why political disputes among the branches of government are never decided by direct, extraconstitutional appeals to the people. In effect, the people have no existence outside of the Constitution, or more precisely, outside of the moral law embodied in the Constitution.[12] It is only by elections and by political competition among the branches, therefore, taking place *under* the provisions of the Constitution, that the people's rational will may be expressed.

THE PROGRESSIVES' ASSAULT ON THE CONSTITUTION

Nothing could be further removed from the reverence for the Constitution recommended by the Framers and encouraged by the separation of powers than the tone adopted by the chief architect of the administrative state, Woodrow Wilson. In his first book, *Congressional Government*, published in 1885, he acknowledged that "opposition to the Constitution as a constitution, and even hostile criticisms of its provisions, ceased almost immediately upon its adoption; and not only ceased, but gave place to an undiscriminating and almost blind worship of its principles. . . ." Reverence for the Constitution would be "blind worship" only if reason's say in political life had been gravely underestimated by the Framers, and the Constitution's rationality greatly overestimated. This was exactly Wilson's position. He attributed "the charm of our constitutional ideal" to a kind of "political witchcraft," and advised his countrymen to undertake an unsentimental and "fearless criticism" of the Constitution. "The more open-eyed we become, as a nation, to its defects, and the prompter we grow in applying with the unhesitating courage of conviction all thoroughly tested or well-considered expedients necessary to make self-government among us a straightforward thing of simple method, single, unstinted power, and clear responsibility," he counseled, "the better."[13]

Rejecting the Separation of Powers

Wilson's political thought, like that of many of the leading American political scientists and reformers in the Progressive era, rejected the separation of powers in favor of the allegedly more fundamental and modern separation between politics and administration. Separation of powers, in his view, was the product of an outmoded theory of politics. At the time of the founding, men thought of politics on the model of Newtonian physics, imagining that the departments of government could be held in place by the countervailing forces of interest and ambition, even as the stars and planets were kept in their orbits by the force of gravity. The "theory of checks and balances" was at bottom "a sort of unconscious copy of the Newtonian theory of the universe."[14]

A century or so later, however, the limitations of this eighteenth-century world view were apparent. Government is "not a machine, but a living thing," wrote Wilson, in lines that he would incorporate into his presidential campaign speeches in 1912. "It is accountable to Darwin, not to Newton." Consequently, government must constantly adjust to changes in its environment; its purposes and structure are not ordained by "the laws of Nature and of Nature's God" or limited by a written constitution.[15] In particular, government has no use for separated powers. "No living thing can have its organs offset against each other as checks, and live," he declared. "There can be no successful government without leadership or without the intimate, almost instinctive, coordination of the organs of life and action."[16]

Wilson's efforts to overcome the separation of powers occupied his entire life, from his student days at Princeton through his career as a professor to his years in politics. Concerning the specific reforms that would be necessary to achieve this "coordination of the organs of life and action," his own thoughts underwent an evolution. As a young man, he favored a series of constitutional amendments designed to make congressmen, senators, and the president serve roughly concurrent terms, so as to increase the probability that one political party would gain control of the whole elective part of the government. In addition, he proposed that the president be required to choose his cabinet from the leaders of the majority party in Congress, who would be authorized to introduce legislation on the Hill, thus obviating the committee system. These are essentially the same proposals advanced today by Lloyd Cutler and the Committee on the Constitutional System, though their view of the costs and consequences of superimposing them on American government is not so clear as Wilson's.

In any event, later in his career Wilson decided that there was an easier way. Strong presidential leadership combined with a highly developed and centralized administrative apparatus would succeed in liberating the national government from the straitjacket of separated powers. Today's constitutional reformers have had a similar change of mind but in reverse order, starting out with an enthusiastic embrace of strong presidential leadership (Roosevelt, Truman, Kennedy, Johnson), but eventually deciding that progress will not come to America without far-reaching constitutional change. Whatever the strategy, the goal of these political reforms is the same: to deliver up American government to the salutary currents of progress, rather than allowing a superannuated Constitution to keep the country drydocked.

Redefining the Role of the Executive

In rejecting separation of powers in favor of the separation of politics and administration, Wilson reformulated the terms of political debate. "Democracy" now meant the last and most perfect stage in the evolution of the state, in which the people's will was directly responsible for setting public policy. But the immediate expression of their will could be whimsical, and so was not to be taken as authentic, as conveying their permanent instinct for progress—the Darwinian impulse. Therefore, the people's will had to be mediated by *leadership,* a word that assumed a new prominence and respectability in the vocabulary of American politics. As compared to the masses, leaders were more closely attuned to the spirit of the age; they were able to distinguish the faint but swelling notes of progress from the background noise of history. Their task was to prepare the people for the future, to act as interpreters and spokesmen for the spirit of the age; and, of course, actually to lead the way. But they went only where the "common thought" and "common impulse" were destined eventually to take the people. The leaders' function was to mediate between the people and the future, not to educate or elevate the people's will to a rational or trans-historical, much less a constitutional, standard.[17]

What did this mean for American politics? Whereas "energy" in the executive had come mainly from the president's position in the constitutional order, leadership in the executive would depend entirely on the president's personal traits—his charisma, as we say today. Around his personal appeal to the voters and his "vision" of the future, he would build a political movement, perhaps even a "Reagan Revolution." But the important point for our purposes is that his principal role in office would be the same as in campaigning for office: he would be first and foremost a political or party leader, not the country's chief executive. The constitutional function of chief executive officer, which in Wilson's scheme falls under the rubric of administration, would be largely transferred to the Congress.

The reason for this, in Wilson's blunt words, is that the president "cannot execute laws." In practice, it now takes a dozen or so departments and millions of executive branch employees to execute the laws. "It is therefore becoming more and more true, as the business of the government becomes more and more complex and extended," Wilson wrote, "that the President is becoming more and more a political and less and less an executive officer." His executive powers drain away into the bureaucracy while "his political powers more and more centre and accumulate upon him and are in their very nature personal and inalienable."[18] In the new dispensation, it is not our rights but our charisma that is inalienable. Even as, in Wilson's considered view, it is inevitable for society to become more complex and in need of governmental regulation, so it is inevitable that the president must take more and more of the responsibility for leading the country into the future, and less and less for executing the laws.

Presidential leadership has therefore a certain hollow ring to it, of which Wilson was well aware. The president is the only truly national leader, chosen by the whole people; and if he rightly interprets the people's inchoate desire for progress, "he is irresistible," for the people's "instinct is for unified action, and it craves a single leader." Therefore, in Wilson's famous phrase, the president's office "is anything he has the sagacity and force to make it."[19] But this means that in ordinary times, with ordinary men in the Oval Office, the presidency will not be the center of affairs and the dictator of events. Largely bereft of constitutional rights and duties, the office will be as small as the men who occupy it. And even on those occasions when the president is a man of great "personal force," his leadership will depend absolutely on his connection to the people, on his ability to read their thoughts and stir them to action. Far from being the energetic and independent executive the Framers sought, the president in the routine operations of his office will be a hostage to popular opinion.[20]

The Rise of Administrative Lawmaking

Perhaps the deeper reason why the president cannot execute the laws, however, is that few laws in the old sense—general rules and measures directing action toward the common good—will be necessary. The assumption of the Progressives is that *history* ultimately will direct human action toward the common good. To put it differently, the Darwinian imperative does not require human legislation to see to it that the fittest will survive. That outcome is guaranteed; those who survive are by definition the fittest. The task of law, in Wilson's view, is only to see to it that the inevitable growth of society be as evenly distributed as possible among classes and sections of the nation. Thus, law regulates and redistributes the inevitable; it is not based on a choice between competing opinions of the common good or clashing views of justice. In this sense, law is not political but administrative; the main purpose of law in modern times is not to defend the country, punish wrongdoing, and inculcate principles of justice. It is to administer progress—in short, to create the administrative state.

"Legislation is but the oil of government," as Wilson put it. "It is that which lubricates its channels and speeds its wheels; that which lessens the friction and so eases the movement." What is now important about law is not so much its purpose or claim to justice, but its execution or implementation, its effect on the process of government. "It is even more important to know how the house is being built than to know how the plans of the architect were conceived and how his specifications were calculated. It is better to have skillful work. . .than a drawing on paper which is the admiration of all the practical artists in the country."[21] Yet how is it possible to know whether a house is being well built without comparing it, implicitly or explicitly, to the *idea* of a well-built house? Although Wilson implicitly rejected Aristotle's claim that politics is the architectonic art, he could not abolish the need for a "literary theory" or a model to act as a guide for skillful craftsmen. He simply replaced prudence or practical wisdom as that guide with the notion of a leader's "vision," the revelation that history vouchsafes to him.

Replacing Traditional Notions of Good Government

To regulate or administer progress, not to secure men's inalienable rights, is therefore the basic function of the modern state. Such regulation is necessary because progress brings with it problems, or more precisely, progress exposes as "problems" what had once been regarded as unhappy aspects of the human condition. Selfishness, poverty, war, as well as many lesser evils—these became social problems in the modern sense when the assumption was made that they could be solved, that man did not have to content himself with alleviating or enduring them. What made their designation as social problems plausible, in turn, was the assumption that the future would be very different from and much better than the past. From that tenet it was easy to conclude that the distinction between "progressive" and "reactionary" ought to replace the distinction between good and evil, because the former distinction was not only the functional equivalent of the latter but was historically demonstrable, hence unassailable.

The dichotomy between politics and administration, which Wilson did as much as anyone to popularize, meant ostensibly that the ends of government ought to change easily with the changing sentiment of the majority, and that the means to those ends ought to be efficiently, scientifically determined by a specially trained class of nonpartisan civil servants. But underlying and bridging the dichotomy was his faith that history was progressive, was good. Both politics and administration served the cause of progress—the one through leadership, sounding the trumpet of advance; the other through pacifying and reorganizing the newly won territory. For that reason, administration was not as "value-free" or "value-neutral" as Wilson and the reformers let on. In truth, the administrative class was intrinsically hostile to anyone who did not accept the rationale of its own existence, namely, the progressive theory of history.

Publius had stated in *Federalist* 68 that,

"Though we cannot acquiesce in the political heresy of the poet who says: 'For forms of government let fools contest—That which is best administered is best,'—yet we may safely pronounce that the true test of a good government is its aptitude and tendency to produce a good administration."[22]

The difference between Publius's and Wilson's positions could not be more significant. For Publius, the poet utters a heresy because there is a connection between a properly constituted republic and good administration: republican government under the Constitution will have a greater "aptitude and tendency" to produce good administration than would any other form of government. But what is good administration? Certainly it comprises energy in the executive and all those other means to the public good of which Publius speaks. The crucial point, however, is that the Constitution is part of the public good, according to Publius. Whereas Wilson treats public policies abstractly, as ends in themselves to be determined by a progressive people, Publius emphasizes that public policies and laws are themselves only means to the ends set out in the Constitution. Therefore the people can err, and the powers of government ought to be separated both to protect against governmental—or popular, that is, legislative—tyranny, and to provide the time and institutions necessary to decoct "the cool and deliberate sense of the community" from its "transient impulse[s]" and "temporary delusion[s]."[23]

For Wilson, however, the people always (not "commonly") express the historical forces working for good, and the leader's task is only sifting the timely from the untimely impulses at work in them. In practice this means that all popular impulses are regarded as ultimately rational, that neither popular nor governmental tyranny is seen as a fundamental danger anymore, that separation of powers may safely be dispensed with, and in particular that the Congress may be—must be—entrusted with "complete and convenient" authority over the executive agencies.[24] "Complete" is not the same as "exclusive," of course, and Wilson did not envision the executive surrendering all executive authority. But with the advent of the administrative state, whatever power the executive retained over the agencies was bound to atrophy. To this development Wilson could not imagine an ethical or political objection, for the principle governing the distribution of powers within the administrative state, like the Darwinian ethic as a whole, admitted no appeal from the order of things determined by the triumphant forces of history.

The Demise of Constitutional Government

The administrative state was born to replace an outmoded constitution with a new one, organized around a powerful centralized government retaining, at most, only the independent judiciary as a holdover from a principled separation of powers. The new government would feature a closely integrated executive and legislative, dominated in partisan matters by a president who could influence Congress through his leadership of public opinion, and dominated on the administrative side by a Congress whose committees could control the executive agencies. On many levels, this is a description of American national government today. From the Framers' point of view, this picture represents a critical breakdown in the separation of powers. From the viewpoint of Woodrow Wilson and the advocates of the administrative state, it represents a stupendous breakthrough for enlightened political theory and practice.

The Constitution defended in the *Federalist* presumed that in order to be respectable, republican government had to be good government. It had, that is, to secure private rights and the public good, rather than simply obey the majority's will. Furthermore, it presumed that man, as a creature of passions as well as reason, would often act rashly and unjustly if he were not taught or habituated to respect the moral law superior to his own will, the law embodied in the Constitution.

But the progressive architects of the new order assumed that history itself would guarantee the victory of reason in politics. Granted, this victory would not be direct but dialectical, employing men's passions as the vehicle by which reason would progress. Actually, however, the doctrine encouraged the belief that in political life there was no compelling need for self-restraint, for the moderation of political passions, for the accommodation of prejudices to reason. Practically speaking, no respect was owed to anything except the future—that was the new meaning of idealism, in whose name leaders and experts of all sorts were (in effect) to claim the right to rule ordinary citizens.

The success of the politics of progress was, on its own terms, the token of reason's ascendancy over passion. Man seemed, so to speak, to be reducing the distance between himself and God, as his reason worked itself out in the life of the administrative state. This is a strange, unholy justification for bureaucratic rule, but perhaps, in the final analysis, it is the only compelling one.

Notes

1. See, in general, W. B. Gwyn, *The Meaning of the Separation of Powers* (New Orleans: Tulane University Press, 1965), and M. J. C. Vile, *Constitutionalism and the Separation of Powers* (Oxford: Clarendon Press, 1967).

2. See the excellent discussion in Harvey C. Mansfield, Jr., *Taming the Prince* (New York: The Free Press, 1989).

3. Alexander Hamilton, James Madison, John Jay [Publius], *The Federalist Papers* (New York: New American Library, 1961), 47, p. 301.

4. See Harry V. Jaffa, *How to Think About the American Revolution* (Durham: Carolina Academic Press, 1978), pp. 131-32; George Anastaplo, "The Declaration of Independence," *St. Louis University Law Journal*, vol. 9 (1965), p. 390.

5. *Federalist* 48, p. 308; 51, p. 322.

6. *Federalist* 48, pp. 308-10.

7. *Federalist* 48, p. 308; cf. 37, p. 227; 39, p. 241; and see Aristotle, *Politics* IV.14-16.

8. *Federalist* 9, p. 72. For examples of the "deadlock" thesis, see Woodrow Wilson, *Constitutional Government in the United States* (New York: Columbia University Press, 1908); James MacGregor Burns, *The Deadlock of Democracy: Four-Party Politics in America* (Englewood Cliffs, N.J.: Prentice-Hall, 1963); and Robert Dahl, *A Preface to Democratic Theory* (Chicago: University of Chicago Press, 1956).

9. *Federalist* 68, p. 414.

10. *Federalist* 10, p. 82; 73, pp. 442-46.

11. *Federalist* 49, pp. 314-315.

12. *Federalist* 49, p. 317.

13. Woodrow Wilson, *Congressional Government: A Study in American Politics* (Baltimore: Johns Hopkins University Press, 1981; orig. ed., 1885), pp. 27, 215.

14. *Constitutional Government*, pp. 54-56.

15. *Constitutional Government*, pp. 56-57.

16. *Constitutional Government*, pp. 56-57.

17. See Woodrow Wilson, "Leaders of Men," in *The Papers of Woodrow Wilson*, ed. Arthur S. Link, 43 vols. (Princeton: Princeton University Press, 1966-83), 6:644-71.

18. *Constitutional Government*, pp. 66-67.

19. *Constitutional Government*, pp. 68-69.

20. Consider in this connection *Constitutional Government*, pp. 80-81.

21. *Congressional Government*, pp. 197-98.

22. *Federalist* 68, p. 414.

23. *Federalist* 63, p. 384; 71, p. 432. See Paul Eidelberg, *A Discourse on Statesmanship* (Urbana, Ill.: University of Illinois Press, 1974), pp. 296-304. On the people's goodness, cf. Federalist 71, p. 432: "It is a just observation that the people commonly *intend* the PUBLIC GOOD," he writes in *Federalist* 71. "This often applies to their very errors. But their good sense would despise the adulator who should pretend that they always *reason right* about the *means* of promoting it."

24. *Congressional Government*, p. 203.

2. Executive Authority Under the Separation of Powers

DOUGLAS A. JEFFREY

Professor Jeffrey argues that while the power exercised by the legislative branch is derived from the constitution, the executive branch enjoys undelegated powers, powers that inhere in the nature of a sovereign state. One of the functions of the separation of powers was to preserve those powers, especially those dealing with foreign policy, from encroachment by the legislative branch. To preserve efficiency in foreign policy, and to permit the involvement of the legislative branch in the details of administration, the Progressives, led by William Graham Sumner and then Woodrow Wilson, sought some form of legislative-executive amalgam, along the lines of the parliamentary model.

As the Congressional committees investigating the Iran-Contra Affair drew their public hearings to a close on August 3, 1987, one of the more spirited, articulate defenders of the "Reagan Doctrine" in the 100th Congress delivered concluding remarks that were primarily remarkable for showing what he—along with most of his fellow conservatives—still didn't understand with regard to what is called, in the subtitle of this book, the "crisis in the separation of powers." Reflecting on "psychology," he suggested that the major actors in Iran-Contra—John Poindexter and Oliver North—had sought to bypass the democratic processes of American government because they distrusted politics; they had learned this distrust when our political system let them and their comrades-in-arms down during the Vietnam War.

Leaving aside Vietnam, this hypothesis simply doesn't pan out. It fails to descry the larger purpose of the theoretical attack on the separation of powers that began in the "progressive era": to replace politics in our country with the administrative or bureaucratic state. It fails to observe that the actual attack on separated powers, specifically on presidential power, that began in earnest with Watergate has gone far toward realizing this goal. Thus it fails to perceive the highly political (as opposed to revolutionary or anticonstitutional) character of any struggle to blunt such attacks.

By their covert actions as executive branch members, and in their televised testimony, Poindexter and North did certainly demonstrate a lack of trust in the 100th Congress and in its predecessor. Understanding the important difference between this conviction-driven behavior and the desperate lack of trust unfairly imputed to them requires first, a discussion of the purposes of and arguments for the separation of powers, particularly with regard to foreign policy; and second, a consideration of how and why these purposes and arguments have been undermined in recent years, and what this subversion portends.

THE PURPOSE OF SEPARATED POWERS

Too often the separation of powers is taught and understood simply as a way to arrange democratic governments in order to help keep them limited. As Publius wrote in *Federalist* 47, echoing Montesquieu, "The accumulation of all powers, legislative, executive, and judiciary, in the same hands, whether of one, a few, or many, and whether hereditary, self-appointed, or elective, may justly be pronounced the very definition of tyranny." This was self-evident to America's founding generation, and remains largely so among Americans today; jealous of our liberty, few would be willing to place all governmental power in the hands of one man or one body of men. But the question remains: Why the separation as constituted in 1787? And on this there is no longer a consensus. Many indeed argue that the original relationship between the executive and legislative branches should be amended, in order to ameliorate the increasingly rancorous strife between them. Some suggest making Congress the president's electoral college, for instance, and allowing its members to serve in the president's cabinet, that the government might again be able to act in unison.[1]

The sense in which the separation of powers is commonly taught and understood today—simply as a libertarian bulwark—lends itself, as above, to an argument for a decisive shift toward parliamentary government; the very sort our founders experienced first-hand as British subjects, and roundly rejected in 1787. They must have understood that the purpose of separated powers went beyond limiting government. And indeed, just in terms of foreign policy, two other ways of understanding it are discernible in their writings—and in the books of the theorists of liberal democracy who influenced them—by which the separation appears other than libertarian; it appears in fact to reflect a teleological concern for the public good. The first approach to understanding the separation of powers involves the different roles intended for and proper to the executive and legislative branches of government; insofar as these are recalled at all today, they are recalled badly. The second approach entails the extraordinary importance of the executive power in a liberal democracy, which has for all intents and purposes been forgotten in our time.

Achieving Just Government

The American separation of powers was intended to promote rational, or good, in addition to limited, government. Whereas Publius opens his treatment of the separation, as we have noted, by invoking the danger of tyranny, this is far from his final word. In *Federalist* 49, discussing how effectively to separate the political branches, he insists that "it is the reason, alone, of the public, that ought to control and regulate the government. The passions ought to be controlled and regulated by the government." And in the last of his five general articles on the subject, *Federalist* 51, he proclaims justice "the end of government," warning that a civil society ruled by an oppressive majority is as anarchic as the state of nature. A government with its political powers separated, these passages in context suggest, is somehow better able to reflect the reason of the people, and therefore better lends itself to just policy-making than one built upon the parliamentary model.

One argument supporting this proposition is that the distinct powers of government entail different duties, themselves requiring different character traits to perform them properly. Separating the powers, then, makes it more likely that the character of the man or body of men wielding each power would befit the specific duties required; for it makes it possible to assign the corresponding institutions various compositions, and different modes of election and lengths of term.

Tapping the Strengths of Each Branch

Under the American Constitution, executive power is to be wielded by one man, elected by a national majority of citizens to serve a four-year term. As a single chief executive he is best able to make decisions and to act upon them with speed, as well as to keep secrets. ("Decision, activity, secrecy, and dispatch," Publius writes in *Federalist* 70, "will generally characterize the proceedings of one man in a much more eminent degree than the proceedings of any greater number.") Being elected by a national majority empowers him to speak and act for the nation, as head of state as well as of government, both within the nation and to the world. And having a relatively long term in office best allows him to carry out policies with a view to the country's long-term interests.

The word most used by the architects of our executive is "energy." Not coincidentally, as we will see below, energy is above all necessary in the conduct of foreign policy.

Consider the character of the American legislative power in contrast; endowed differently by the Constitution, it lends itself to quite different excellences. Congress's many-headed composition best suits it to deliberate. As the proper objects of congressional deliberation are general laws by which all in our extended republic will live, its many constituencies are local, comprising fractions of the national majority. In order for any compromise or consensus the body reaches to be at once effective and democratic, its members must keep close ties with their constituents; to ensure that they do, or that they are honestly representative, their assigned terms of office (in the case of the House of Representatives) are short. As for congressional secrecy, such is neither likely in so large a body, nor on the whole desirable. To be effective, laws must be universally promulgated and widely understood; thus they ought to be debated and enacted in the light of day.

In sum, the very makeup of Congress, which suits it well for the purpose of producing domestic legislation—slow to enact and, like conditions in society, slow to change—precludes the ingredients of energy, and thus those virtues proper to operating on America's behalf in an unpredictable, fast-changing, and dangerous world.

Early on under the Constitution, in 1793, James Madison (writing as "Helvidius") and Hamilton (as "Pacificus") exchanged arguments on the constitutional propriety of President Washington's pledge of American neutrality in a war between England and France (with whom we had a Treaty of Alliance). Hamilton's was a powerful brief for broadly construing the president's foreign policy-making powers. Those powers assigned constitutionally to the legislative branch, he argued—participation by the Senate in making treaties and appointing officers, and Congress' right "to declare war and grant letters of marque and reprisal"—should, as exceptions to the plenary grant of executive power in Article II, be strictly construed.

A critical point of contention concerned the relationship between treaties and laws. If, as Madison suggested, treaties are equivalent to laws, "to be carried into execution, like all other laws, by the executive magistrate," any claim of preeminence for the president's foreign policy making role is rendered suspect. But in arguing that "a treaty is not an execution of law," Madison injected the notion that neither do treaties "presuppose the existence of law."[2] And that turns out to be the rub: Hamilton rightly understood this to illustrate the marked difference between laws and treaties, hence between domestic and foreign affairs. On this basis he insisted that the legislative branch cannot act as an international organ.

Laws enacted by Congress do presuppose the existence of law—the Constitution—by which they (and Congress itself) are legitimated. But the international theater, wherein sovereign nations conduct business, is for all practical purposes lawless. These nations recognize no common constitution, being rather notable for encompassing radically different ways of life. As a consequence, they stand a much greater chance of entering into conflict, one with another, than do fellow citizens. And in such conflicts the stakes are very high.

Americans were perhaps more familiar with this theme when the Western movie was in vogue. The best of these—for example, *The Man Who Shot Liberty Valance*—often depicted in sharp contrast the executive virtues that won the West, wresting it from badmen and savages, and the legislative virtues that came to govern the West once won. Of course, even under the rule of law there remain those to whom such rule is foreign, reminding us always of what foreign relations are like; and the importance of the executive power (as opposed in this case to the judiciary) in dealing with them is well depicted in films like *Dirty Harry*. But it is in history above all that the inadequacy of legislation and adjudication on the world stage should have been driven home to us in the twentieth century. Could Madison still—or we ever—equate treaties with laws, having experienced the behavior of Hitler's Germany, or of Stalin's Russia and its many proxies and imitators around the world?

Preventing One-Branch Domination

The executive power, by virtue of its apparent similarity to the power of the crown under the English constitution, was an object of suspicion from the outset in our nation. Thus within the state governments formed in 1776, with the notable exception of New York, executive power was weak by design and ineffective across the board when it existed at all. With regard to Virginia's Constitution, Thomas Jefferson wrote of this problem in 1781:

> All the powers of government...result to the legislative body. The concentrating of these in the same hands is precisely the definition of despotic government. It will be no alleviation that these powers will be exercised by a plurality of hands, and not by a single one.[3]

And when the Constitutional Convention opened in May

1787—to reconsider the Articles of Confederation, which constituted a Congress of States incorporating no separation of powers and a national government woefully inadequate to perform its requisite functions—the experience gained within the states proved invaluable.

The Framers understood that what Publius called "parchment barriers" between the powers of government would not do; that "unless these [powers] be so far connected and blended as to give each a constitutional control over the others, the degree of separation. . .essential to free government, can never in practice be duly maintained" (*Federalist* 48). The result: Our system of mixed but separated powers, mixture being the key to effective separation that had been lacking in theoretical models.

The experience in the states also demonstrated that the legislative branch was most problematic in terms of corruption. Madison expressed this on the floor of the Constitutional Convention, presaging his later arguments in the *Federalist*:

> Experience had proved a tendency in our governments to throw all power into the legislative vortex. The Executives of the States are in general little more than cyphers; the legislatures omnipotent. If no effective check be devised for restraining the instability and encroachment of the latter, a revolution of some kind would be inevitable. The preservation of Republican Government therefore required some expedient for the purpose, but required evidently that in devising it the genuine principles of that form should be kept in view.[4]

Thus the constitutional checks as addressed in *Federalist* 51 all aim at weakening Congress: it is divided into two houses, the weaker of which is designed to share long-term interests with the executive, and the executive is given what amounts to one-sixth of the legislative vote in the qualified presidential veto.

THE CONSTITUTIONAL CASE FOR AN INDEPENDENT EXECUTIVE

One of the greater inadequacies of the national government under the Articles of Confederation was its incapacity to defend the nation. Here the lack of an independent executive was key. Thus some of the president's constitutional foreign policy powers, are enumerated, as are those of Congress. He is to act as commander-in-chief, make treaties with the Senate's advice and consent, and receive ambassadors. But these by no means are meant to limit his ability to act as chief of state. We have already alluded to the different wordings of the first sections in Articles I and II of the Constitution; whereas the former states that "All legislative powers *herein granted* shall be vested in a Congress of the United States" (emphasis added), the latter simply states that "The executive power shall be vested in a President of the United States of America." Of equal significance to this plenary grant is the president's uniquely prescribed oath, also in Article II, Section 1, requiring him to "faithfully execute the office of President of the United States" and to "preserve, protect, and defend" the Constitution.

Let us acknowledge that the dividing line between executive and legislative foreign policy powers in the Constitution is unclear. For instance, while an early draft of Article I, Section 8, assigned Congress the power to "make war," in the final version this became the right to "declare war." Does this mean that the power to make war, whether declared or not, remains with the president? This is left ambiguous, apparently by design. But if the dividing line is unclear, the president's plenary grant of executive power and prescribed oath are enough to show that his office was intended to be strong and independent in this area. Indeed, they suggest that the Constitution incorporates something like John Locke's "executive prerogative."

Incorporating the Executive Prerogative

As Locke explained it, prerogative meant that the executive may rise above the law, for the sake of the law, in times of crisis.

This is partially a matter of common sense: In order to execute and enforce the law, and thus to preserve the peace, any executive must be free of detailed restrictions and preserve for himself great latitude of action. Furthermore, in a nation of laws such as ours, the executive could hardly remain independent were he constitutionally bound to obey every jot and tittle of the laws as made and as interpreted by Congress; he simply would be its puppet in this case. (For the same reason, "Pacificus" argued that it is the president's responsibility to interpret treaties once ratified, bringing to bear an independent "right of Judgment in the execution of [his] own functions."[5] Thus, writes Publius of the executive, "It is one thing to be subordinate to the laws, and another to be dependent on the legislative body. The first comports with, the last violates, the fundamental principles of good government" (*Federalist* 71).

Whereas in Locke's writings, prerogative remained outside the Constitution, the American system in effect "constitutionalizes" it by requiring the president (and not congressmen) to swear to preserve, protect, and defend the Constitution as the highest duty of his office. At the same time the "genuine forms" of republicanism are kept in view; for ultimately, the American executive power is contingent not on the president's own will, but on that of those for whom he acts. This is clear from a consideration of the two great checks upon the executive provided in the Constitution: the requirement that he stand for reelection at four-year intervals, and the impeachment power that is vested in Congress.

On the one hand the impeachment power reflects the fact that the legislative branch will predominate within any democratic government; but on the other hand it ensures that the legislature will be forced, in taking power from the national majority's representative, to defend its actions publicly, since its members would be loath to impeach a president whom they could not simultaneously make the people despise. Thus Congress was not to be able to encroach upon the executive power with stealth. An impeachment battle cuts both ways: It compels both Congress and the president to make their cases in public, leaving the people to pass ultimate judgment as they do in periodic elections.

The president's power is not, then, the prerogative of despots. Despots can not rise above the law, for they are the law. But the people are the ultimate source of ordinary law in America, and the extraordinary power of the American executive—like his ordinary powers—is a function of his ability to muster and maintain popular support.

Insuring Responsibility

One further attribute of the single executive, as opposed to the many-headed Congress, is responsibility. In one sense this means accountability. Congressmen can escape accountability for even the most consequential disasters. (Who ever was held responsible for the fall of South Vietnam in 1975, which Congress forbade President Ford to prevent? Nobody.) The president, assuming he can act, lacks this luxury. It is useful in this context to contrast Congress with England's Parliament: While the Prime Minister serves at its pleasure, he also takes genuine authority from it. The majority in Parliament supports or abandons the Prime Minister, fully knowing that its composition, and the seats of each of its members, are entirely at risk. Authority and responsibility are thereby shared in equal proportions, and accountability to the people is preserved. Not so in Congress, whose majority can—and do, as we shall see—avoid the second, and destroy the third, if they can steal the first.

But there is another, albeit related, sense of the word, as Harvey C. Mansfield, Jr., has pointed out: "Responsibility is a term apparently coined by Madison (see his use of it in regard to the Senate, *Federalist* 63) to mean, not only 'accountable' or 'responsive,' to the people, but also to take responsibility out of their hands on their behalf: responsible politicians in this sense do for the people what they cannot do for themselves but can form a judgment about."[6] And what better example of this could there be than an executive bringing prerogative to bear at a time of great danger to the nation's security?

Using Executive Prerogative

The precedents most fitting in this regard must be distinguished from repeated assertions of executive power in our history that have gone without serious challenge. When President Truman, for example, ignored Congress in initiating the Korean War, he no doubt ruffled some congressional feathers. But in most times, as in his, no crisis will ensue from such executive behavior because the policy itself will be judged right by an essentially unified government. But this was not the case when, in the year between the fall of France in 1940 and the German invasion of Russia in 1941, Britain's defeat by Hitler appeared probable. At that time, the American Congress, holding to its policy of neutrality, had acted to prevent President Roosevelt from aiding Churchill's Britain in its embattled and lonely cause. The president deemed that the loss to Germany of Britain's fleet, combined with the German alliances then in effect and the German conquests theretofore, would render the defense of our country untenable. So he arranged, by a simple executive order which many considered illegal, to transfer 50 American destroyers to Britain. He believed this his duty, statutory prohibitions notwithstanding; he risked impeachment by his action, but took that risk to fulfill his oath of office.

An even greater example of prerogative, exhibited in America's greatest crisis, was set by President Lincoln who, with Congress out of session in 1861, called up troops, had Southern ports blockaded, and suspended the writ of *habeas corpus*. In the last, he refused to accept a writ issued by the Chief Justice of the United States, defending this in terms of his duty to preserve the Union: ". . .are all the laws but one to go unexecuted," he asked, "and the government itself go to pieces, lest that one be violated?"[7]

The Constitution clearly allows such actions by its vagueness about the limits of executive power. But it does not, and it could not, do more. It does not read like directions for assembling a cart because it was not constituting a government to act as a machine. In the end, the constitutional right of any president to wield great authority—whether over foreign or domestic policy—is his right to engage on behalf of the nation's majority in such political struggles as befit a democratic regime; his right and his duty.

In 1936, President Roosevelt was challenged for banning the sale of weapons to warring countries in South America. The Supreme Court, in *U.S. v. Curtiss-Wright Export Co.* turned back this challenge, citing a "very delicate, plenary and exclusive power of the president as the sole organ of the federal government in the field of international relations"—and acknowledging in the process that this foreign policy power would exist even if the Constitution were silent on it, as it arises of necessity from nationhood. The relationship between necessity and the executive power was the theme as well of a letter by Thomas

Jefferson in 1810, responding to the query, "whether circumstances do not sometimes occur, which makes it a duty in officers of high trust, to assume authorities beyond the law. . . ." Of higher obligation than "strict observance of the written laws," Jefferson answered, are "the laws of necessity, of self-preservation, of saving our country when in danger." Sacrificing the requirements of the latter to those of the former, he continued, entails "absurdly sacrificing the end to the means."[8]

Necessity, self-preservation, the salvation of our liberal democracy. Even the anti-Federalists—one of whose great concerns regarding the Constitution during the debates over ratification was the single, independent executive—by and large ended up supporting ratification, as they could see no alternative to it in light of these requirements. Returning to the topic of Iran-Contra in this light, it would be a far more interesting (not to mention difficult) psychological task to determine the motivations of those in recent congressional majorities, than those of the men who did what was needed to forestall the entrenchment of a Soviet-proxy state in Central America—an entrenchment, as the president had stated, that could render null and void America's capacity to react to Soviet invasions of Western Europe or the Middle East, by tying us down in a defense of our own borders.

THE EXECUTIVE UNDER SIEGE

On May 25, 1988, after his team's second straight romp over the Dallas Mavericks in the final round of the NBA Western Division play-offs, Los Angeles Laker backup center Mychal Thompson remarked: "When the Lakers make up their minds to do something, we're like congressmen, we get it done"; not the country, or the president, but congressmen. Everyone seems to know the score in Washington today. How did it come about?

Foreign Policy by Committee

In the area of foreign policy, of course, the War Powers Act looms large in any such discussion. Passed over President Nixon's veto in 1973, its specific provisions are generally well known: it sets limits on the president's ability to send troops into imminent danger of hostility without Congress's prior approval; within or without those limits, it requires the president to consult with Congress when possible, and to report to Congress in any case; it requires the president to disengage troops from hostilities within 60 or 90 days in the absence of a war declaration; and it requires such removal upon a concurrent resolution by Congress, not subject to a presidential veto. Many have argued that certain of these provisions—particularly the latter—are unconstitutional. But in a sense such arguments are irrelevant; the larger significance of the War Powers Act, too little remarked on, is its implicit (and gloriously unconstitutional) assumption that Congress, as opposed to the Constitution itself, is the fount of presidential power.

The War Powers Act's chief congressional sponsors acknowledged openly during floor debate that it represented a break with precedent going back to the first years of the republic. Indeed, in at least 317 cases, between 1798 and 1970, "the president sent troops into imminent hostilities or transferred arms or other war materials abroad without any congressional authority."[9] The backdrop for this momentous break was formed by Watergate on the one hand, and the waning of the Vietnam War (by that time unpopular) on the other; rightly or wrongly, each acted to undermine public confidence in the executive branch.

Given this setting, it is not surprising that Congress kept coming. The Bingham Amendment in 1974, for instance, gave congress veto power over arms sales involving more than $25 million. (In 1976, this figure was reduced to $9 million.) And whereas in the past only a few members of Congress had even the slightest idea about the CIA's budget, strict regulations requiring congressional oversight and control of America's intelligence operations were soon imposed. Over the next decade, former Senator John Tower noted more than 150 constraints placed by Congress on the exercise of executive power.[10]

Unprecedented use of the power of the purse to control foreign policy left its mark as well. In the 30 years prior to 1973, our country was engaged in three wars and numerous other conflicts involving military force; during that period, no appropriation for military purposes was denied the executive by Congress. But since 1973, it has been very difficult for the president to obtain even the smallest amounts of money from Congress.

In terms of foreign policy, congressional government has resulted in precisely what one would expect, given the arguments for separation of powers and an independent executive as outlined above. The government has neither the capacity to act with dispatch, to present a united front to the world, nor to keep secrets.

Congress's capacity for keeping mum has become an international joke, even (if not especially) with the most delicate security considerations involved. As the executive reports the CIA's doings to congressional intelligence committees, for instance, they become quickly known to the Washington press corps, an act that can be accomplished either under the table or blatantly: Consider the surreal spectacle of the protracted debates in the early 1980s—in public sessions of Congress, through the newspapers, and on TV talk shows—over the question of "covert" action in Central America.

Nor has Congress shown itself capable of steadiness in policy. In contrast to President Reagan's unflagging support of the Contras, Congress altered its Nicaraguan policy over a decade as if by whim. In 1977 and 1978, it appropriated aid to President Somoza. When the communist Sandinistas came to power, it sent them $100 million in 1979 and 1980. In 1983 it appropriated $24 million to the rebel Contras, but in 1984 blocked such aid with the notorious Boland Amendment. In 1985 it waffled, voting first against and then for Contra aid, repealing Boland. In 1986 it voted to send the Contras $100 million, but backed off from its support throughout 1987, until in early 1988 it again withdrew support and effectively appeared to end the Contra cause.

As for dispatch, consider the following paradigmatic scenario in November 1986: The Sandinista government in Managua was moving troops into southern Honduras to attack the Contra's main camps before the $100 million Congress had voted for the Contras could be translated into arms, and new SA-14 ground to air missiles were arriving in Nicaragua from Moscow; but the CIA was holding up military shipments to the Contras to ensure that all congressional requirements were met, and representatives of the Government Accounting Office were sent in their stead to inspect the Contras' financial records.[11]

Who Controls the Bureaucracy?

When the Department of Foreign Affairs (soon renamed State) was created by the First Congress in 1789—as one of the two original executive departments, along with Treasury—it was placed unambiguously at the president's bidding. But as recent Congresses have stridently insisted on their right to scrutinize every aspect of executive policy, and to impose limits upon and guidelines for it at will, the executive bureaucracy—now comprising many departments, each bloated in size—has become Congress's tool. In the foreign policy realm, for instance, the State Department has come increasingly to depend on and respond more to Congress than to its titular boss. Consider the following newspaper account from the early days of Iran-Contra: "In blunt and highly unusual congressional testimony, the State Department's second-ranking official, John Whitehead . . .sharply questioned the wisdom of shipping arms to Iran, [and] contradicted Mr. Reagan himself on many key points." Perhaps even more shocking is that Whitehead "called [on Congress] for a review of the extent to which the [National Security Council, or NSC] which traditionally advises the President, should be involved in operations."[12] Of course the State Department, in inviting Congress to investigate the president's office, plays in part an old game. The foreign service—professional and tenured—has always felt itself the fixed guardian of our foreign relations and has sought independence from executives who come and go. But coupled now with the onslaught of congressional government, it amounts to open rebellion. This new political dispensation once led President Nixon to describe State Department personnel as "the striped-pants faggots in Foggy Bottom."[13]

The Executive Response

It should come as no surprise, then, that the NSC—established by the National Security Act of 1947 to help coordinate foreign, domestic, and military policies in the executive—has risen to prominence in the White House, or that it is now under attack by Congress. Presidents have been increasingly compelled to resort to quasi-official or even unofficial channels in order to carry out their constitutional functions; thus President Nixon's famous "plumbers," originally set up to stop and even circumvent the plethora of "leaks" from official executive branch agencies. Thus too the use of the NSC in carrying out controversial presidential policies—an NSC which is largely insulated both from congressional oversight and from the larger executive departments. Its staff, as aides to the president, are not subject to Senate confirmation, are not normally called before congressional committees. Its files are kept separate from the central White House files. As NSC Advisor, for example, Henry Kissinger was able to lay the groundwork for President Nixon's opening of relations with mainland China during a secret trip in 1971; similarly, President Reagan used the NSC to prepare his presentation of the Strategic Defense Initiative to the American people without the prior knowledge of those in the bureaucracy—not to mention Congress—who opposed it, and who could and would very likely have undermined it in advance.

If the truth be told, clandestine operations by the NSC staff closely resemble the mode of the older executive branch, and so from a constitutional perspective are more a bugbear than a problem. But as an obstacle to congressional government, they have come under fire.

In October 1984, when Congress discontinued Contra aid and the president remarked that America must still not "break faith" with the Contra cause, it was only certain members of the NSC who took him at his word. This precipitated the Iran-Contra "scandal," in the wake of which many arguments were made in Congress for curtailing the NSC's independence. Some said the appointment of the National Security Advisor should be made subject to Senate confirmation; others that its charter should be amended to restrict the NSC to a purely advisory role. (Presently, the NSC is free to perform "other such functions as the president may direct.") But these moves will likely be unnecessary; Congress has many weapons at its disposal already—including especially its use of the criminal law to punish executive branch members who thwart its will—that serve very effectively to intimidate such members who may not yet know their place.

THE IDEOLOGICAL DIMENSION OF CONGRESSIONAL ENCROACHMENT

What explains the battle over control of foreign policy that crowns the attack on the American executive branch? In a sense it reflects a tendency of Congress foreseen by the Framers, a tendency to confuse opposition to its own will—even by a man elected by a national majority—with despotism. "The representatives of the people, in a popular assembly, seem sometimes to fancy that they are the people themselves, and betray strong symptoms of impatience and disgust at the least sign of opposition from any other quarter" (*Federalist* 71). But in another sense it reflects a development the Framers could not possibly have foreseen.

The War Powers Act would not have prevented American involvement in Vietnam, which received congressional sanction in 1964. But what of the liberation of Grenada in October 1983? Had there not been American medical students on that island— allowing the president to claim that American lives were in imminent danger—it could not have occurred under the terms of the Act without prior congressional consent. Considering the criticism of the invasion at the time by leaders of the congressional majority—criticism quickly stifled by the uprising of public delight in the operation's success—it is debatable whether this approval could have been obtained. But the more important question concerns the highest purpose of the Grenada invasion: Was it to rescue American medical students, or was it to deny Cuba (and its Soviet sponsor) another base in the Caribbean from which to threaten U.S. security? Why should the president be free to act independently for the one, but not the other? Do not such questions suggest that congressional limitations on the executive are born of a disagreement concerning the ends of national policy—in this case of foreign policy—rather than, as most of those involved would have us believe, a disagreement over procedures or means? Indeed, only in a government so morally divided could one imagine Congress treating a chief executive with the adversarial vigor we have witnessed in recent years.

The End of Bipartisan Consensus

At the U.S.-Soviet Summit in May 1988, General Secretary of the Communist Party Gorbachev reportedly made many "favorable references to the role of Congress in impeding the war efforts of presidents."[14] This ought to remind us of the backdrop for the institutional struggle over foreign policy within our government: a world divided between noncommunist nations, many of whom are formally allied with the United States, and the Soviet Empire, which comprises not only the Warsaw Pact countries but also many of the so-called "nonaligned nations." America's place in this division became firmly secured in February 1947, when Great Britain in effect passed the torch: Greece was devastated by war and facing a communist revolution supported from without; Turkey was extremely weak economically and facing a direct threat from the Soviet Union; and England's government informed America it would no longer be able to help these two of its traditional allies. Thus was initiated one of the most remarkably successful periods of American foreign policy, encompassing passage of the Greek-Turkish aid bill, the political intervention in Italy to prevent a communist takeover, the Berlin blockade, the organization of NATO, the Marshall Plan, and the Truman Doctrine.

With the help of Republican Senator Arthur Vandenberg, President Truman gained bipartisan support for his policy of containing communism; this meant disengaging the Republican Party in Congress from its longstanding commitment to isolationism—an isolationism rooted, many have noted, in the American tradition going back at least to George Washington's Farewell Address.

President Washington had advised his countrymen to steer clear of entanglement in the European power struggles of the time, counsel clearly predicated on two circumstances: the weakness and immaturity of the United States, and its physical isolation. That we were weak meant that such entanglement could spell our doom; that we were immature meant that our national character and institutions might be corrupted by it; that we were physically isolated meant that we could be isolated politically and militarily, while increasing commercial ties with all. "With me," Washington wrote,

> a predominant motive has been to endeavor to give time for our country to settle and mature its yet recent institutions, and to progress without interruption, to that degree of strength and consistency, which is necessary to give it, humanly speaking, the command of its own fortunes.[15]

Truman was able to gain bipartisan support for containment largely because, by the mid-twentieth century, two world wars had made clear that the circumstances holding sway in the early years of the republic were no more. The United States was no longer physically isolated, given technological advances in such fields as communication, transportation, and weaponry; American institutions were settled and mature; and America was suddenly very powerful, having indeed "command of its own fortunes." In addition we were confronted with necessity: the specter of universal tyranny had arisen with modern ideologies, made all the more fearsome by modern technology, and the United States was the only world power equal to the challenge.

The spectacle of an American Speaker of the House of Representatives opening private negotiations with a communist president of a Central American Soviet client-state—in fact advising him in his adversarial relations with the American president—as we witnessed in the Winter of 1987-88, is but one recent sign that this bipartisan commitment to containment is no more. At present, the Democratic majority in Congress stands in extreme opposition to the Republican president, representing something more than just a different party in the ordinary American sense; for today, as only three or four times previously in our history, the great parties are opposed in regard to the most fundamental political issues—issues that bear upon our very purpose as a nation. One of these is Central American communism. As Jim Wright's machinations with Daniel Ortega indicate, disagreement in this regard is not—as once it was, *vis-a-vis* Asia—a practical matter of where to draw the containing line, or in terms of what America's security demands and what

American capability allows. It is instead the question of the morality of effective anti-communism that divides our parties and thus our institutions.

Rejecting the Founding Fathers

As opposed to George Washington's isolationism, a better model for understanding today's might be that of the early Progressive intellectual and essayist, William Graham Sumner. Briefly stated, Sumner elevated the isolationist argument from the level of prudential counsel based on particular circumstances, to that of imperative principle. Underlying this elevation was a rejection of America's original principles, the rejection itself grounded in moral relativism.

What distinguished American democracy for Sumner, insofar as ours remained different from the many corrupt nations of the earth, was that we lacked the illusory conviction of superiority which might lead us to imperialism. The extent of what we have to learn from our revolutionary origins is respect for the right of national self-determination. We hear clear echoes of such sentiments today, as in claims that we become like our enemies simply by using similar methods—for example, spying, or covertly attempting to topple foreign governments—regardless of how our purposes may differ.

The chief difference between Sumner and present-day isolationists is that he fully understood and acknowledged his abhorrence for the American Founders, and especially for their natural law principles, that underlay his isolationism. "The authority of the fathers of our republic," he wrote in this context, "may well be sacrificed without regret"; and he admitted to being "afraid of the great principles" of the Founding, and that he "would make no fight on their behalf."[16] The Founders—not to mention those throughout our history who were wont to speak of America as a redeemer nation, "a shining city on the hill"—did clearly believe ours superior to other nations, on the basis of its being founded upon self-evident truths, universal principles of right. (This is what justified the American Revolution in their eyes.) And while the example of Washington, for one, demonstrates that such belief in America's superiority does not require foreign adventurism, it is admittedly this belief that would assure us—should we by necessity or choice act abroad, upon our principles and in our interest—that such action is for the good.

One can begin to see the connections between the institutional battle over U.S. foreign policy and the larger attack on executive power that undermines the original purposes of separated powers generally. Consider the argument made during congressional debate over Contra aid in February 1988: While admitting that the communist Sandinista government denies civil liberties, Senator Christopher Dodd (D-CT) recalled that neither has American government been spotless in this regard; and what he mentioned as proof positive was, remarkably, not slavery, which existed counter to constitutional principles, but President Lincoln's suspension of habeas corpus upon the outbreak of the Southern secession. What could better illustrate the aversion at the heart of the attack on the executive's standing within the framework of separated powers—an aversion to morally principled constitutionalism—than the revival of this old Confederate saw by a modern congressional liberal?

The effective exercise of executive power in any regime must presuppose agreement that its ends—and we have suggested that its highest end is the active defense of the regime's constitution against its enemies—are proper and good; that they are worth defending. It is the loss of this type of an agreement that underlies the crisis in the separation of powers outlined above.

STEMMING THE TIDE

The chief characteristic of the modern movement to transform the presidency into a sort of clerkship is its nonpartisan guise— in truth a disguise, for it is nothing if not partisan; and therein lies the key to its possible defeat.

Refocusing the Public Debate

The American government as originally constituted, in order to be effective, must be united in all its parts upon the basic ends of foreign and domestic policy. Only the people can elect a government that is so united, and this only after there is an open and vigorous political battle, during which their allegiance is sought by the contending parties. But here is the heart of the bizarre situation we now face: Although our government is radically divided, the public is not listening to arguments about the rights and wrongs of national policy or the rights and wrongs of separation of powers. Instead, as in Iran-Contra, it sees lawyers being assembled, and courts starting to work, and various administration figures being hounded and harried by congressional committees—all over "nonpartisan" legal or procedural details.

In effect, the congressional majority foreordained something like the Iran-Contra "scandal" by attempting to hog-tie the president with the Boland Amendment. But this fateful and significant law was passed without public debate, tacked onto a gargantuan continuing budget resolution, allowing Congress to maintain the pretense that the president was responsible for any consequences: at the outbreak of Iran-Contra, Senator Robert Byrd remarked with what must have been feigned indignation, "What this says is that nobody seems to be really in charge of the foreign policy of this country."

One can observe similar tactics, and thus begin to grasp the congressional majority's strategy, on several other battlegrounds as well. Take, for example, bureaucracy. Since 1968, national majorities have consistently elected presidents who campaigned against bureaucracy. But in the meantime bureaucracy has flourished, because Congress has thwarted any and all presidential attempts to act against it. And yet members of Congress—and here, in particular, of the House of Representatives—are not held accountable for this; indeed, when they return to their districts every two years, they criticize the bureaucracy and present themselves as the indispensable instruments by which the red tape associated with it can be overcome. They have assembled for themselves large personal staffs and budgets, and they are now the expediters of social security checks, welfare payments, student aid applications, farm subsidies, etc. And a grateful electorate short-sightedly rewards this cynical game in election after election.

Thus Congress is—and most members of Congress are—able to avoid responsibility for the most important things that it does and they do.[17] (The stunning success of this post-1965 congressional strategy was confirmed again in the 1986 election, in which a record 98 percent of all incumbents running in the House of Representatives were reelected.) It has found a way to perpetuate its rule without persuading the people by doing public battle over controversial issues with the president—who, in "Washingtonese," is cut out of the policy loop. As a result, the national majority is left with no one to act for them and with no one to blame for inaction (or bad action, as the case may be). Increasingly frustrated, they vote in ever decreasing numbers, retreating instead into the sphere of simply private concerns—a development that is no accident.

The assault on executive independence is inseparable from the struggle to replace political government with bureaucracy—with the administrative or welfare state (see Chapter 3). As Tocqueville described it, this state—which has proved perfectly compatible with so-called interest group liberalism, reflected by the above-mentioned appeals of congressmen—seeks to cultivate private, to the detriment of public, concerns within the nation. Indeed, undermining public spiritedness is the *sine qua non* of its ascendancy. As Tocqueville presented it, the administrative state would become "an immense, protective power which is alone responsible for securing [the people's] enjoyment and watching over their fate. ... It likes to see the citizens enjoy themselves, provided they think of nothing but enjoyment;" yet it "daily makes the exercise of free choice less useful and rarer, restricts the activity of free will within a narrower compass, and little by little robs each citizen of his own faculties."[18] In other words, the architects and rulers of this new state will trade the people absolute security, along with what appears to be complete private freedom (to those who "think of nothing but enjoyment"), for the sort of political freedom embodied in the American system of representation.

Reviving the Separation of Powers

In thinking about how to stem the tide of these developments, we must see first that what stands between American democracy and the administrative state—or the victory of interest group liberalism in redefining the country's character—is the separation of powers. For the concerns about which the executive and legislative branches will clash, given a healthy separation, will necessarily go beyond pluralistic concerns to questions of principle; questions about what America stands for as a whole. In the deepest sense, the battle to squash the executive—to get beyond separated powers and establish legislative-administrative supremacy—is a battle to get beyond these questions of the principles of public right. So long as they persist—and here foreign policy is paramount; for as Sumner understood, the ability of the American executive to act energetically abroad hinges in every instance on the understanding that the nation is worthy of whatever defense is necessary, based on these very principles— politics itself will persist.

Second, we must understand that only a president is in a position to lead a defense of the separation of powers—that is, a defense of the constitutional standing of his own office within the separation of powers—under prevailing circumstances. This would require inciting a political brouhaha, forcing those who have undermined his office to show their partisan hand, and involving the people once again in affecting national policy. Specifically, it would require refusing to have his office investigated (and thus intimidated) by "nonpartisan" independent counsels when controversies arise.

Imagine, for instance, if the president had addressed Congress this way, at the outset of Iran-Contra in November 1986:

> The reported operations of those within my compass were in accord with my stated policies and absolutely within the bounds of my constitutional power as chief executive. I take responsibility for them without apology. There is no more reason under the sun, then, for further investigations of how things occurred, or of who knew what when, within the executive branch of government, which is my domain. I have revealed what I can within the constraints of national security. Your argument is thus with me, and you are left with an obvious path of action. You can, and should, attack me politically, in speeches before the people. You can conduct your hearings into the operation of the executive branch. My people who customarily appear before Congress will continue to come and explain my policy and as many of the details as the nation's interest will permit. But these hearings will not be of the judicial character that you now propose.

Or perhaps you wish this to be a judicial, as well as a political quarrel. In that case you have your impeachment power, and if you are so inclined, you may surely use it. But to do so in a manner that is clearly partisan and political will display a spirit to our people that you may not wish to defend in public. And remember that whatever you do, I will be taking my case to the people, and debating you on its political merits.

Needed: Uncommon Courage

It would take uncommon courage today for a president to act in this fashion. All of the established powers in society, after all, would work in concert against him. (Consider, for example, how the media now feels itself ripe to decide whether what a president chooses to say in a speech to the nation deserves broadcasting; and how members of the congressional opposition are given equal time to respond to presidential addresses, as was not the case—for instance, after FDR's fireside chats—when the president's standing as chief of state was understood and respected.) But surely to wage political warfare is not too much to ask of a man in his station, given the high stakes involved. Certainly it is what the Framers would have expected; it is fair to say that while they may not have been confident that a future president would have sufficient constitutional firepower to withstand the encroachment of a corrupt and despotic Congress, they never imagined that he would simply acquiesce in the emasculation of his office, as has been the recent pattern.

A serious student of the psychology of American politics today would have to explain this pattern of acquiescence in addition to the spirit of rancor directed at executive power on the other side. Both perhaps involve a loss of will, resulting from forgetfulness or rejection of the moral purposes of constitutional government (not to mention life itself). Something on that order might have to account for how in America—where not that long ago the cowboy served as a symbol of independence and virtue—the term "cowboy operation" has taken on a derogatory connotation not just among bureaucrats, but among most of our leaders; how paperwork, and the tedium and delay it imposes, has become the mark of American government; how the distinction between government and bureaucracy has become clouded, so that the proper role of the president, the active arm of our government, evokes such angst-ridden debate.

We have suggested what is needed. It may be added that even should a resolute executive lose in a head-on battle with his foes, he might still have served the nation in exemplary fashion. By forcing the congressional majority to become openly partisan or political, and thus controversial, he will have given it a face, and those within it names. Even in victory, they would be held accountable for the consequences of their actions from then on; the people would have a vista upon which to look and be pleased, or to look and be angry, and act to rectify. The assertion of the Founders would be vindicated in their conviction that in case of conflict between the legislative and executive branches, the people shall judge.

The prerequisite for a defense of the American executive is a revival of candid and manly partisanship—understood not in a narrow sense, but as partisanship to the moral principles at once reflected in and served by the American Constitution—both at home and abroad. Its domestic revival is necessarily prior, however; for when all is said and done, the highest purpose of defending the presidency is not so much that we reenable it to preserve our mere existence, but that, live or die, we will do so as free citizens of the American republic, and not—as Tocqueville described the subjects of the administrative state—"a multitude of men. . .constantly circling around in pursuit of. . .petty and banal pleasures," of whom "one can say [they have] not got a fatherland."[19]

Notes

1. See "A Bicentennial Analysis of the American Political Structure," issued by The Committee on the Constitutional System, Washington, D.C., January 1987.

2. James Madison, "Helvidius Letter No. 1," in *The Mind of the Founder: Sources of the Political Thought of James Madison*, ed. Marvin Meyers (Hanover: Brandeis University Press, 1981), p. 204.

3. Thomas Jefferson, *Notes on the State of Virginia*, in *The Portable Thomas Jefferson*, ed. Merrill D. Peterson (New York: Penguin, 1977), p. 164.

4. Max Farrand, ed., *The Records of the Federal Convention of 1787*, Vol. II (New Haven: Yale University Press, 1966), p. 35.

5. Alexander Hamilton, "Pacificus No. 1," in *Selected Writings and Speeches of Alexander Hamilton*, ed. Morton J. Frisch (Washington: American Enterprise Institute, 1985), p. 401.

6. Harvey C. Mansfield, Jr., "Republicanizing the Executive," in *Saving the Revolution: The Federalist Papers and the American Founding*, ed. Charles R. Kesler (New York: The Free Press, 1987), p. 181.

7. See Harry V. Jaffa, "What President Reagan Ought to Do," an article syndicated by Public Research, Syndicated, in *The New Federalist Papers*, Claremont, 7 January 1987.

8. Thomas Jefferson, *The Writings of Thomas Jefferson*, ed. Andrew A. Lipscomb, Vol. XII (The Thomas Jefferson Memorial Foundation, 1904), p. 418.

9. See the list appended to L. Gordon Crovitz, "Presidents Have a History of Unilateral Moves," *Wall Street Journal*, 15 January, 1987.

10. Cited in John Norton Moore, "The Constitution, Foreign Policy, and Deterrence: The Separation of Powers in a Dangerous World," The Heritage Lectures No. 82, 1986, p. 3.

11. Doyle McManus, "Contras Leader Complains of Delays in Arms," *Los Angeles Times*, 21 November, 1986.

12. Robert S. Greenberger and Jane Meyer, "Schulz's Top Aide Blasts Reagan Staff," *Wall Street Journal*, 25 November, 1986.

13. Hedrick Smith, *The Power Game: How Washington Works* (New York: Random House, 1988), p. 600.

14. Fred Barnes, "Friendly Gambits," *The New Republic*, 27 June, 1988, p. 12.

15. George Washington, *George Washington: A Collection*, ed. William B. Allen (Indianapolis: Liberty Classics, 1988), p. 527.

16. William Graham Sumner, "The Conquest of the United States by Spain," in *The Conquest of the United States by Spain and Other Essays*, ed. Murray Polner (Chicago: Regnery Gateway), p. 166.

17. For a fuller account of this revolution in American politics, see Morris Fiorina, *Congress—Keystone of the Washington Establishment* (New Haven: Yale University Press, 1977).

18. Alexis de Tocqueville, *Democracy in America*, ed. J.P. Mayer (Garden City: Doubleday, 1969), p. 692.

19. Ibid, p. 692.

3. Bureaucratizing the American Government

JOHN ADAMS WETTERGREEN

Conservatives have often charged that the great centralizing tendencies in American government were a product of the New Deal. As Dr. Wettergreen shows in this essay, the true culprit was not FDR but LBJ, as the full bureaucratization of American government did not take place until the 1960s. Dr. Wettergreen makes a further useful distinction, grounded in the writings of Alexis de Tocqueville and Max Weber, between "governance" and "administration." In Dr. Wettergreen's view, the centralization of governance is justified, but the centralization of administration is terribly threatening to the liberties of Americans.

Conservative Americans, almost as commonly as those on the left, are inclined to believe that bureaucracy is a necessity of modern government. According to this conventional wisdom, the bureaucratization of America has been going on—inevitably—for over a century. This conviction is decidedly pessimistic: after all, "bureaucracy" is a pejorative term. No matter how much we might try to use it with a neutral sense, its connotations of vapid formality, mindless routinization, and obtuse impersonality shine through. Even the greatest defender of bureaucracy, Max Weber, confessed that this form of rule is inhuman. In considering bureaucratization, then, we must ask whether modern government can be good government. Nevertheless, American government today is more highly bureaucratized than ever before, and it is likely to become more so. American government today, due to this, is not good government. By practical standards, the United States has been well governed throughout most of its history. In the past, we have had a government which, by and large, sought the consent of the governed on the great issues of the day. We were blessed by national statesmen—Washington, Jefferson, Madison, Lincoln, Theodore Roosevelt, Franklin Roosevelt, and many others—who actively sought political responsibility before the electorate for what they proposed to do, because they intended to do great things, and great things were done. Among these accomplishments were in particular, the ending of the scourge of slavery, the building of a great modern nation unrivaled for civil and religious liberty, and the victory in a global war against barbarism. Moreover, the nation's great injustices could at least be recognized as such, because such public principles as "all men are created equal" were popularly venerated.

Today, however, we have a government skilled in obfuscation. Elected officials are so intent upon avoiding responsibility that even the "regular Statement and Account of the Receipts and Expenditures of all public Money," which the Constitution directs to "be published from time to time," is a multi-volume monster—one so huge that it requires yet another volume to interpret it authoritatively. Representatives and senators freely admit that they do not know what was in the 1987 Omnibus Continuing Resolution, Our office holders are so far from accomplishing grand objectives that America cannot even protect its borders from drug runners, much less seal them against migrant workers or other foreign elements. Moreover, even if our public principles of right are still popularly venerated, we now have an injustice unmatched since the days of slavery, a national policy of systematic racial inequality called Affirmative Action, which goes virtually unopposed in the highest public counsels. If this catalog of governmental ills does not fit the political taste of all educated people, it could be amended to satisfy almost everyone, for almost all people today understand that our country is not well governed. For example, James L. Sundquist of the left-liberal Brookings Institution has been maintaining since 1980 that American government is "incompetent."[1]

Of course, not all would agree with the thesis of this essay: that the most serious ills of American government are due to bureaucratization; to what political scientists call "centralization of administration." Beyond that, and contrary to what is ordinarily supposed, centralization of administration in the United States is not a century-old, inevitable trend, but a creature of the choices made well within living memory. It is important to understand, in other words, that the "Great Society" of Lyndon Johnson is the true father of our present troubles, far more than is the New Deal of Franklin Roosevelt. This point is important, not because Johnson is more easily despised than Roosevelt, but because it correctly explains what is the root of bureaucracy in America.

WHAT IS BUREAUCRACY?

The two most common definitions of bureaucracy need to be understood, and rejected before we can see some of the simple truths of contemporary American government. First is the notion that any large, public organization is a bureaucracy. This definition misses the universal disapprobation that goes to the heart of the bureaucratic phenomenon. Furthermore, it is relativistic in the extreme: how large is large? Tacitus tells us that the Roman Empire, at its peak during the reign of Augustus Caesar, was administered by 1,800 officials, fewer than the state of Nevada. Was imperial Roman administration large enough to be bureaucratic? Furthermore, we all have had experience with very small organizations—the registrar's office at almost any college or university, for example—that are as bureaucratic as the Internal Revenue Service. Conversely, vast public organizations—Napoleon's army at its best, or Tammany Hall or the Mormon Church—are said to be remarkably nonbureaucratic, for reasons which will soon become clear.

The second standard definition of bureaucracy is usually associated with a twentieth-century ideologue by the name of Max Weber. In one form or another, this is the definition preferred by today's intellectuals. Weber thought of bureaucracy as *the* modern form of political organization. Every aspect of modern everyday life is cut to fit the bureaucratic framework.

Bureaucracy is, Weber supposed, always the most rational type of rule, because under the bureaucratic form of rule all must be treated the same, without any preference given on account of kinship, friendship, neighborliness, or other forms of personal attachment. Such "neutralization" is the bureaucratic ideal of fairness.

Furthermore, bureaucratic administration is professional, both in the sense that being a bureaucrat is a career and in that specialized training, knowledge, and experience, rather than kinship, election, or any other form of subjective preference form the basis for appointment and tenure in office. To meet the needs of modern society, Weber held, bureaucratic administration is completely indispensable. To suppose otherwise is to be guilty of "dilettantism."[2]

To Weber, bureaucratization was "the most crucial phenomenon of the modern Western state."[3] He conceived of bureaucracy as the modern system of rule, not merely a part of government (e.g., a "fourth branch") or a part of society (i.e., an interest group, vocation, or profession). As Weber saw it, bureaucracy is the final or ultimate form of rule, the expression of the highest Western value, "rationality." If there are any problems with bureaucratic rule (and Weber thought there were many), they only reveal what are, to Weber, the ultimate, insoluble problems of human existence.

Weber's Bureaucracy Meets Reality

The power of Weber's argument for bureaucracy is easily underestimated. In the political and governmental world as well as among intellectuals, today's models of bureaucracy are invariably Weberian. Yet, almost anyone who has had to contend with bureaucratic rule will tell you that this understanding barely accords with reality. Characteristically, bureaucracy is not rational, but arbitrary; it is neither efficient nor objective, but officious. Our purpose here does not permit a demonstration of the theoretical unsoundness of Weber's understanding of bureaucracy. Instead we consider a massive practical misjudgment, which identifies the inadequacies of Weber's (and the common) view and illuminates Alexis de Tocqueville's more adequate understanding of bureaucracy.

Weber admired very much the moral type that is peculiar to bureaucracy: the professional administrator, whose personal interests are objective, universal, scientific. This admiration caused him to misconstrue American political reality. "As late as the early 1900s," Weber remarked in deep puzzlement, ". . . American workers of English origin. . .allowed themselves to be governed by party henchmen who were often open to corruption." Looking at the big city party machines like Tammany Hall in New York, Weber assumed that they were mass parties like those he knew in Europe:

> The increasingly bureaucratic organization of all genuine mass parties offers the most striking example of the role of sheer quantity as a leverage for the bureaucratization of a social structure. In the United States, both parties since Jackson's administration have developed bureaucratically.[4]

In other words, Weber thought that the American parties were "under the leadership of professionals or experts" as distinguished from "traditional notable rule based upon personal relationships and personal esteem."[5] Thus, a dogmatic political assumption bred Weber's conviction that bureaucracy is the ultimate form of rule: "Bureaucracy inevitably accompanies modern mass democracy. . . ."[6]

The Importance of Nonbureaucratic Authority

Like his idea that nineteenth-century American democracy was "mass democracy," Weber's view of American parties as bureaucratized, mass parties is wrong.

He examined nineteenth-century American (democratic) decentralized administration, but he could not see its nonbureaucratic character, perhaps because the nonbureaucratic rulers he was looking at were not "local notables" with titles of nobility but rather leading men of the people. Seeing the unprofessional patronage system that they operated, Weber concluded that American nonbureaucratic rulers were corrupt, partisan henchmen. This judgment does an enormous injustice to such partisans as George Washington Plunkitt of Tammany Hall, a classic example of a modern American machine politician and also a local notable whose rule was based upon personal relationships and personal esteem.

At the root of Weber's misjudgment is his disjunction of professional or specialized leadership from nonbureaucratic authority. This disjunction excludes the possibility that there could be rulers who make a living by acquiring personal relationships and personal esteem. This, of course, is precisely what the urban machine politicians did.

Consider Plunkitt's description of how to begin a career in politics:

> Did I get up a book on municipal government. . .? I wasn't such a fool. What I did was get some marketable goods. What do I mean by marketable goods? Let me tell you: I had a cousin. I went to him and said, "Tommy, I'm goin' to be a politician, and I want a followin', can I count on you?" He said, "Sure, George." That's how I started in business. I got a marketable commodity—one vote.[7]

The vulgarity, greed, brutality, and ambition of the American party machines ought not be allowed to conceal the fact that these parties were founded on personal attachments of kinship, friendship, and neighborliness. Accordingly, their hatred of bureaucracy was absolutely intransigent, as a quick look at Plunkitt's work would show.

The machine politicians were also antibureaucratic in their contempt for scientific learning and professional expertise and in their abiding hostility to civil service, with its examinations. Yet their opposition was not merely selfish or irrational. Indeed, nothing puzzled Plunkitt more than bureaucratic moral values. He could not comprehend why bureaucratizers condemned "honest graft," or the officeholder's legal use of his office for his private benefit. Nor could he understand why the bureaucratizers insisted that high marks on civil service examinations, rather than the esteem and gratitude of one's fellow citizens on election day, qualified one for public office. He could not understand because his moral perspective was radically different both from the bureaucratizers and from Weber's. Plunkitt's morality is what Weber calls "traditional," a morality founded upon those personal attachments which can never be the basis of bureaucracy. Weber, however, was unable to recognize Plunkitt's type of morality as traditional, perhaps because he was not accustomed to a society in which democracy, not aristocracy, is the tradition.

Weber's misconception also caused him to mistake as irrational some of the very qualities which produced effective, efficient administration in early American industrialized society. If one considers the administrative tasks accomplished by Plunkitt and his fellow "henchmen" of Tammany Hall, one sees the inadequacy of the Weberian judgment that bureaucratic organization is administratively superior.

Decentralized administration is superior even in a merely technical sense. Certainly, even with its superior financial resources, today's welfare bureaucracy does not solve the problems of social and economic welfare any more successfully (to say nothing of the inefficiency, nepotism, personal subjugation, and capricious and uninformed judgments that it spawns) than Tammany did in turn-of-the-century New York. Moreover, at that time, some of the most magnificent adornments of that city—its museums, parks, bridges, and boulevards—were constructed. Most importantly, all of this was accomplished continuously, with a minimum amount of unlawful violence, and by popular consent.

Tocqueville's Understanding of Bureaucracy

Tammany Hall's remarkable success in building up New York City is inexplicable in Weber's terms, but it is well within Alexis de Tocqueville's understanding of bureaucracy. Even a century and a half ago, Tocqueville could see that all the details of individual citizens' lives—their vocations and professions, their education, their entertainments, the disposal of their estates, the organization of all professional, civic, and commercial associations—were in danger of being subjected to the uniform, deadening regulation of bureaucracy. In fact, he wrote, even "religion is in danger of falling under government control."

> It is not that the rulers are overzealous to fix dogma themselves, but they are getting more and more of a hold over the wills of those who interpret it, . . .and with their help they reach right down into the depths of each man's soul.[8]

Tocqueville concluded that every aspect of modern society— especially industrialization with its vast scale, its novel social relations, its economic instability, and the inherent danger of its work to health and life—might be an occasion for further "centralization of administration," as he called bureaucratization. Moreover, Tocqueville already could see that the most corrupt form of industrial society—namely, socialism—would also be the most advanced or disciplined form of bureaucracy.[9]

Tocqueville thought that the chances of success in the battle against the universal tendency toward bureaucracy were slim:

> The only public men. . .who favor decentralization are, almost invariably, either very disinterested or extremely mediocre; the former are scarce and the latter powerless.[10]

Yet, unlike Weber and most American intellectuals, he refused to despair, and accordingly devoted his considerable talents to finding ways to keep free politics alive within great modern nations:

> I am certainly not the one to say that such inclinations [toward bureaucracy] are invincible, for my chief aim in writing this book [*Democracy in America*] is to combat them.[11]

Tocqueville trusted that human nature was opposed to bureaucratization. By nature, all humans have some taste for liberty, in the form of "an instinctive tendency, irresistible and hardly conscious, born out of the mysterious sources of all great human passions." This "common source not only of political liberty but of all of the high and manly virtues" is present in the souls of all humans. Bureaucracy violates this "instinct." "To me, human societies, like individuals, become something worthwhile only through their use of liberty."[12]

Because of his estimate of human nature, Tocqueville instinctively denied the superiority of bureaucratic administration. He had no doubts that, in the absence of sound democratic statesmanship and citizenship, bureaucracy would thrive, but he did not think that administrative centralization was inevitable, much less superior in rationality, in capacity to deal with complexity, or in scientific expertise.

Distinguishing "Administration" from "Government"

To understand bureaucracy correctly, one must grasp Tocqueville's distinction between *administration* and *government*, which he made in this famous passage on centralization:

> "Centralization" is a word in general use, but much misunderstood. It is necessary to discriminate between the two distinct kinds of centralization which exist.
>
> Certain interests are common to all parts of the nation, such as the enactment of its general laws and the maintenance of its foreign relations. Other interests are peculiar to certain parts of the nation, such as local enterprises. When the power that directs the former or general interests is concentrated in one place or in the same persons, that is centralized government. To concentrate in like manner the direction of the latter or local interests, I call centralized administration.[13]

Here Tocqueville indicates that administration and government are two distinct kinds of political activity or rule. The one—administration—is proper to personal or parochial interests, and the other—governance—to general or national interests. So, contrary to American constitutional law and politics, "administration" is not synonymous with "execution," e.g., with the powers of the presidency. Rather, both administration and governance are characterized by deliberation or legislation, by adjudication, as well as by execution. Nevertheless, the one kind of politics cannot be reduced to the other. That is, administration is not a type of government (or vice versa), because the principle of administrative authority is essentially distinct from the principle of governmental authority.

Administrative authority is personal or partial, not to say partisan; it is rooted in the personal attachments of kinship, friendship, and neighborliness. These are the very things which Weber supposed to be irrational, or subjective. In contradistinction, governmental authority is impersonal or general, not to say nonpartisan: it proceeds from ideas or such universal truths as "all men are created equal, [and] endowed by their Creator with certain unalienable rights." Thus government, as Tocqueville distinguished it from administration, is rule in accord with reason. The principle of governmental authority is distinguished from the principle of administrative authority by its generality, and so government is distinguished from administration as the universal from the particular. Tocqueville's portrait of the moral character of the administrator and the government official shows just how far Tocqueville's judgment of bureaucracy departs from that of Max Weber and our contemporaries. Administration, as understood by Tocqueville, requires common sense and moral integrity, because the administrator—whether he is a bureaucrat or a noncentralized administrator—must judge and act upon particular people in particular circumstances. So the scientific expertise and professionalism which Weber and our contemporaries believe to be essential for administration are almost the opposite of the virtues preferred by Tocqueville in administrators. Tocquevillean governors, on the other hand, must have intelligence and education to be able to recognize and act upon social and political circumstances in a generalized and impartial way. Their need for the prudence of the administrator would be secondary or derivative.

Of course, if one remains ignorant of Tocqueville's moral-political distinction of administration from government, one will insist, as did the great bureaucratizers of the 1960s and 1970s, that "all levels of government. . .share the responsibility to promote the general welfare."[14] Bureaucratizers believe that the Tocquevillean virtues of a governor should prevail at every level of politics, but especially at the local level. The virtues of the administrator, as Tocqueville understood them, would then appear to be merely the low cunning of the elected politician. Tocqueville is hardly the first or the last social scientist to praise highly the ability to judge soundly individual men and affairs. But he is perhaps the best available corrective for that overappreciation of wholly formalized merit—of certificates, diplomas, titles, and licenses—that informs bureaucratic ages.

Tocqueville's Formula: Decentralized Administration and Centralized Government

Bureaucracy is modern democracy's worst ill, according to Tocqueville. To cure it, he prescribed decentralized administration and centralized government. In the American context, this prescription does not necessarily advise the execution of national policies by the states, as is commonly supposed. Instead, when Tocqueville discussed governance, as distinguished from administration, he referred primarily to the governments of the states, not to the national government.

In the early nineteenth century, the state governments were the centralizers of administration, threatening the vital, albeit parochial, political life of the townships of early America. So too, it was the states that, he thought, threatened genuinely centralized or national government. Of course, Tocqueville saw that the states, in the face of a powerful central government of the nation which was bent on national centralization of administration, might be defenders of decentralized administration. In general, however, Tocqueville feared that if national politicians did not guard local liberties, no one would.

Incidentally, Tocqueville suggests that the national government might have a stronger antibureaucratic interest than the states. This might seem strange to us, for we are use to lumping state and local government together against the national government. He was not absolutely opposed to powerful central government. The moderation of Tocqueville's antibureaucratic stance can be contrasted with that of Justice Louis D. Brandeis, who wrote in 1933, "If the Lord had intended things to be big, he would have made man bigger—in brains and character."[15] Tocqueville was in favor of "Big Government," to accomplish big things, but he did not think it could also accomplish little— petty or parochial—things. For that, administration is most definitely necessary.

Tocqueville's idea that government ought to be centralized but administration decentralized was based upon his knowledge of the limits of human moral and intellectual capacities. Only the divine mind is unlimited, in the sense that it does not need to distinguish the universal from the particular, but " [w]ith one glance. . .sees every human being separately and sees in each the resemblances that make him like his fellows and the differences which isolate him from them."

No human being, not even the greatest scientist, can see himself or the world as God can. If humans could think like the Deity, Tocqueville would have to admit, both government and administration could be, and ought to be, centralized. In that case, humans could govern themselves and the whole world providentially, providing at one and the same time for the general interest and for the particular interests in a perfectly harmonious manner. However, since there are limits to the human intellect, two kinds of political order ought to be established: one—government—with authority over humans insofar as they are alike or similar; and two—decentralized administrations—to rule men insofar as they are different. A "central power, however enlightened and wise one imagines it to be, can never alone see all the details of the life of a great nation. . . . [S]uch a task exceeds human strength."[16]

The great success of Tammany Hall, George Washington Plunkitt, and his ilk in New York, confirms Tocqueville's understanding: particular attachments, not general ideas however rational, are the basis of administrative authority. The all-too-common notions about the superior efficiency and rationality of bureaucracy seem to be just as dogmatic as notions of bureaucracy's moral superiority.

However, there are few superstitions in modern public life more powerful than the belief that the exercise of all public functions can be improved by appointing and promoting officials who are professionals, who possess "impersonal, rational, and objective" merit. Certainly, this is still the case in American government today: if there is some agency which is particularly troublesome, if it is a bone of partisan contention, then likely there will be a bipartisan consensus that it should be made an independent agency—in order that it be "nonpolitical and objective."

HOW ADMINSTRATING REPLACED GOVERNING IN AMERICA

When did the bureaucracy become a significant part of American political life? Some believe that it has always been important, but this opinion is based upon an unsophisticated definition of bureaucracy, which equates it with any large governmental body with executive power. Of course, Tocqueville got a whiff of the bureaucratization of America as early as the 1830s, but if we take bureaucracy in Tocqueville's sense of centralized control of the details of daily life, then one must conclude that there was very little bureaucratization of American national life until the 1960s.

There was, of course, quite a lot of sentiment in favor of bureaucracy among the Progressives. Theodore Roosevelt proposed, "a national industrial commission" with "complete power to regulate and control all the great industrial concerns engaged in interstate business—which practically means all of them in this country." This regulation would have been by bureaucratic fiat, not by law: "Any corporation voluntarily coming under the commission should not be prosecuted under the antitrust law as long as it obeys in good faith the orders of the commission."[17] And in 1913 the Progressive Democrats under Woodrow Wilson tried to establish such a monstrous bureaucracy, calling it the Federal Trade Commission. Senator Cummins, who managed the Federal Trade Commission Act for President Wilson, did not fear bureaucratic indiscretion and arbitrariness: "The whole policy of our regulation of commerce is based upon our faith and confidence in administrative tribunals."[18] This meant that the FTC should be trusted to define its own regulatory objectives, powers, procedures, and limits.

Although it was created with virtually unlimited regulatory authority over all of American commerce, the FTC was in fact a regulatory non-entity—even a laughing stock—until it was revived by the great wave of bureaucratization that swept the country after 1964.

Almost immediately after its creation and from the 1920s through the early 1960s, the FTC was frustrated in the courts, by presidential appointments, and in appropriations. For almost half a century, public opinion of the FTC was summed up by a remark of Federal Trade Commissioner Edward F. Howrey that it was "common gossip that the Commission met in solemn session to assign parking spaces in the garage and things like that."[19]

Before and after the passage of the FTC Act, Congress never deliberately created regulatory agencies with broad, vaguely defined purpose and purview. Never, that is, until the late 1960s and early 1970s, when it created society-wide regulatory agencies with intentionally vague purposes after even less deliberation than when it created the FTC. (For a detailed discussin of this regulatory agency phenomenon, see Chapter 11.)

Perspectives on The New Deal

Did bureaucratization start with the presidency of Franklin Roosevelt and his New Deal, as American conservatives often insist? The leading New Dealers, and Franklin Roosevelt himself, expressed misgivings about bureaucracy far more than the Progressives, and they did so in a political culture that was far more willing to accept bureaucratization.

When Big Business wanted laws of national incorporation and automatic seats in the highest counsels for the heads of the largest corporations and of the securities markets, Roosevelt and the New Deal gave them the Securities Exchange Commission to ensure that corporations were freely organized. When Big Labor wanted government organized and sponsored unions (and a Labor Party), a measure which would certainly have compromised the principle of free labor, Roosevelt gave them the National Labor Relations Board to ensure that unions were freely organized. To be sure, the National Industrial Recovery Act was not only unconstitutional, it was the source of the National Recovery Administration, one of the greatest advances for bureaucratization imaginable, if it had lasted. It did not last, however, and even the New Dealers themselves did not consider it a permanent measure, but rather a temporary, emergency expedient which could be abandoned once commercial recovery had been accomplished. In this respect, the wartime Office of Price Administration and the War Production Board were much the same: not permanent bureaucratic reforms, but emergency measures for the most difficult times.

The New Deal undoubtedly made many massive errors in coping with the Great Depression, not the least of which was the NRA, but the New Dealers certainly did not believe that bureaucratization was desirable. Perhaps the clearest expression of this view was Roosevelt's when he stated that:

We need trained personnel in government. We need disinterested, as well as broad-gauged, public officials. This part of our problem we have not yet solved, but it can be solved and it can be accomplished without the creation of a national bureaucracy which would dominate the national life of our governmental system.[20]

The New Deal certainly was willing to accept a degree of bureaucratization that went beyond what was desirable to Calvin Coolidge, for example, who had a very clear view of what was necessary in this regard. But neither the New Deal nor Roosevelt was willing to allow bureaucracy to dominate politically.

Can bureaucratization be accepted on a limited basis? Once it is accepted, can it be stopped short of dominance? So long as the principle of bureaucracy is not publicly accepted, the rule of scientific professionals and experts cannot replace constitutional self-government. Since almost all of the New Deal bureaucratization was undertaken as temporary, emergency, stopgap, or experimental measures, it never accepted the principle of bureaucracy; only one highly centralized administration was established permanently, the Social Security System, and it was created and defended as an insurance system, not as the rule of scientific experts on retirement. Furthermore, Roosevelt insisted on presidential administration. Even before he became president, Roosevelt understood that if there had to be bureaucracy, it ought to be under the authority of the executive. Otherwise, bureaucracy becomes dominant; it cannot be responsible to the people. In particular, from his experience as Governor of New York, he knew that "all responsibility shall be lost" when the legislature tries to share in administration.[21]

Roosevelt's Faith in Constitutional Government

Did the New Deal prepare the way for the dominance of bureaucracy indirectly, by undermining the ethic of individual responsibility and the ideas of limited or constitutional government which are so beautifully and authoritively expressed in the Declaration of Independence?[22]

Certainly, Roosevelt did attack the excesses of individualism and he did claim that the constitutional limits on the government's power, to regulate national commerce for example, had been drawn too narrowly by the Supreme Court. Nevertheless, in what is crucial for the maintenance of constitutional forms, the New Deal was conservative of the American political tradition. Roosevelt never attacked the moral principles that are the foundation of constitutional government. In fact, he spoke and acted to sustain the traditional American doctrine of individual rights in the face of the anti-individualism of some of his own supporters.

Because of contemporary intellectuals' inability to conceive of any principled means between individualism and socialism—between laissez-faire capitalism and communism—Roosevelt's moderate attack on individualism appears to be a break with the American tradition to conservatives, and an unprincipled "chaos of experimentation" to the left.[23]

Nevertheless, from beginning to end, Roosevelt appealed to the American faith in constitutional government—to the Constitution itself, to the Declaration of Independence, and to the examples of Washington, Jefferson, Lincoln, Jackson, and Theodore Roosevelt. Never did he argue, as did the Progressives and above all Woodrow Wilson, that modern circumstances had made the Constitution a relic. He did not regard the problems of constitutional government as merely eighteenth-century problems. Instead, Roosevelt viewed the economic and social nightmare of the Depression (and World War II) as a great challenge to free institutions, and he saw his own project to be the preservation of free institutions in the new circumstances of industrial society.

Roosevelt understood quite well the connection between free institutions and human rights. For this reason, he could never be an outright opponent of individualism. Even as the United States approached something like class war between labor and management in 1935, FDR declared that "individual effort is the glory of America."[24] Thus, he could never be simply a socialist. He could never be a simple individualist either. He believed that the nation's economic crisis revealed the limits of individualism. In a speech devoted to the excesses of individualism, Roosevelt argued that industrial society is fundamentally different from the society of 1787. Individualism as a social and economic policy had run its historical course for the nation, but, Roosevelt insisted, the moral principle of individual rights and the economic necessity of relying upon individual initiative could never become obsolete:

> Let me emphasize that serious as have been the errors of unrestrained individualism, I do not believe in abandoning the system of individual enterprise. The freedom and opportunity that have characterized American development in the past can be maintained if we recognize the fact that the individual system of our day calls for the collaboration of all of us to provide, at the least, security for all of us. Those words "freedom" and "opportunity" do not mean a license to climb upwards by pushing other people down. [25]

Roosevelt adhered to the political principles which follow from the moral doctrine of individual rights. There are really only two forms of government: one which protects the rights of its citizens and one which does not:

> Our common life under various agencies of Government, our laws and our basic Constitution, exist primarily to protect the individual, to cherish his rights. . . [26]

Congressional Resistance to Central Administration

Nor was it only Roosevelt who attempted to provide against the dominance of bureaucracy. There were powerful antibureaucratic elements in Congress, who understood that once administration was centralized, Congress would either have to leave it to the president, which could be politically dangerous, or else spend its whole day ministering to the petty personal cares of the folks back home. These legislators believed that their duty was the deliberation of the great course of the nation, not just negotiating the partial or parochial interests of their constituents with bureaucrats.

The party-purging primaries of 1938 brought home to Congress, especially the House, the political dangers of centralized administration. In these elections, beneficiaries of unemployment insurance programs and of the Works Progress Administration had helped the president against members of his own party. Moreover, with the prospect of a third term for Roosevelt, Congress believed that, even with a merit system, a nationalized bureaucracy could not help but favor and work for the incumbent president, insofar as it was under his authority.

The Hatch Acts of 1939-40 were an attempt to remedy this situation by strictly curtailing the political activities of federal bureaucrats (including those at the state and local level who were covered by the Social Security Act's 1939 amendments). That is, for the protection of the legislative branch, the federal bureaucracy was removed from its dependency upon the executive. This was done in the name of the morality of civil service reform, as the Hatch Acts were said to guarantee the professionalism, objectivity, and non-partisanship of the bureaucracy.[27]

Through the 1940s and 1950s, Congress continued to cope with the political problem posed by centralized administration by insisting upon the Hatch Acts' ideal of "neutral administration." That ideal was the heart of civil service reform. Of course, it was very much in the congressmen's interest to check centralized administration, unless they were interested in devoting their whole public lives to ministering to the petty interests of their constituents. And that attitude on the part of congressmen was actually fairly common right up into the early 1970s.

Consider Representative Gillis Long's remarks applauding the Supreme Court's decision in *Immigration and Naturalization Service* v. *Chadha* (1983), which ruled the legislative veto unconstitutional:

> It appeared to me that with the application of an extreme type of legislative veto . . .we were turning ours from an institution that was supposed to be a broad policymaking institution with respect to the problems of the country and its relationship to the world, into merely a city council that overlooks the running of the store everyday.[28]

For the same reason, Speaker Sam Rayburn, as great a partisan of congressional power as anyone, did not care to administrate the nation either. As Representative Bolling remarked, "He fought this idea . . .step by step."[29]

The Rise of the Bureaucratic Class

The ideal of a politically "neutral" administration proved to be merely a stopgap measure against a greater danger of bureaucratic dominance. In fact, the Hatch Acts allowed a propagation of the principles of bureaucracy, which permitted the consolidation of the interest of bureaucracy in the form of nationally organized public employees' unions at all levels of politics. By 1958, on its seventy-fifth anniversary, the Civil Service Commission could proclaim that its principal task was no longer combating the evils of patronage. Instead its purpose had become "public personnel management."

Four years later, President Kennedy formally recognized the national consolidation of bureaucratic interest by issuing Executive Order 11491, which encouraged collective bargaining with public employees' unions. When this order was written into law by the Civil Service Reform Act of 1978, the Civil Service Commission was replaced by the Office of Personnel Management and two (soon to be three or more) other independent agencies; none of them is principally charged with combating the evils of patronage.

In the decade since, the Hatch Act has been continuously rewritten to give lower level bureaucrats (GS-15 and below) more and more political rights while protecting them from the wrath of the politicians against whom they may work. Thus, civil service reform—the elimination of machine politics—has been accomplished by the creation of a bureaucratic class, a class which, as shall be shown, is strongly allied with the Congress.[30]

As Richard Nixon foresaw in 1960, the really substantial centralization of administration began, not with Franklin Roosevelt and the New Deal, but with John Kennedy:

> . . . [T]here was no difference between [Kennedy and me] in "caring" about the problems of less fortunate people. We had the same ultimate goals. . . . The great gulf of difference between us . . .was that of a bureaucratic society vs. a free society.[31]

The Great Society

According to Lyndon Johnson's 1964 presidential campaign, centralization of administration was a chief objective of the Great Society.[32] And among the intellectuals, the fashionable idea was that the "public sector" (that is, the federal bureaucracy) was starving.[33]

The rise of the public sector in the late 1960s and early 1970s had three principal features: (1) the assumption of vast new authority by the central government; (2) the establishment of regulation as the typical political activity of the United States government; and (3) the assumption (*de facto* and *de jure*) by Congress of administrative functions, with a consequent increase in conflicts with the Presidency.

When the American government, in principle, assumed responsibility for the socioeconomic well-being of every American, it also had to introduce programs for managing, in detail and from the center, the relations between the races, the sexes, employees and employers, electors and elected, state and local governments and their citizens, consumers and producers, husbands and wives, parents and children, and so on. New Deal programs, such as Social Security and Aid to Families with Dependent Children, were drastically reformed, so that they became enormously burdensome on the taxpayer, rickety, and perhaps even socially corrosive.[34]

Equally important was the enormous extension of the federal bureaucracy's regulatory apparatus from 1964 to 1974. The size of the commercial regulatory apparatus alone more than doubled in that period, In particular, not only did the number of commercial regulatory agencies increase from fifty to seventy-two, but thirty-five of the fifty established agencies were substantially reformed. For the first time, agencies with "economy-wide" (in fact, "society-wide") purview and vast administrative discretion were established, so that after 1975, government's primary function was to regulate.

Indeed, a report on the reformed federal regulatory apparatus issued by the House Government Operations subcommittee in the spring of 1975 remarked approvingly: "In its broadest sense, everything the government does is regulation. . . ." That means, as we shall soon see, that very little of what the government does is legislating, executing, and adjudicating—the normal functions of constitutional government.

Measuring the Growth of Bureaucracy: Debt, Employment, and Spending

In the United States, Big Government really became big after 1964 (between the election of President Johnson and the resignation of President Nixon). "Bigness" in this sense means centralization of administration, the assumption of power at the national center over the details of the citizens' lives. Such bigness brought with it the more conventional kind—huge government workforces, vast public expenditure, and vast public debt.

The fact that for over two decades state and local debt, employment, and spending have been larger and growing faster than federal debt, employment, and spending is commonly cited as evidence that centralization of administration is no danger. But how much of this state and local activity is commanded by the authority and leveraged by the finances of the central government? This is the crucial question for measuring centralization. It cannot be fully answered, because the necessary statistics are not reported. Moreover, the reliability of the commonly accepted measures of the central government's spending, employment, and debt are questionable.

Over the past two decades, federal civil service employment has remained relatively stable. Employment in the executive departments and independent agencies, the heart of the federal bureaucracy, was 2.35 million in 1960, rose to 2.91 million in 1970, and declined to 2.83 million in 1980. However, these official measures of federal employment are extremely deceptive. They do not include the beneficiaries of social programs, like CETA or Job Corps, even though they receive taxable income from the federal government. Nor do they include workers who, although formally employed by some state or local governments or educational institutions, receive part or all of their incomes from the central government. Official figures exclude the vast army of independent contractors and administrators in the "Third Sector," and also research and management consultants, even when their sole source of income is the federal government. Nevertheless, the working conditions of these employees are overseen by the House Committee on Post Office and Civil Service.[35]

How large is this unofficial federal workforce? Donald Lambro seems to be the only researcher who has followed its development with any care.[36] Depending upon what standard of federal employment is applied, Lambro estimates that the unofficial federal *civilian* workforce is between 9 and 13 million. Thus, together with the official workforce, federal employment is at least equal to state and local. This unofficial federal workforce has emerged almost entirely in the past two decades.

Such a level of federal employment is dangerous to constitutional government. In *Federalist* 45, Publius explains why, in practice, the central government cannot dominate the state and local governments under the Constitution of 1787:

> The members of the legislative, executive, and judiciary departments of the thirteen and more states, the justices of the peace, officers of militia, ministerial officers of justice, with all the county, corporation, and town officers, for three millions and more people, intermixed, and having acquaintance with every class and circle of people, must exceed, beyond all proportion, both in number and influence, those of every description who will be employed [by the central government].

Only in the mid-1960s or early 1970s did the employees of the central government "of every description" come to equal or exceed state and local employees. From the point of view of 1787, this development would appear to doom the American union: the central government would dominate all. In fact, however, because bureaucratic government is big, it is fat, and therefore, ineffective.

The enormous size and growth of federal debt and expenditure need not be detailed here. It should be noted, however, that measures of aggregate federal spending are not very accurate. For beyond the federal budget, there is off-budget spending and debt, which has mushroomed since 1974. The fact that an off-budget agency, the Federal Financing Bank (FFB), had to be created in 1974 to move debt on- and off-budget is a measure of the enormity and complexity of federal obligation. (By 1982 it was the second largest bank in the United States.) Moreover, the FFB helps to market state and local debt, so that not only the distinction of off- from on-budget federal debt, but also the distinction of federal debt from state and local debt have become obscure.

In addition, federal investment guarantees to private enterprises (estimated at $509 billion for 1983) ought to be somehow included in federal debts, even though this does obscure the distinction of private from public debt. Considering this maze of federal obligations, the oft-reported guess that the central government has leveraged one-half of the market for capital does not seem extreme.[37]

The Reach of Centralized Administration

The simple (and comforting) contrast of federal spending, debt, and employment to state and local spending, debt, and employment is deceptive, because these traditionally sensible and useful measures of government activity have been rendered inaccurate by bureaucratization. This obfuscation is symptomatic of centralized administration itself. Bureaucratization requires that there be no sources of authority independent of the center. In principle, that means that no enterprise—certainly no public enterprise, but ultimately no private enterprise either—can be undertaken without authorization from a center. In the United States, where reliance upon central administration is still new, and where the bureaucracy is insufficiently armed, the central authorities must buy compliance. That is, the centralization of administration has required an enormous financial and patronage apparatus, which must be hidden because the centralization of administration as such lacks political authority.

Bureaucracies exercise enormous public authority in relation to their financial resources and patronage. In public education, for example, Thomas H. Jones observes that the relatively small federal contribution (about 8 percent) to the public schools' financing commands their policies on "equity in educational procedures" totally, and, in important part, their curricular content, administrative costs, and educational goals.[38] Then how much authority does the federal contribution to state and local budgets purchase, when it has averaged 20 to 25 percent over the past decade? Obviously, the overall answer defies quantification, but many particulars are available. Consider that every mile of new sewer line laid down by a local government today is authorized by the Environmental Protection Agency, and so the EPA somehow participates in the financing of every mile. Similarly, since 1974, virtually all state and local policing of occupational hazards proceeds pursuant to the Occupational Safety and Health Administration's authority, and so (by law) from 50 to 90 percent of the costs of this function are paid by OSHA. Schools, occupational safety, sewer lines: until twenty years ago, the administration of these very important matters was completely decentralized.[39]

Although the growth of federal, state, and local government over the past two decades has been so convoluted that traditional statistical measures of political and governmental activity at each level are almost meaningless, even if they could be known with any accuracy, this very convolution is a measure of the vast centralization of administration which has taken place only in the past generation.

THE CONSEQUENCES OF CENTRALIZED ADMINISTRATION

This maxim of Tocqueville's should always be borne in mind, if the bureaucratization of American government is to be understood:

> A central power, however enlightened and wise one imagines it to be, can never alone foresee all the details of the life of a great nation. Such a task exceeds human strength.

Until humans become gods, or at least angels, bureaucracy will be unable to rule well though nothing prevents it from being pursued. In fact, beginning around 1970 and increasingly thereafter, the central government has been compelled to reform itself in order to cope with bureaucratization. The result of these reforms has been characterized by John Marini as "decentralization of government". Making the central *administration* more powerful has actually made the central *government* weaker.

Shifting Centers of Power

Over the past two decades, centralization of administration has necessitated a reorganization of the central government. The result of this division of central government against itself is the crippling, if not the death, of unified national political authority. Most of this reorganization took place between 1970 and 1975, but the trend continues to this day. Thus, in the 1970s, the executive bureaucracy shrank by a third while the independent bureaucracy more than tripled. The trend toward divided executive power is particularly conspicuous since many of the agencies which are responsible for strictly internal governmental management (such as the Office of Personnel Management, the Governmental Services Administration, and the National Archives and Records Administration) are independent of the presidency, if not dependent upon Congress. Indeed, Congress regards the independent agencies not as truly independent, but only as independent of the executive branch, and perhaps as arms of the Congress. (See Chapter 11.)

Although almost every one of the independent regulatory agencies is itself a highly centralized administration, the organization among them is highly decentralized. None takes precedence over another, so not only can several agencies demand compliance from citizens based on different and sometimes conflicting regulations, but also they can demand compliance from one another.

The result is a net of federal regulation—minute, but not uniform, and not subject to much legal scrutiny since the reforms of the 1976 Administrative Procedures Act.

The same trend is even more obvious when one considers the executive, legislative, and judicial staffs. From 1970 to 1986, employment by the Executive Office of the President declined by about two-thirds, while the equivalent employment by the legislative branch increased by about one-fifth. These employees are especially significant, because they are available to do the political work of the officeholders, including the work of one branch against another.

However, these numbers are merely symptomatic of more fundamental changes in the form of political authority that occurred when members of the legislative branch began to be preoccupied with administration.

Congressional Attempts to Rule the Administrative State

The political necessity for the legislature to increase attention to administration was already beginning to become obvious to members of Congress as early as 1967, when the Legislative Reorganization Act was introduced and rejected. However, the need for detailed reorganization that would follow the lines drawn out in the federal bureaucracy and restrict presidential authority over central administration came only after the Democratic Congress experienced a Republican president who was determined to gain and maintain control of domestic and foreign administration.

Beginning in late 1969 with the Legislative Reorganization Act of 1970, Congress has continuously reorganized itself by committees and subcommittees so that congressmen, individually, can better oversee and intervene in the details and day-to-day operations of independent and executive branch agencies. Thus, "closed *ex parte* dealings . . .emerged" as a principal activity of government in those parts of the central administration which were of special concern to representatives and Senators."[40]

Important changes in the Administrative Procedures Act of 1946 had to be made in order to make appeals to courts of law against the bureaucracy more difficult and *ex parte* relations acceptable under the rubric of "public participation in the regulatory process." Such relations had formerly been unethical, if not felonious, for congressmen, but they are now the essence of the new bureaucratic politics.[41]

Beyond this, beginning in 1973, congressmen also began to develop new kinds of formal power over administration. The so-called legislative veto, the best known of these devices, was included in over 295 public laws, the vast majority of which were passed after 1973.

The *Chadha* decision did stop the further development of this device for administrative control, which would have allowed even individual members or congressional staff to void agency actions, but it could not prevent the development of many new means by which members of Congress can participate directly in the day-to-day administration of the nation. Such devices include reprogramming agreements between agencies and committees or subcommittees or individual members, and prior notification of agencies' spending and personnel decisions. More importantly, "any number of informal, nonstatutory substitutes for the legislative veto exist. . . ,"[42] consisting of private (or secret) agreements between congressmen (or their staff) and bureaucrats, agreements which have no legal status but are the main basis upon which the public business is conducted.

In addition to these rather straightforward attempts to gain administrative power, Congress also began in 1973 and increasingly thereafter to attack presidential authority by developing new institutions of criminal and civil procedure, notably the so-called "independent prosecutors" and the Office of Government Ethics. Recently, the Supreme Court upheld the prosecutors in *Morrison, Independent Counsel* v. *Olson* et al (decided June 29, 1988). (For more discussion of the *Olson* case and the "independent prosecutor" issue, See Chapter 10.)

These institutions are primarily diversionary. So far, their operations and investigations, which can be ordered by congressional committees and subcommittees, have seldom resulted in court trials, but they can throw into confusion any executive office or agency at which they are directed.

From these few facts, upon which it would be possible to expatiate at much greater length, one can see the political difference which centralization of administration has made over the past two decades. It has created a paradise for the deal-cutting congressman who pays attention to the myriad of bureaucratic snares into which his constituents are bound to fall. The fact that the congressmen themselves, in their legislative capacity, are the producers of these snares does not impress the voters, who are grateful for the relief from bureaucratic arbitrariness that their congressmen as ombudsmen provide. Thus, in addition to or in place of the "pork barrel," congressmen can offer their constituents "regulatory relief" from the demands of the federal bureaucracy. No wonder congressmen have forsaken the old-fashioned work of legislation in order to serve as ombudsmen.[43]

The Effect on the Separation of Powers

Centralization of administration has also brought about an extraordinary deadlock of democracy among the branches. The president and Congress no longer undertake their traditional, healthy, and constitutional rivalry, which is the consequence of separation of powers, but instead the Congress seeks to subject the presidency to its will and the president struggles to be free.

The presidency, as the only truly national elective office, is ultimately subversive of central administration, while Congress, especially the House, has a natural sympathy with administration because of its closer ties to narrower interests. This point may seem novel, if one believes—as is common—that "administration" is synonymous with "execution." In fact, as noted above, administration is legislating, adjudicating, and executing for private and parochial interests; it is what is today called "regulation" or "the regulatory process."

Continued attacks on executive authority by Congress will be necessary if Congress is to become administrator. Of course, neither congressmen nor the president really want to have responsibility for central administration. No elected politician would want to take responsibility for a task that exceeds human strength. However, representatives and senators do wish to be able to exercise decisive influence upon administration, whenever they wish to relieve one of their constituents of bureaucratic arbitrariness.

When administration moves to the center, it does not naturally fall under the authority of any one branch. Contrary to common opinion, bureaucracy does not by nature belong to the executive branch. Instead, once administration moves to the center, it becomes a bone of contention among the branches, and especially between the powerful "political" branches.

So far, as we have seen, central administration has been divided between the president and Congress, with Congress getting the better of the division because of its superior attention to localized interests (and its superior skills in deliberations). Before centralization, congressmen constantly watched the president to protect non-national interests from the untoward effects of national executions. The ultimate protection enjoyed by Congress was its refusal to make laws touching parochial interests on the ground that they were not national interests.

Similarly, before centralization, the president watched Congress with an eye to the national (or, at least, trans-sectional) interest, if only because his political interest required a broader coalition. So, before the choice to centralize was made, separation of powers was an important prop for decentralized administration, in which congressmen had an interest (even during the New Deal), and for centralized governance, in which the president had a special interest. In sum, the whole central government had a common interest in deliberating the national interest, and in distinguishing it from narrower interests.

The Great Society's policies of centralization did not subordinate private and parochial interests to the national interest, as the proponents of bureaucracy believed would happen. Instead, centralization brought all the partial, petty, and parochial interests to the national center, where they do almost nothing but try to compromise national legislation and national execution of the laws.

Accordingly, bureaucratically promulgated regulations have replaced public laws as the typical expression of public authority. After centralization, the president still has a political interest in central governance, but Congress has lost its interest in decentralized administration. Therefore, the conflict between the two branches is no longer the result of differing opinions of the national interest, but, at best, is merely the expression of the conflict between the public interest and private interests and, at worst, of the conflict among the vast variety of private interests. Laws, and the passing, enforcing, and judging of laws, are no longer the central focus of government.

In the past, separation of powers did not deadlock national governance on national issues; instead, it discouraged deadlock by making the cooperation of the two branches necessary. However, administration does not require that cooperation. So today, the branches stand divided against themselves, one wishing to govern and the other to administer. As such, both private or parochial interests and the national interest are neglected. The result is bad government.

The Effect on Traditional Politics

This partisan division of the president from Congress colors the division of the Republicans from the Democrats. The Democrats, because they created and appointed the bulk of the federal bureaucracies, have succeeded as the representatives of private and parochial interests; the more bureaucratized those interests are the more strongly they support the Democratic party.

Accordingly, that party's dominance at the state and local levels in the House, and usually in the Senate, has grown. At the same time, the national appeal of the Democratic Party has been feeble; at best, it is still addressing the problems of the Great Depression. Since the rise of centralized administration, the Republicans have articulated the national interest. By emphasizing the problems of national defense, national economic growth, and the burdens of taxation and regulation upon social and economic life, they have managed to remain more than competitive for the only genuinely national office.

In 1980 and 1982, they managed to gain and maintain a slim majority in the Senate by nationalizing the campaigns for certain key seats. However, Republican national success cannot diminish or neutralize the Democrats' advantage with the bureaucracy. For example, Ronald Reagan's policies of deregulation and spending limitations have failed, but his tax policy (the passage of which did not affect Congress' command of administrative details), has been relatively successful.

It may be that the Republicans have replaced the Democrats as the national party, but, unlike in the past, the national party no longer necessarily holds national hegemony. Bureaucratization has changed that by dividing the national government against itself, such that one part is essentially concerned with ministering to the vast variety of private and parochial interests that fall under the federal bureaucracy and the other is concerned with the national interest. The president and Congress, Republicans and Democrats, no longer contend directly and politically over the national interest, because bureaucratization has confounded private and parochial interests with the national interest. Therefore, for the foreseeable future, the partisan political question ought to be whether central administration is really in the national interest.

TOWARD FULL BUREAUCRACY OR RENEWED SELF-GOVERNMENT?

"A house divided against itself, cannot stand " Abraham Lincoln said in 1858. Either the contemporary forces of bureaucratization will push forward, and elect a president of their own, who, by unifying the federal bureaucracy under his authority, will combine central administration with central government; or the opponents of central administration will gain the hegemony over national government which is necessary to begin the long, difficult task of de-bureaucratization.

Although it does not seem likely that the current regime can endure permanently while half-bureaucratized, a crisis point has not yet been reached. Probably any catastrophe which requires a genuinely national exertion (a major international war, another Great Depression, or a great inflation) would cause the collapse of this regime. Yet national crises can be temporized indefinitely. In the meantime, one can monitor the disparate forces, and point to the political issue.

A national majority composed of the bureaucracy and the interests closely associated with it could be formed today, if any political leaders were willing to organize it. Such a majority would make nonsense of representative democracy. In such a case, the government would literally represent itself. That government could claim democratic legitimacy, because more would have voted for than against it. However, when the government itself is the majority, and representative of itself, then it is just one more private interest group—albeit the largest—among the many demanding a piece of the pie; except that such a government demands this of itself. Thus one can appreciate why the partisans of bureaucracy have refrained from making a political case for bureaucracy: the private interest of the bureaucrats depends upon government not appearing to be just another special interest.

With the beginning of the end of the Reagan era, centralizers have taken to arguing that bureaucracy is "pervasive," and, therefore, a "necessity." An argument from necessity, however, is an argument from force and can only be proven (or disproven) by force. So, this political position, which has been taken by George Will and Irving Kristol as well as many liberals, shows that there is no *reason*, in the present circumstances, to chose bureaucracy. In sum: the fully bureaucratized order cannot yet be established by a free popular vote. Indeed, the fully bureaucratized order could only be established by popular vote if the American people were so demoralized that they lacked the capacity to rule themselves politically.

Two decades of aggressive centralization have already undermined that capacity to some extent. However, the continued success of the antibureaucratic appeal at the national level is a sign, at least, that the longing for self-government is not yet dead in the American soul.

Notes

1. James L. Sundquist, "The Crisis of Competence in Our National Government," 95 *Political Science Quarterly*, p. 183ff.

2. Max Weber, *The Theory of Social and Economic Organization*, trans. A.M. Henderson and Talcott Parsons (New York: Free Press, 1964) p. 337.

3. Weber, *The Theory of Social and Economic Organization*, p. 337.

4. Max Weber, "Bureaucracy," From *Max Weber*, trans. and ed. H.H. Gerth and C. Wright Mills (New York: Oxford, 1970) pp. 211, 225.

5. Weber, "Bureaucracy," pp. 211, 225.

6. Weber, "Bureaucracy," p. 224 (original emphasis).

7. George Washington Plunkitt, *Plunkitt of Tammany Hall: Plain Talk About Practical Politics*, ed. William L. Riordan (New York: Dutton, 1963), p. 8.

8. Alexis de Tocqueville, *Democracy in America*, trans. George Lawrence (New York: Doubleday, 1970), p. 681.

9. de Tocqueville, *The Old Regime and the French Revolution*, trans. Stuart Gilbert (Garden City, N.Y.: Doubleday, 1955), p. 164.

10. *Democracy in America*, p. 735.

11. *Democracy in America*, p. 671.

12. de Tocqueville, *"The European Revolution" and Correspondence with Gobineau*, ed., trans. John Lukacs (Gloucester, Mass.: Peter Small, 1968), p. 309.

13. *Democracy in America*, p. 87.

14. Testimony of Senator Edmund Muskie, *Intergovernmental Personnel Act of 1966*, Senate Committee on Government Operations, 89th. Cong., 2nd sess. (1966), pp. 2, 5.

15. *Letters of Louis D. Brandeis*, eds. Melvin I. Urofsky and David W. Levy, (New York State, 1971) V, 527.

16. *Democracy in America*, p. 91.

17. *Purposes and Policies of the Progressive Party*, Speech of Hon. Theodore Roosevelt before the Progressive Convention at Chicago, Ill., August 6, 1912, Senate Document No. 904 (19120), p. 21.

18. *Economic Regulation of Business and Industry: A Legislative History of U.S. Regulatory Agencies*, ed. Bernard Schwartz (New York, 1973), III, 1763.

19. *The Organization and Procedures of the Federal Regulatory Commissions and Agencies and Their Effect on Small Business*, House Select Committee on Small Business, 84th Cong., 2nd sess. (1955), p. 53.

20. *Public Papers and Addresses of Franklin D. Roosevelt*, ed. Samuel I.Rosenman (Government Printing Office), III, 122.

21. *Public Papers* I, 343.

22. See Chapter 1 above.

23. Richard Hofstadter, *The Age of Reform: From Bryant to FDR* (New York: Knopf, 1955), p. 305.

24. *Public Papers* IV, 405.

25. *Public Papers* IV, 341.

26. *Public Papers* IV, 406.

27. See, above all, *Amending the Social Security Act* ..., Senate Committee on Finance, 75th Cong., 3rd sess. (1938), pp. 1-5, 27, and also *Social Security Act Amendments*, Senate Committee on Finance, 76th Cong., 1st sess. (1939), pp. 26-27, 31, 32, 34-35, 137, 140, 290-91.

28. *Legislative Veto After Chadha*, House Committee on Rules, 98th Cong., 2nd sess. (1984), p. 182.

29. *Regulatory Reform and Congressional Review of Agency Rules*, House Committee on Rules, 96th Cong., 1st. sess., (1979), Part 1, p. 217.

30. *Federal Employees Political Activities Act of 1977*, House Committee on Post Office and Civil Service, 95th Cong., 1st sess. (1977), p. 138.

31. Richard M. Nixon, *Six Crises* (Garden City, N.Y.: Doubleday, 1962), p. 339.

32. See, e.g., Eric F. Goldman, "Too powerful?" *New York Times* (Mar. 1, 1964), VI, 22 and "Senator Humphrey Charges Goldwater Has Deep Misunderstanding of American Federalism," *New York Times* (Aug. 13, 1964), 17:7.

33. See John Kenneth Galbraith, "The Dependency Effect and the Social Balance," *Private Wants and Public Needs* (New York, 1962), pp. 13-36.

34. See Charles Murray, *Losing Ground: American Social Policy*, 1950-1980 (New York, 1984) and Daniel Patrick Moynihan, *Politics of a Guaranteed Annual Income* (New York, 1972).

35. See Theodore Levitt, *The Third Sector: New Tactics for a Responsible Society* (New York, 1973), pp. 72, 77; *Non-Profit Organization Participation in the Federal Aid System. . .*, Senate Committee on Governmental Affairs, 96th Cong., 2nd sess. (1980).

36. Donald Lambro, *Fat City: How Washington Wastes Your Taxes* (South Bend, 1980), pp. 11-15.

37. See James T. Bennett and Thomas J. Dilorenzo, *Underground Government: The Off-Budget Public Sector* (Washington, 1983), pp. 137, 143, 152, 146 and Theodore Lowi, *Nationalizing Government* (Beverly Hills, 1978), pp. 23-24.

38. "Federal Mandates and the Future of Public Schools," in *Nationalization of State Government*, ed. Jerome J. Hanus (Lexington, 1981), pp. 106-7.

39. See Environmental Protection Agency, *Environmental News* (June 28, 1982), p. 1.

40. *Legislative Veto After Chadha*, House Committee on Rules, 98th Cong., 2nd sess. (1984) p. 459.

41. See *Public Participation in Government Proceedings Act of 1976*, Senate Government Operations Committee, 94th Cong., 2nd sess., (1976) and *Public Participation in Federal Agencies Proceedings*, Senate Judiciary Committee, 94th Cong., 2nd sess. (1976).

42. Louis Fisher, "The Administrative World of Chadha and Bowsher," 46 *Public Administration Review*, 213.

43. The importance of these new functions of congressmen was already understood in detail by the mid-1970s; see Morris Fiorina, *Congress: The Keystone of the Washington Establishment* (Washington, 1977).

The Imperial
Congress
at Work

Introduction by

GORDON S. JONES

*I*n the preceding section, we examined the theoretical basis for and the historical development of the constitutional separation of powers. The approach was historical and philosophical. The next section will provide a bridge between the theory and the real damages in terms of the policies that affect Americans directly. It will show how Congress, in crossing the line into the territory of the executive, poses real threats to the liberties of our citizens.

In recent years a cottage industry has developed criticizing Congress for failing to get its job done. That there is some disagreement about exactly what its job is may have contributed to the criticism, but the consensus persists.

The story can be told numerically: Congress is doing less at a higher cost and with more people than ever before in history. Here are just a few illustrative figures:

• In the last 30 years, congressional staff has tripled, growing from 3,500 to 11,200. There are further staff resources available to Congress through the General Accounting Office, the Library of Congress, and the Office of Science and Technology;

• Since 1946, the congressional budget has climbed from $54 million to almost $2 billion. The overall cost of living has grown 450 percent over that period, yet Congress's expenses have grown at *six times* that rate;

• In 1975-76, the House of Representatives met 311 days and held almost 7,000 committee hearings. In 1985-86, the House met only 281 days, and held only 4,222 hearings.

Or one can point to the extraordinary number of laws imposed by Congress on others, from which it has exempted itself. I am indebted to Richard Miniter of the National Journalism Center for the following list. He may have missed some:

- Social Security Act of 1933 (Members of Congress and their staffs paid no Social Security taxes until 1983; the law changing the system continues the exemption from SS taxes for all members and employees eligible for the generous congressional retirement program prior to 1983);

- National Labor Relations Act of 1935;

- Fair Labor Standards Act of 1938;

- Minimum Wage Act of 1938;

- Equal Pay Act of 1963;

- Civil Rights Act of 1964;

- Freedom of Information Act of 1966;

- Age Discrimination Act of 1967;

- Occupational Safety and Health Act of 1970;

- Equal Employment Opportunity Act of 1972;

- Title IX of the Higher Education Act Amendments of 1972 (covers educational opportunities for women);

- Rehabilitation Act of 1973, which covers the handicapped;

- Privacy Act of 1974;

- Age Discrimination Act Amendments of 1975;

- Ethics in Government Act of 1978;

- Civil Rights Restoration Act of 1988 (on this bill, popularly known as the Grove City Bill, Congress, despite years of consciousness-raising, rejected a specific amendment to include itself in coverage).

In the chapters that follow, a number of experts on the Congressional system will discuss its failures in some detail. They will discuss such distortions in the traditional congressional operations as micromangement, the hypocrisy of Congress, its lack of account-ability, its thirst for power. Some of these authors will differ in their analysis of the problem, or about the proper remedies. That is as it should be. But all have first hand experience with the deformations in the separation of powers as provided by the Constitution, and real insight into the concrete effects of these deformations.

4. Congressional Micromanagement: National Defense

HERMAN A. MELLOR

Any organization with 535 chief executive officers would have serious problems. This chapter shows that for all practical purposes, that is the situation with the Department of Defense. Unfortunately, the Department of Defense is not an ordinary organization, but is the largest executive branch agency, charged with defending the nation. Congressional interference prevents the Department of Defense from accomplishing its job. The result of congressional micromanagement is waste, inefficiency, and absurdity. The author speaks with the authority of one who has spent years working at the Department of Defense and with congressional leaders of both parties.

THE DEPARTMENT OF DEFENSE: A WHOLLY OWNED SUBSIDIARY

The Golden Rule: He who has the gold makes the rules.
—Anonymous

The following true story describes the recent imbalance between the legislative and the executive branches of the federal government, especially between Congress and the largest executive agency, the Department of Defense (DOD).

Public Law 99-550 annoyed the Secretary of Defense. As he signed a letter to accompany the quarterly report to Congress required by that law, he took the extra time to scribble a note at the bottom of the page to the chairman of a Senate committee and his House counterpart:

> One of the frustrations of this job...is that I must spend time on this kind of an issue instead of the larger problems that haunt us. This is not good management.

Public Law 99-550 requires agency heads to report to Congress a quarterly list of those employees who are authorized to receive home-to-work transportation at government expense. It is a well-intentioned law aimed at limiting an apparent luxury to those who can justify it for, as an example, security.

Nonetheless, it is quintessential micromanagment because: (1) The Secretary of Defense is forced to waste valuable time on an issue of microscopic proportions; (2) mere publication of this report encourages other congressional committees to get into areas traditionally reserved to the Armed Services Committees; and (3) Congress absorbs a constitutionally delegated function of the executive branch. Too often, the executive branch merely provides the staff and middle management which seemingly exist only to report to, and carry out the managerial decisions of Congress.

The Congress today proves the truth of the Golden Rule quoted above. There has been an explosion in the number of reports required by Congress. In hundreds of instances, Congress mandates in law the purchase of specific equipment or the funding of particular research projects, even those specifically declared unnecessary by the Department of Defense (invariably, the requirement for such items is constituent-based). An increasing number of committees lay claim to oversight of the defense budget, giving rise to a growing burden in terms of congressional requests to testify in committee and subcommittee hearings, legislatively required reports, official letters, phone calls, debates, explanations, and other time-consuming efforts.

Democrat Senator Sam Nunn of Georgia, chairman of the Senate Armed Services Committee, has been particularly plain-spoken on the issue:

. . . [T]he extent to which we have wrapped ourselves around the budget axle is exacerbated by the growing tendency to examine budget proposals in even finer, almost microscopic, detail. The Armed Services Committee now authorizes almost every element of the defense budget each year, down to almost the last screw and bolt.

Evidence to support Sen. Nunn's assertion is abundant. Congress *does* budget to the last screw and bolt. But first, they expand the number of overseers and then they usurp management prerogatives in order to pave the way for microbudgeting. This has led to an inevitable and dramatic increase in the size of congressional staffs, a trend chronicled by Michael Hammond and Peter Weyrich in Chapter 9.

EXPANDING OVERSIGHT

In 1960, when defense commanded a much greater share of the United States' national wealth than it does today (9.5 percent of Gross National Product in 1960, versus 5.7 percent for Fiscal Year 1989), spending came under the oversight of just two committees in each chamber of Congress.

Nonetheless, today the tendency is toward increasing oversight. In large part, this is because defense represents an opportunity for landing federal contracts within a member's state or district. Defense also has come to be viewed as an opportunity to gain political attention. Attacking the defense budget had become a very popular pastime by the mid-1980s, for both Democrats and Republicans. Final FY 1989 numbers will represent the fourth consecutive year of decline in the inflation-adjusted defense budget. Public opinion polls currently support members' suspicions that defense is the cheapest political cut.

Cutting the defense budget also increases pressure for oversight since it increases scrutiny of every defense spending decision. Thus, reprogramming, once a very routine management action approved by Congress, has been transformed into a substantial political debate. Together these factors—the desire to oversee an agency that commands such a large portion of the budget, and the political benefit in cutting defense—have contributed to increased oversight.

Who's in Charge?

In the late 1970s, four committees wrote defense legislation. Today, 24 committees and 40 subcommittees oversee defense. By actual measurement, current law and regulation on defense procurement fill 1,152 linear feet of law library shelf space. Thousands of pages are added during each legislative cycle with few, if any, being removed.

Numerous thoughtful observers, from administration officials to congressional leaders, universities and think tanks, have exhorted Congress to end the current chaos of subcommittee micromanagement and reassert order in the process.

Indeed, Congress acknowledges the problem. As Senator John Tower, former chairman of the Senate Armed Service Committee, observed in 1984:

> If we look at the area of national security, most committees in the Senate have an involvement with some aspect of the subject. The involvement of the Armed Services, Appropriations, and Budget Committees is obvious. The Foreign Relations Committee has jurisdiction over arms control, foreign aid, security assistance, war powers, and many aspects involving the use of military force outside the United States. The Small Business Committee injects itself in the breadth of the procurement process on the basis that it is concerned about small business opportunities to participate in defense contracting. The Veterans Affairs Committee has jurisdiction over a series of benefits available to those who have previously served in the armed forces, though this benefit package may have an impact on military recruitment and retention.
>
> The Governmental Affairs Committee asserts a claim, which I strongly dispute, that it has primary jurisdiction over procurement policy, including procurement policy in the Department of Defense. The Banking Committee has jurisdiction over the Cost Accounting Standards Board, which sets the fundamental-ground rules for the manner in which defense contracts are paid.

That committee also has jurisdiction over the Defense Production Act, which is a critical legislative tool for ensuring an adequate defense industrial base. The Banking Committee also has jurisdiction over the Export Administration Act, which is the primary legislative tool for stopping transfer of militarily sensitive technologies.

The Commerce Committee has jurisdiction over NASA, which plays an integral role in providing access to space for the Department of Defense. The Commerce Committee also has jurisdiction over the Merchant Marine, which has an important national defense function, as we learned in the Falklands War. The Intelligence Committee has primary jurisdiction over the gathering of intelligence though that is inextricably linked to military posture.

This is simply an illustrative list of the extent to which aspects of national security are divided among a huge number of standing committees. I might add that in the House the situation is even worse, in that the House Energy Committee has shared jurisdiction with respect to the Department of Energy nuclear weapons program.

Endless Inquiries

Increased oversight has been reflected in an increasing demand for DOD officials' testimony before the various committees and subcommittees. The number of requests for DOD testimony in the 10-year period between 1975 and 1984 was three times higher than between 1965 and 1974. Example: Assistant Secretary of Defense for International Security Affairs Richard Armitage was personally called upon to testify some 154 times over a seven-year period during the Reagan Administration.

The Pentagon receives more than 100,000 official written congressional inquiries each year; an average of 200 written requests per year from each of the 535 members of Congress. The last presidential campaign year, 1984, saw some 123,130 written requests sent from Capitol Hill to the Defense Department. Now, calendar year 1988 threatens to set a new record, as the inquiries always reach their peak before the November presidential election.

The cost of responding to such inquiries has not been tabulated, but amounts to many millions of dollars per year. There are additional costs for the preparation of official testimony for up to 500 hearings. This does not include the increasing number of reports which DOD must research and write each year for members of Congress.

Expanding oversight has slowed the process in other ways. As members, and their staffs, gain expertise in some facet of defense for which they have some oversight responsibilities, they write and offer more detailed amendments to the defense authorization bills each year. The sheer number of amendments offered each year has helped to slow a budget process that already fails to meet the deadlines specified in law. To illustrate, Senator Nunn has pointed out that the five-year period of 1975-80 brought an average of 15 House and Senate amendments offered to the annual authorization bill, with an average of three days spent on floor debate. Between 1981 and 1985, however, the averages jumped to 75 amendments and nine days of debate. During the FY 1989 authorization bill for national defense, for example, the House considered 120 amendments that required nine days of debate; in the Senate, where the efficiency-conscious Senator Nunn was manager of a bill that attracted some 92 suggested amendments, six days were spent on debate. Table 1 charts the number of amendments and days of debate concerning authorization bills for Fiscal Years 1975-89.

Mountains of Paper

The increases in congressional oversight result in mountains of additional reports. Members can slow the process considerably by asking for a formal report to Congress as a prerequisite to almost any action.

Both the number and types of reports required are nearly unfathomable. Example: In April 1987, in accordance with a requirement set out in the Goldwater-Nichols Department of Defense Reorganization Act of 1986, DOD identified some 319 periodically recurring reporting requirements placed upon the Department by Congress. The Goldwater-Nichols Act required DOD to identify those reports and make recommendations on

Table 1 Floor Debate on DOD Authorization Bills

Fiscal Year	House Days of Debate	House Amendments	Senate Days of Debate	Senate Amendments
1975	3	15	6	29
1976	2	12	4	16
1977	3	0	2	6
1978	3	0	2	18
1979	5	33	3	11
1980	4	17	3	18
1981	8	49	3	16
1982	8	78	7	61
1980	12	64	13	72
1981	6	52	10	107
1985	9	140	9	107
1986	9	137	6	108
1987	9	103	7	84
1988	11	130	16	118
1989	9	120	6	92

Source: Department of Defense

those reports that the Department believed could be repealed or modified. The Defense Department has presented draft legislation to repeal 97 of the requirements and modify another 16, leaving some 206 recurring reports, even assuming that Congress will accept every DOD recommendation for repeal or modification. Thus far, Congress has accepted only a minimal number of the Department's recommendations. A cursory review of the reports suggested for repeal illustrates the detail Congress demands from its coequal branch of government. DOD has suggested repeal of reports on:

• Acquisition of power-operated collators for use in facilities other than printing plants.
• Advance notice and reporting of acquisition and/or installation of printing equipment.
• Status of an automated technical order system for printing purposes.
• Notification relating to the repair, restoration, or replacement of damaged or destroyed military facilities.
• Notification on military exercises.

Table 2 Congressional Reporting Requirements In Defense And Military Construction Authorization And Appropriations: Committee Reports

Fiscal Year	Number of Reports/Studies
1970	36
1976	114
1977	129
1978	153
1979	177
1980	231
1981	223
1982	221
1983	325
1984	422
1985	458
1986	676
1987	680
1988	719

Source: Department of Defense

- Notification on the transfer or gift of any obsolete, condemned or captured vessels.
- Agreements with the Department of State regarding use of that agency's housing by Department of Defense personnel.
- Annual report on the cataloging of stock and supplies.

These recurring reporting requirements only suggest the whole list. One-time, non-recurring reporting requirements that are written into law may well represent the fastest growth industry within the U.S. government. Table 2 shows the exponential growth in this category of reports.

The record 719 non-recurring reports required as part of the FY 1988 process will require an estimated 300 man-years to complete, and will cover an estimated 25,000-plus pages, at an approximate cost of $25 million. As the table shows, since 1970, reporting requirements have increased an astounding 1,900 percent. Concurrent with this explosion in time-consuming reporting, Congress has illogically mandated reduced staffing of management headquarters.

Reaching Absurdity

In FY 1985, the Defense Department was required to report on the retirement benefits for Philippine scouts. Such nonsense moved Senator Nunn to take to the floor of the Senate in the fall of 1985 and say:

> Each of these studies could be justified on its own merits. But when you add up all of them and look at the total of what we are directing the Defense Department to do, the sum total is absolutely absurd. The micromanagement problem is out of control.

Included among the one-time reports required for FY 1988 are the following:

- Plans for manning and operating DOD tugboats.
- Proposed survey questions pertaining to parental and family leave policies.
- Quarterly updates on the above survey.
- Final report on parental and family leave policies.
- A concept plan and procedures to comply with congressional guidance on funding for morale, welfare, and recreation.

• Prior to signing a lease for facilities at Oakland, California, a report on the terms of that specific lease.

• A separate report explaining the terms of a lease for land in Oakland.

• Long-range plans for modernizing a specific research facility.

• Reporting and justifying the number of military bands.

• Details of a proposed contract to sell DOD land in various locations.

• A report on demonstrating the training of machine technicians in a production facility.

• A report on the demonstration and testing of the basic configuration of the safety device on the Stinger anti-aircraft missile launcher.

• A separate report on the demonstration and testing of the reprogrammable microprocessor configuration of the safety device on the Stinger.

• A report on what techniques can be used to measure "readiness."

• A report on how DOD intends to structure and conduct a demonstration project on the management of health care in areas within a 30-mile radius of certain DOD health care facilities.

• A follow-up report to the above discussing the methodology to be used for evaluating results.

• A third report to describe any results during the first 12 months and a final report describing the results, and cost/benefit comparisons to incorporate the demonstrated technique throughout the military health care system.

• A comparison of civil service and military household goods moving benefits.

• An overall procurement strategy for mortar time fuses.

• A five-year budget plan and acquisition strategy for purchasing an intrusion detection system.

Big Brother Is Watching

Congress also has required DOD to submit internal management reports dealing with acquisition programs and long-term budget planning. The Defense Department uses various methods to track the progress of major acquisition programs. Over the years, the reports evolved into what now are called Selected Acquisition Reports (SARs). The SARs detail the various elements of the Department's largest contracts. SARs track contract negotiations, provide schedule and cost-estimate updates, and compare the current program status with the original plan. SARs had been a valuable management tool. They allowed Defense Department management to receive confidential assessments of progress, or the lack thereof, on critical acquisition programs. Congress decided in 1975 that it should begin receiving such reports through the Armed Services Committees. Long-time career civil servants in the Defense Department maintain that the value of SARs plummeted dramatically once they became public documents. Confidentiality and candor disappeared. The reports became more bland and less informative, since report authors feared being sacrificed to the press for presiding over troubled programs. To bar internal confidential reporting is to leave any management severely hamstrung. Indeed, even Congress allows itself confidential, internal meetings and planning sessions.

Congress in 1987 similarly weakened the DOD's internal Five-Year Defense Plan (FYDP). The FYDP is an internal planning document by which the various levels of management within DOD are supposed to be able to take a longer-term view and ensure that today's programs are moving the Department in the proper direction. It is essentially a list of thoughtful alternatives from which choices are made. Congress, however, decided to demand such management information. Again, career budget specialists in DOD fear that the utility of the FYDPs will be sharply diminished as the reports begin to be prepared primarily for a critical public rather than as internal management tools.

Congress's management hand reaches into the personnel realm as well. Since the Defense Department's inception in 1947, Congress has specified how many special assistants (today called "assistant secretaries") the Secretary of Defense may have. And Title IV of the DOD Reorganization Act of 1986 is full of very specific personnel rules. Congress, for example, specifies tour duty length, the criteria that must be employed in deciding if someone can be nominated for certain positions, and similar detailed personnel matters.

Other congressional initiatives even threaten to affect DOD operations. For example: a new intelligence oversight bill passed by the Senate in 1988 requires the administration to notify Congress within 48 hours of all covert activities. Potentially, such oversight even could extend to DOD efforts to mislead the Soviets as to the location of our nuclear deterrent.

MICROBUDGETING

Many stimuli, from Watergate to the federal deficit, have prompted Congress to react with more detailed management. Another factor is the budget process itself, as discussed in detail in Chapter 6. A 1985 staff report for the Senate Armed Services Committee entitled "Defense Organization: The Need for Change" explicitly spelled out congressional management of defense spending:

> The annual review process, together with an increasing desire to control details, has led the Congress to a preoccupation with detail....There has been a steady and dramatic increase in the extent of congressional involvement in the annual defense budget submission. In 1970 the defense authorization act totaled 9 pages, with a 33-page conference report accompanying the bill....The fiscal year 1985 bill was 169 pages and the conference report totaled 354 pages.

Although this trend has exploded dramatically in the years following the 1974 Budget Act, it began many years earlier. In fact, like some other major federal government trends, this one can trace its beginnings to a well-known Democrat who believed in an activist role for government: Lyndon Baines Johnson.

In 1958, then-Senator Johnson chaired the Preparedness Investigating Subcommittee of the Armed Services Committee. His subcommittee launched an investigation into a perceived "missile gap" between the Soviet Union and a lagging United States. The issue ultimately was a factor in the 1960 presidential election.

The perception of that gap also gave rise to a legislative change in 1959 when the Senate began to require annual authorizations for DOD purchases of missiles, aircraft and naval vessels. Before 1959 and the missile gap, the House and Senate Armed Services Committees simply authorized types of activity on a permanent basis, and let the Appropriations Committees determine specific amounts.

The Irresistible Pork Barrel

Once started, the metamorphosis was unstoppable. It was only in 1982 that Congress began to require annual authorization for procurement of ammunition. Today the level of micromanagement continues to expand. The authorization process, for example, has been used to legislate DOD purchases of millions of tons of anthracite coal. As a result, at the end of FY 1988, the Defense Department will have on hand some 700,000 tons of anthracite coal, more than a 12-year supply. Despite contentious debate on the issue, this year the Senate reported a bill directing purchase of 300,000 more tons of anthracite coal, at a projected cost of $21 million.

The Defense Department has been required ever since 1962 to burn only U.S. coal at its European military installations. Further, there have been various legislative prohibitions over the years against converting the obsolete and inefficient heating systems at those bases to burn any other kind of fuel. Although DOD did gain permission in both FY 1987 and 1988 to convert some heating systems to other energy sources (after much diplomatic pressure from a West German government driven by environmental concerns), the House-passed FY 1989 Defense Authorization bill included an amendment by Pennsylvania Democrat Paul Kanjorski to prohibit further conversions for one year until a study was done by DOD and submitted to Congress. The Army owns a huge supply of an uncompetitive energy source, and at this time, is being forced to stockpile acres of anthracite coal as a monument to the way an overly detailed budget process can be used to serve the interests of powerful legislators.

The Heavy Expanded Mobility Tactical Truck (HEMTT)

provides another example of microbudgeting. The HEMTT is a 10-ton, eight-wheeled truck that costs about $130,000 per unit. The truck is the primary product made by the 1,700 employees of the Oshkosh Truck Corp. of Wisconsin. The Army entered into a five-year contract with Oshkosh Truck in 1981, under which it ultimately arranged to purchase more than 8,500 units. But the Army opted in 1987 to terminate future purchases of the HEMTT in favor of a larger capacity vehicle, called a Palletized Loading System (PLS).

Congress had other plans, however, and the FY 1988 Continuing Resolution required the Army to purchase another 4,737 HEMTTs from Oshkosh beginning in FY 1988 and continuing through the next three fiscal years. This despite the fact that the Army projected a total need of only 2,300 additional HEMTTs, and preferred to develop the 16.5-ton PLS. Congress effectively foreclosed that option by denying development funding for PLS in FY 1987, and granting only a small portion of the amount requested for PLS testing and evaluation in the next fiscal year.

As DOD attempts to find a more capable vehicle, with open competition between Oshkosh Truck and others for the contract to produce it, the issue will persist. And it will persist in large part because the budget process is so susceptible to specific line-item tinkering by members of Congress.

While the politics of authorization and appropriation allow for legislative micromanagement, the process also is susceptible to broad and unworkable prescriptions that are written for political rather than national security reasons. Precisely because the defense bills are so important to the nation, it is always difficult for a president to veto them. That means politically inspired provisions with little relation to promoting national security can be grafted onto one of those bills and signed into law. The FY 1989 Authorization bill provided a textbook case of just such an attempt.

A Freshman's Debut

Freshman Representative Joe Kennedy (D-MA) authored an amendment to the Authorization bill which presumed to change the laws of other countries. Mr. Kennedy's proposed amendment stated that:

> the Secretary of Defense may not award a contract to be performed in a foreign country to any contractor (foreign or domestic) if, as determined...by the Inspector General of the Department of Defense, such contractor would be in violation of an equal employment opportunity law or order...in the United States.

Oklahoma Democrat Dave McCurdy quickly modified the amendment to eliminate specific reference to U.S. law, substituting instead language to make it illegal to allow a contract if the Inspector General's office found that a given contractor "discriminates, on the basis of race, color, religion, sex, or national origin, in its employment practices."

In opposition to the Kennedy-McCurdy amendment, Representative William Dickinson (R-AL), the ranking minority member of the Armed Services Committee, noted that requiring foreign suppliers to comply with all U.S. laws (or even broad social policies) only invites a destructive round of reciprocal treatment and retaliation from the national legislatures of our allies. What Mr. Dickinson did not mention is that requiring the DOD Inspector General to ascertain whether or not any present or potential overseas suppliers are guilty of any kind of discrimination in their hiring practices is a hugely expensive, subjective, and impossible task. The only practical redeeming factor of such a proposal is that it would mean greater sightseeing benefits for a globetrotting Inspector General's staff. Small wonder that it was quickly tabbed by many pundits as the worst amendment offered in the FY 1989 budget cycle.

Changing the Rules

Such involvement in the details of the DOD budget represents an infringement on the traditional territory of the Appropriations Committees. As mentioned above, for many years the authorization process approved only the broadest categories, leaving the appropriators to decide the details. So, as a kind of counterpoint to this infringement upon its turf, both Appropriations Committees began to appropriate funds that had not been specifically authorized.

The Appropriations Committees now feel free to appropriate whatever dollar amount they desire for any authorized activity as long as the total for all the line items in a given account does not exceed the authorized overall amount for that account. The authorizers may have specified an amount for a particular line item, but the appropriators do not consider themselves bound. Increasingly, the appropriators are engaging more in policy than in pricing.

Thus, a growing feud has developed between the authorizing Armed Services Committees and the Appropriations Committees. As the president's Blue Ribbon Commission on Defense Management (the Packard Commission) noted in its June 1986 report to the president:

> ... [T]he Department of Defense (DOD) now finds itself involved in a new congressional budgeting phenomenon in which the Appropriations Committees have funded programs that the Armed Services Committees have not authorized. In fiscal year 1986, the DOD Appropriations Act included over 150 line items, valued at $5.7 billion, that were authorized at a lower level or were not authorized at all . . . . Under these circumstances, the Secretary of Defense and the Military Departments find themselves in the position of making final decisions in formulating a budget for the next fiscal year while Congress is still debating its own wide-ranging differences on the budget that was submitted for the ongoing fiscal year.

In the Senate, this jurisdictional problem was addressed by an agreement in 1985 between Armed Services Committee Chairman Goldwater and Chairman Stevens of the Appropriations Committee's Defense Subcommittee. The senators agreed to sit in on each other's respective conferences with their House counterparts. In 1986, when the Democrats resumed majority status in the Senate, the problem was mitigated by the fact that Senator John Stennis of Mississippi was serving as both a member of the Armed Services Committee and as chairman of the Defense Subcommittee of the Appropriations Committee. Unfortunately, Senate rules now forbid such dual service, effective upon Senator Stennis' retirement at the end of the 100th Congress. Thus, the Senate may find itself revisiting the Armed Services vs. Appropriations turf battle.

In the House, a similar battle between committees simmered until the FY 1989 budget cycle was underway. It was then that Armed Service Committee Chairman Aspin and Representative Bill Chappell of Florida, chairman of the Appropriations Committee's Defense Subcommittee, agreed to respect each other's turf.

Exposing the Smoke and Mirrors

Into this less than ideal process, Congress threw the Gramm-Rudman-Hollings (GRH) deficit reduction act, which served to further expose the micromanaging boondoggles of Congress.

GRH effectively uncovered the "smoke and mirrors" of congressional budgeting: Congress appropriates money for some multiyear programs, so that in any given year the money actually expended (outlays) is comprised of money appropriated not only in the immediately preceding year, but also from earlier years. In other words, before a dime is appropriated in the annual budget cycle, the Defense Department must allocate money for outlays appropriated in earlier years. In recent years, roughly 40 percent of the defense outlays have been comprised of dollars appropriated years earlier for multiyear programs, leaving about 60 percent for new appropriated outlays.

The GRH approach to deficit reduction dealt only with controlling outlays in the immediate year. To meaningfully reduce defense outlays, therefore, given that 40 percent of the outlays were from previous years, requires either cancellation of ongoing multiyear programs (in effect throwing away an investment already made) or sharp reductions in the areas of the Defense budget that are not multiyear (primarily personnel and operations).

For years, the Appropriations Committee staffs played technical games to meet the numbers prescribed by Budget Resolutions. But these numbers were, and are, very political. In the House in particular, Democrats wanted a defense number lower than the administration's in order to lay claim to reducing the deficit, yet high enough to avoid the charge of being "soft on defense."

One of the ways in which defense is deftly shrunk relative to the rest of the federal budget, without making anyone look bad, is by utilizing the current services baseline to compare domestic spending to defense spending. This is an inaccurate and misleading comparison. (See also Chapter 6.)

In contrast to the domestic programs in the federal budget, defense is budgeted in a straightforward way: increases are carried as increases, and cuts as cuts. But the entitlement programs that dominate the domestic portion of the budget are measured by the current services baseline. The baseline consists of a series of amounts that would have to be spent in future years in order to maintain a constant level of services in a particular budget category. Because the cost of these services continues to rise with inflation, and the number of people using these services continues to increase, the current services budget assumes a status quo requiring rapidly increasing government expenditures. Therefore, even if a given program is expected to double in cost for either of these reasons in the coming year, it is not considered an "increase" if the level of spending does, in fact, double. Worse still, if the anticipated spending is cut so that rather than doubling, the program is increased only 50 percent, that 50 percent increase is scored as a "cut."

Congress uses such baseline shenanigans to argue that domestic spending has been "cut" dramatically while defense spending has increased. In fact, since such a "current services" approach does not lend itself to the defense budget, these comparisons are bogus.

Budget resolutions have often made such deep cuts in defense outlays that many House Appropriations Committee members balked on the grounds that national security would be severely damaged. Instead, they instructed staff to find creative technical changes. "For years," explains one House staff director, "we went through a smoke and mirrors routine to 'create' outlay savings: we reduced inflation estimates, pretended there would be no foreign currency fluctuations, reduced the amount of cash on hand, and so on. About the time we ran out of smoke and mirrors, along came Gramm-Rudman-Hollings."

As a result, GRH today hangs like a sword of Damocles over the Defense Department and Congress. If GRH's deficit targets are not met by the regular budget process, it requires across-the-board cuts in current year outlays to meet the targets, with half of them to come from defense.

Breaking Agreements

Faced with meeting the GRH deficit targets, leaders of Congress and the Reagan Administration sat down in November 1987 in a budget summit and hammered out an agreement (a handshake, really) to control DOD outlays. They also agreed on an FY 1989 defense budget of $299.5 billion.

On May 20, 1988, Deputy Secretary of Defense William Taft issued instructions to strictly curtail DOD outlays since the Department felt "every effort should be made to conform" to the budget summit agreement. His memo announced several technical outlay controls along with the deferral of all new research, development, technology, and engineering contracts, disallowance of all overtime pay, an end to educational assistance, limits in all new civilian hires to one hire per every two attritions, and deferral of all contracts for a long list of equipment and supplies.

The Department quickly received scores of letters from legislators concerned not about the effect of this sudden curtailment in spending on national defense, but on the harm caused to constituent contractors. The Deputy Secretary was summoned before a congressional committee, where it became evident that not only did many congressional defense experts not know they had limited outlays, but some did not even understand the difference between budget authority and outlays. At the same time, some in Congress were virtually ignoring the budget summit agreement. During the consideration of the Defense Authorization bill in the House, an amendment was offered and passed that took $475 million out of the Strategic Defense Initiative, and gave it to the Navy with express orders to give $410 million of it to the Coast Guard in the form of cost-free equipment for 10 years. The cause was worthy, since the equipment was a variety of aircraft and sea vessels for use in drug interdiction. But it clearly represented a $400 million-plus reduction in the funds available for DOD. While this effort did not survive the conference, it reflects the fact that Congress willingly breaks its agreements.

Likewise, in the Senate appropriations process, several Senators persuaded their colleagues to take $600 million from the defense budget for NASA purposes. If this decision becomes law, it will represent a violation of the White House budget summit. That action aside, consideration of the FY 89 defense bills seems to show that a handshake at a White House summit has more staying power than all the processes of Congress.

In the rush to cut, to save face, and to manage, procedure has suffered if not died. The House, in its consideration of the FY 1989 Defense Authorization bill adopted a rule for floor debate that sets out the rule for debating the Chairman's substitute which states: "[A]ll points of order against said substitute for failure to comply with the provisions of section 303(a)(4) of the Congressional Budget Act of 1974...are hereby waived." This represents the method by which the Caucus controls the end product of a committee whose members represent a position other than the House Democratic leadership.

Trivial Pursuits

More important than the procedural shortcomings of micromanaging is how it affects the nation's ability to defend itself. All of the above would be tolerable if we could still be assured that the real and serious national security needs of the United States were still being met. Unfortunately, that is not the case. In this atmosphere, Congress cannot find the time to address the necessary questions of threat analysis, military requirements and strategy. Instead, the size and shape of the defense budget are driven by an artificially achieved top line, narrow constituency issues, self-serving political manuevers and an unwieldy, expensive and overregulated bureaucracy. This assumes everything goes as well as possible. As Senator Nunn stated:

> The budget process distorts the nature of congressional oversight by focusing primarily on the question of how much before

we answer the key questions of what for, why and how well . . . .
Members of Congress and the staff are focusing on the grains of
sand on the beach, while we should be looking over the broad
ocean and beyond the horizon . . . . The current congressional
review of the defense program would make a fitting version of
the popular game 'Trivial Pursuit.'

Proof of the accuracy of Senator Nunn's assessment is everywhere. Precisely because Congress rarely wrestles with major
policy questions, it has no moorings when they arise. The Senate Armed Services Committee has attempted to remedy this
deficiency with strategy hearings, but, while cogent, they have
not had an impact on the system.

Burden Sharing and Base Closings:
Congressional Contradictions

"Burden sharing" is a current catchword. It means that the
U.S. and its allies should bear fair shares of the cost of the defense of the West. While the United States spends a greater
percentage of its wealth on national defense than do our allies,
the U.S. level of 5.7 percent of GNP for fiscal year 1989 is low,
relative to what our country has historically expended for defense. So, as Secretary of Defense Carlucci always maintains,
"we can all do more."

Nonetheless, in this age of large federal deficits, burden sharing represents to many members of Congress an opportunity to
reduce the defense budget while at the same time claiming to
favor defense spending. In this case, the proposed spending is
by an ally, and it may never materialize, given the politics of
most of our allies.

In such an environment, the administration proposed to sell
some Aegis cruiser technology to Japan so that it could use that
technology to defend itself and strategically important portions
of the North Pacific. The first sale in 1988 would have been for
$526 million and would have provided some 5,400 work-years
to the U.S. economy. The additional sales planned over the next
decade would have resulted in adding billions of dollars to the
U.S. economy and increasing defense capability in the North

Pacific, as Japan had agreed to be responsible for defending the airspace and sea-lanes out to 100 miles from her shores. But various members of Congress, including some of those calling for greater burden sharing by our allies, refused to support this cooperative effort, and used the FY 1989 Defense Appropriations bill in an attempt to effectively cancel the sale by requiring the technology sale to include the purchase of a U.S. hull.

Base closing is another example of conflicting signals from Congress. Despite Congress's constant inveighing against waste, and excessive defense spending, no major base has been closed since 1977, despite changing force structure, force requirements, and missions. As a result, billions upon billions of dollars are wasted keeping unnecessary military bases open and operating.

A July 1988 ABC-TV news broadcast by Pentagon correspondent Bob Zelnick made exactly this point. He called some of DOD's outdated bases "a national joke." As examples, Zelnick pointed to Fort Monroe, a moat-encircled base built in Virginia shortly after the war of 1812, and to Fort Douglas, built near Salt Lake City to protect stagecoach routes from hostile Indians. Zelnick described for his viewers the standard sequence of events when DOD has suggested closing unnecessary bases: closure is proposed, lawsuits are filed, an anticlosure citizens group is formed, and political pressure is applied that ultimately results in specific legislation mandating certain steps before a given base closure can even be studied or considered.

Recently, amid declining dollars for defense, the pressure for frugality became great enough that Secretary of Defense Carlucci worked out a procedure with congressional leaders that he thought would be acceptable. There appeared to be a general agreement that pressure from diminishing resources was enough to get people to accept the perceived pain of closures. (In fact, the pain, mostly unemployment in the surrounding community, is probably chimerical. In 100 communities experiencing base closings between 1961 and 1981, there was actually an employment gain, due to DOD assistance.)

Again, because Congress had not dealt with this subject for so long, it acted contradictorily. Members who decried DOD's inefficiency and waste were quick to defend the bases in their state or districts. They paid lip service to the idea of closing bases, but added such legislative impediments as calling for a study of all bases worldwide before domestic bases could be closed. The cost of all these amendments dwarfs the alleged wasteful spending of DOD on overpriced hammers, coffee pots, and toilet seats.

TOWARD A NEW PARTNERSHIP?

The final irony in the struggle between Congress and the executive branch is that, were Congress to more evenly share its responsibilities, treating the executive as a coequal, rather than as a servant, many of these problems would disappear. Members of Congress would be freed from the entangling detail of the budget to discuss real policy issues. And members would find that every administration, Democrat or Republican, employs an army of policy people anxious to discuss substantive issues. Members would find management professionals in every agency capable of making the necessary decisions on details.

The prospects for such a partnership, however, are dim, because as things now stand, Congress has all the gold and doesn't need to change the rules.

5. Congressional Micromanagement: Domestic Policy

JOHN HIRAM CALDWELL

This chapter discusses one example of the impact of congressional meddling in the administration of domestic programs, particularly agriculture. As in the area of defense, congressional interference is idiosyncratic, inefficient, and sometimes just petulant. The costs are very real in terms of failing to help people in need, and in terms of taxpayers' dollars wasted. The author's expertise comes from years on Capitol Hill and in senior positions in the executive branch.

Every day, Americans see newspaper, magazine, and television stories about ways in which congressmen, senators, and the legislative branch as an institution are administering more and more details of American life and government. The Speaker of the House acts as if he were Secretary of State, and thus encourages his colleagues to impose their personal agendas on affairs of state traditionally outside the legislative process. It is not wholly in jest that pundits speak of 536 Secretaries of State—the president's appointee and each member of Congress.

In truth, the charge can be repeated for every cabinet department and agency in the federal establishment. The Pentagon, for example, is prevented from closing scores of obsolete military bases to save $5 billion annually because Congress has written such detailed requirements into the closing procedures to make it impossible, for all practical purposes (see Chapter 4). And, not content to micromanage just the programs of the federal government, Congress now seeks to enact "plant closing" laws, imposing congressional judgment on the management of private firms. These practices are no longer aberrations. Legislative micromanagment of programs is rapidly becoming the norm. It has become such a significant factor in government as to render national policy objectives secondary to the narrow interests of individual legislators and their most vocal constituents. The result is wasteful and unnecessary spending, and serious harm to our constitutional principles of self-government.

New innovations in micromanagement by the legislative branch are underway. These innovations will extend the prerogatives of Congress and congressional bureaucracies at the expense of the president and the executive branch, not to mention virtually every other jurisdiction in America, public and private. The question is whether micromanagement makes our liberties more secure or less secure.

THE ADMINISTRATIVE CONGRESS

Congressman Jamie L. Whitten, Democrat of Charleston, Mississippi exemplifies how a legislator's good intentions can have serious repercussions on the way Americans are governed.[1] In many ways his actions illustrate the extent to which Congress has come to disregard traditional limits on its power, to a degree which threatens our constitutional system of government.

Having spent the past 48 of his 79 years in Congress, Mr. Whitten is the longest serving of all House members. Since 1979 he has been Chairman of the House Committee on Appropriations, and serves simultaneously as Chairman of its Subcommittee on Rural Development, Agriculture, and Related Agencies, a post he has held for all but two years since 1949.

Over the years he has built a reputation as a rascally and secretive curmudgeon who fancies himself as something of a "permanent Secretary of Agriculture." He has never had much affection for the agriculture secretaries of any administration, apparently viewing them as "uninformed" competition standing in the way of his efforts to have Congress provide as much assistance as possible to farmers.

His personality, style, convictions, and alliances combine to make him a powerful character whom few care to cross, and whom most try to accommodate. In the opinion of many, he has established absolute control over his agriculture appropriations subcommittee. The members of the subcommittee permit him to dominate the commitee with their indulgence. He produces agricultural appropriations bills in a closed system of rigorous secrecy without much real participation by other members, and certainly with no meaningful participation by the public. So tight is his control over the appropriations bills and accompanying report language that rarely does anyone outside his closest circle have any idea what exactly may be in an appropriations bill until after it passes the entire House. Indeed, under the new continuing resolution process, few know what Mr. Whitten has mandated until a copy of the enrolled bill has been enacted and signed into law by the president.

The "Rule" of Law

Upon the 125th anniversary of the Department of Agriculture in 1987, in recognition of the considerable role he has played in the history of agriculture over almost 50 years, and perhaps out of some hopeful expectation of an improvement in the relations between him and the executive branch, Mr. Whitten was invited to deliver an address. The celebration was held in the Jefferson Auditorium at the imposing edifice of the Department of Agriculture located on Independence Avenue just across from the Washington Monument. In attendance were all the worthies and notables of the Department, many lobbyists and hangers-on, and other friends of agriculture.

Mr. Whitten used the occasion to complain that those in the executive branch responsible for administering farm programs did not have sufficient appreciation for the importance of agriculture, simply were not doing the job Congress intended, and were generally uninformed about the law as it pertains to farm programs. He summed up his understanding of his role, and that of Congress, by saying, in effect:

> "Don't you see? All anyone ever wants is a special advantage over the next fellow. Understand that, and you've understood the intent of every law ever passed."

In short, Mr. Whitten is an earnest proponent of using the law to give a special advantage to his favored constituency. He cannot understand, and is enormously frustrated by, those who do not agree that showering largesse on farmers is truly helpful to them or to the country. Nor does he appreciate those who share his convictions but who seek some kind of balance or reasonable limits.

With the consent of his colleagues, Mr. Whitten has used his enormously powerful and influential positions to effect major institutional innovations strengthening the role of his committee and subcommittee. These innovations are designed to diminish the opportunity for participation by those who hold other views. They preclude a sharing of power with other entities in Congress or other branches of government. On the one hand, the Whitten innovations, and their analogs elsewhere in Congress, diminish the deliberative functions of the institution; on the other, they increase the administrative role that Congress plays in the governance of the nation.

A New Breed of Political Entrepreneurs

It would be a mistake however, to attribute the pattern of legislative usurpation of executive responsibilities to this one individual. These practices constitute new procedures which are being woven into the fabric of precedent and process throughout the legislative branch.

Like his colleagues, Mr. Whitten is simply operating as a political entrepreneur, taking advantage of every opportunity afforded him, recognizing few if any constraints on his power. The political entrepreneur, adept at taking advantage of opportunities before him, is one of the strongest driving forces behind the new accretions of power to the legislative branch. This new entrepreneurialism is the result of a number of forces that now seem entrenched in our polity, including the decline of the role of party organizations, and the degree to which personality and style determine electoral success.

These factors, and others like them, which cause the legislator to think of himself as an independent entity, push the legislator to seek as much personal publicity as possible, and as many opportunities as possible to "deliver the goods." Under such conditions, legislators, like entrepreneurs in the business world, are constantly exploring the outer edges of what is possible and acceptable to the public. They are frustrated by those who stand in their way. The "imperial" congressman is not content to do the best he can under normal procedures. He must push, even if the limits provided by the separation of powers stand in the way.

New Methods of Lawmaking

There has been fundamental change in the way the House of Representatives and the Senate legislate. The traditional divisions of responsibility in the separate and distinct functions and processes of authorization, appropriations, and oversight have become confused and tangled. While laws have never really been made in the fashion described in the "How Our Laws Are Written" articles popular with school children and political science professors, there was always a predictable process with a regular timetable and deadlines for action that induced resolution of issues.

In recent years, all that has changed; the whole process is subject to instant innovation. Comprehensive, insightful hearings on important legislative proposals are becoming rare. Hearings involving executive branch witnesses have become acrimonious shouting matches in which congressmen ask rapid-fire questions in the tone and demeanor of prosecuting attorneys, cutting off answers that don't suit their purpose. Committees have increasingly diminished the practice of preparing comprehensive spreadsheets so members can compare how different bills under consideration treat similar subjects. The opportunities for members to engage in analysis and deliberation prior to and during legislative drafting sessions are increasingly meaningless. Genuine floor debate on matters of fundamental choice is regarded as an intrusion barely tolerated. Congress appears to have lost interest in developing broad legislative policy for the nation.

The legislative process has become so tangled, confused, and unpredictable that many members seem to find the legislative process tedious, and not very much fun. Further, the decidedly liberal political agenda of the controlling majority leadership and its unrelenting political opposition to virtually every executive branch initiative or point of view is very difficult for most members to sell back home. These factors induce greater attention to the administrative details of government as day-to-day activities for the individual member. Helping their constituents sort through mazes of bureaucratic red tape is what pays off for members at election time. And, of course, such activity is also driven by the desire of members to simply exercise more power and influence, if they can.

Thus, there is an increasing effort by all committees to write greater and greater specificity into laws and statutes. Such specificity allows the executive branch little or no flexibility to deal with changing conditions in a dynamic society and economy. This results in great problems and difficulties which always leads to enactment of more laws, with even greater specificity. The great American folklorist Joel Chandler Harris put it all into perspective years ago when he wrote his famous tale of "Brer Rabbit and the Tar Baby." The more ol' Congress beats on the tar baby of micromanagement, the greater its dismay and the worse its fix. It is simply too risky and difficult to go on record for public scrutiny. Every issue is best worked out behind the scenes, and the intense micromangagement of every detail of programs is best left to the increasingly specialized congressional bureaucracy, which now exceeds 30,000 in number.

ERODING EXECUTIVE POWER

At the heart of legislative indifference to the constitutional separation of powers is the continuing resolution. The CR, as it is popularly called, is a disreputable instrument of law which has transmogrified the legislative process into a caricature of what the Constitution intended for the legislative branch. The CR developed from the concept of "supplemental" appropriations bills. These instruments were used to handle circumstances and needs not contemplated when the regular budget or appropriations bills were passed.

Then came the "emergency supplemental" appropriations bill, which was deemed even more necessary and extraordinary. Sometimes, under the guise of meeting budget constraints, the appropriations committees deliberately created the gridlock that made these supplementals necessary by appropriating insufficient funds to cover entitlements. This has repeatedly been the case in agricultural appropriations bills, including a multibillion dollar under-appropriation for USDA's Commodity Credit Corporation for FY 1989, reported by Mr. Whitten's committee in May 1988. To these instruments was added the increasingly utilized practice of including authorizing language in appropriations bills, contrary to Senate and House rules.

Each little change in the process has seemed so reasonable and desirable at the time that there was virtually no effective opposition from any quarter. The proverbial frog was in the pot with the heat being turned up in very comfortable increments.

The next logical step was the omnibus Continuing Resolution. In this new legislative instrument anything and everything was possible. Careful scrutiny of and deliberation over individual items became impossible. For Fiscal Years 1986, 1987, and 1988, the CR took the place of all 13 regular appropriations bills. As a practical matter, the power of the presidential veto became what our Founding Fathers would have called "nugatory"—of no practical utility. In 1988 it was utterly impossible for any member to have read the bill or even to know what was in all of it.

Because Congress adjourned for Christmas immediately upon passage of the CR in 1987, the president was confronted with the choice of shutting down the government until Congress could be reconvened, or approving the bill. He chose to approve the bill. It was weeks before many details of what was in the bill were made available, and much of what was there, all observers agreed, would never have stood the test of the traditional method of authorizations, appropriations, and oversight. Included was the abolishment of executive branch offices that had challenged Congressional policy, all kinds of pork-barrel boondoggles such as Senator Inouye's (D-HI) $7 million for a school in France and, Senator McClure's (R-ID) $6 million ski resort gondola in Idaho, plus such major substantive laws as Senator Kennedy's (D-MA) ruse to eliminate a critical newspaper in Boston, and scores of others juicy provisions.[2]

The bottom line: the CR has had the practical effect of removing the instrument of the veto from the executive branch. No matter that the Founding Fathers saw the veto as a vital restraint on the legislative branch, and essential to the very concept of the separation of powers.

Two Steps Forward, One Step Back

In an effort to avoid the CR debacle in the future, the Reagan Administration solicited the participation of the congressional leadership in a "bipartisan summit agreement" for the fiscal year 1989 budget and appropriations process. In this further innovation, the executive and the legislative branches agreed to an overall budget number, and established certain understandings as to what amounts would be included in various accounts—a certain amount for defense, for social programs, and so on.

The President's Chief of Staff, the Secretary of the Treasury, and the Director of OMB were to join with the chairmen and ranking minority members of the Appropriations and Budget Committees and other majority and minority members of the Senate and House leadership to resolve differences as the details for the FY 1989 budget were pieced together. There was an understanding that there would be no more supplemental appropriations bills without mutual agreement, and there would be no more omnibus Continuing Resolutions. Each of the 13 appropriations bills would be considered individually, with opportunity for a complete legislative process of hearings, legislative drafting sessions (mark-ups), written reports and full opportunity for consideration, debate, and challenge on the floor of both the House and the Senate, with conferences to resolve remaining differences between the two versions. Moreover, the president was to have full opportunity to effectively exercise his veto of individual appropriations bills as he saw fit.

While one can appreciate the eagerness of the administration to negotiate such a procedure to avoid the kind of collapse of its influence that took place during the fiscal year 1988 appropriations process, one cannot help but feel somewhat disquieted. This agreement is reminiscent of East-West international negotiations, where the Soviet Union is rewarded for withdrawing from a country it has invaded.

In this case, the legislative branch agrees to operate as it should have operated all along. The executive branch, however, made a major concession, agreeing to give up in advance much of its freedom to propose an independent budget. If such a process becomes firmly established in practice and procedure whereby the executive must always negotiate its budget proposal with congressional leaders in advance of sending it forth, the result will be a fundamental change in the way in which Americans are governed. The most aggressive elements of the legislative branch will have new strengths and prerogatives, while the executive branch will be seriously weakened.

A Full Frontal Assault

While Congressional micromanagement has evolved over a number of years, in 1987 it took a particularly pernicious turn with enormous implications for the separation of powers. Congress, through an agricultural appropriations bill, not only mandated how appropriated funds were to be spent, but also eliminated one executive branch office and reduced the size of another at the Department of Agriculture. This, because Congress disagreed with the way these executive offices were doing their job.

Specifically, Chairman Whitten was annoyed that the Assistant Secretary of Agriculture for Natural Resources and Environment refused to request more funding for certain soil conservation programs. The chairman was also annoyed at the department generally, for using cost/benefit analysis in virtually all programs and accounts. So, to extend his power and weaken the executive branch, and in disregard for the constitutional prerogatives of the Senate to advise and consent to the appointment of certain executive officers, his committee did not fund the office of Assistant Secretary for Natural Resources and Environment. Only when senators objected was a compromise reached creating another assistant secretary with unspecified responsibilities. The administration, fearful of the precedents, objected to all this with great vigor, but to no avail.

Likewise, Mr. Whitten was annoyed with the administrator of USDA's Farmers Home Administration for his efforts to establish procedures to assure collection of loans made to farmers. The authorizing laws, written by Congress, authorized the department to make farm loans, not grants. This language certainly seemed to imply some procedure for collecting on the loans, but Mr. Whitten and his committee imposed their will by cutting in half the normal operating funds for the Office of the Administrator of the Farmers Home Administration. The result: the office would no longer have the personnel to produce loan repayment policies and procedures.

These actions were possible because of legislative innovations put in place by Mr. Whitten and his committees over a number of years. Prior to 1980, appropriations for the Office of the Secretary of Agriculture were made as one line item. The Secretary had discretion over how he would use those funds. He could decide how many assistants, secretaries, clerks, and other staff he and his policy team would have. Within certain constraints he could decide how many assistant secretaries he needed and what their responsibilities would be. He could not, of course, exceed the overall appropriation for his office.

But beginning in the early 1980s, Mr. Whitten began to divide up this appropriation into separate segments for each Under Secretary and Assistant Secretary. In that same bill he took the unprecedented step of making a final division for the Office of the Secretary, providing for the first time a special account for the Deputy Secretary separate from that of the Secretary.

The implications of all this have not been lost on other legislators. In a subsequent hearing before another subcommittee on another subject in 1988, an assistant secretary in another department who had made some changes in the organization of one of the agencies for which he had policy responsibility, was advised by the chairman of that subcommittee to reconsider, and to be mindful that if he did not, his fate and the fate of his office might be similar to that of the Assistant Secretary of Agriculture. The executive branch official heeded this warning, with resulting significant modifications to the internal agency's programs.

If Congress continues this practice, and such procedures become institutionalized, how long will it be before assistant secretaries and other senior policy officials appointed and confirmed as officers of the executive branch will feel they are responsible to the Congress, or to congressional committees, or even to individual congressmen, rather than to the president? When and if that day arrives, what will be left of the executive branch?

FARM POLICY: IS THIS WHAT THE PUBLIC WANTS?

In the waiting room of the offices of Senator John Danforth, Republican of Missouri, there hangs on the wall a cartoon spoofing the degree to which the people actually get from Congress the kinds of laws they want. The first panel shows a child's swing with two ropes but three seats, one above the other. This is identified as the "House Version" of the swing.

The second panel shows a single seat, as it should, but there are three ropes: still no room for the child. This is the "Senate Version." The third, fourth, and fifth panels show other versions of the swing situated on the tree in such sophisticated and complicated ways as to make the swing completely useless, even dangerous. These are identified respectively as "The Law as Enacted," "The Law as Administered," and "The Law as the Courts Interpret It." The last little drawing in the series shows "What the Public Wanted," a single rope with a worn out tire hanging from the tree.

So it goes with farm programs. The public wants to give encouragement and support to farmers who may be in financial distress. But the public gets a program that transfers enormous amounts of income to some of the most financially secure and wealthy segments of the population in a way that impacts adversely on almost everyone, including the very farmers who would have first claim to reasonable assistance.

That this can and does happen is a testimony to the degree to which the congressional processes operate in total disregard for the wishes of the executive branch. Every administration, Republican and Democrat, has wrestled intensely with Congress in a struggle to develop a comprehensive farm policy in which the various instruments are mutually consistent. For the most part such struggles have not been successful. This is principally so because the executive has consistently been presented farm bills that it cannot or will not veto. In 1963 Congress enacted a farm bill over President Kennedy's veto, and no president since has even attempted to use the tools provided in the Constitution to counter congressional dominance in farm policy. If the executive branch is unwilling or unable to utilize the veto, it should not be surprising that Congress fills the vacuum of power.

There is little question that almost all Americans feel empathy with farmers and wish them well. Most Americans apparently believe that the government should play a more active role in agriculture than in almost any other area. But it is hard to believe that any sensible person would approve of the manner in which the various farm programs actually operate. Even those who have given their earnest support to the present panoply of farm programs readily acknowledge that such programs are neither sustainable nor desirable. There seems to be universal agreement that policy-makers must construct less intrusive and less costly programs.

A Monument To Micromanagement

The farm commodity programs offer a classic example of how Congress has designed programs with excruciating specificity, flawed in their concept and function, over the most earnest objections of the executive branch. These flawed programs then create conditions which justify even more programs with ever more detail. Such is the ultimate consequence of the imperial

Congress.[3] Much of the continual congressional tinkering deals with problems the original micromanagement created.

Why have farm programs proven counterproductive? The answer is simple: the price supports have been greater than the market value of the crops. But the subsidies aren't paid on the basis of a farmer's demonstrable need or financial stress. The subsidies are paid on the units of production—by the bushel, bale, or hundredweight. The more of a particular crop a farmer produces, the greater his total subsidy. By definition this means that the greatest benefits and subsidies go to the largest farmers, which also by definition means those farmers who need the most help get the least. The small struggling family farm is left in the dust.

Because Congress mandated that USDA must purchase and store whatever farmers could produce, unmarketable surpluses piled up. These surpluses overhang the markets, further depressing prices farmers receive in the marketplace. This results in all kinds of dislocations, such as declining land values and increases in production of other crops and livestock. When the surpluses become so great that there is literally no more physical storage space—as was the case in 1982 and nearly so in 1985—policy-makers are then forced by circumstances to restrict production. The largest acreage reduction program in the history of the world was implemented in 1983 for precisely this reason. Over the past 8 years, more than 250 million acres have been idled through government supply control programs. This has caused tremendous loss of income to farmers and others in the farm economy. And yet, total world production and trade increased, while until very recently, the U.S. share declined. Foreign farmers, and sometimes their Japanese and German financiers, see the U.S. reduce acreage and promptly expand theirs. In 1983, when the U.S. removed 78 million acres from cultivation, total world acreage cultivated actually increased by 13 percent.

Policies that induce more and more production in the face of massive surpluses for which there is no ready market put U.S. agriculture in the position of a dog chasing its own tail. Loan rates and target prices above market levels stimulate production and help turn over U.S. markets to foreign producers. Surpluses accumulate, exerting downward pressure on prices. Land values fall as farmers have trouble producing positive cash flows. Farmers who had not previously participated in these entitlement programs feel compelled to sign up, meaning ever greater government costs and ever greater inducements to excessive production. And then come countless provisions of law trying to protect this or that group from all the dislocations caused by the laws inherently flawed in the first place. The lives of congressional and USDA bureaucrats are consumed with trying to plug all the bulges in the balloon with special exemptions and supplemental payments to compensate for adverse consequences. A language of strange and highly technical terms comes forth: storage payments, advance deficiency payments, PIK-and-roll, certificates, CRP, ARPs, EEPs, haying and grazing, marketing loans, always another term, always another scheme.

Calls come forth for further production controls and even higher price supports in an effort to support the very farm income that was driven downward by subsidies that were too high to begin with. These actions, when taken, induce even greater surpluses, and result in pressure from farmer advocates in Congress for starting the cycle all over again. One important effect of all this, of course, is to further diminish the practical control over policy and administration by the executive branch. Congress has set up a paradox in which it is both the problem and the solution.

Who Loses?

The most startling aspect of all this is that the small- to medium-sized family farmers are the ones most adversely impacted by this bizarre scenario. The larger farmers are generally those whose variable costs of production are the least. They have traditionally had access to the greatest amounts of capital and technology, and can most readily adapt to changing conditions. Because the larger farmers' costs of production are generally lower, they find the price supports to be much more generous than do farmers who are smaller and for whom the unit costs of production are generally higher. Those farmers at the lower end of the cost of production curve simply apply the relatively lucrative price support payments and protections to purchasing more and more inputs and technology. In that way they attempt to increase their net income by selling more and more bushels, bales, and hundredweights—for which they receive more subsidies and payments. Those at the higher cost end of the production curve then find that the surpluses thus created have driven the prices they receive in the marketplace even lower.

The most vocal advocates of the "family farmer" then call for increased price supports, thus creating and exacerbating this perverse cycle all over again. Congress has enacted some kind of farm bill tinkering in these ways in virtually every year for the past decade. The bottom line: the immensely costly provisions of farm programs have very little to do with helping farmers in distress. It is apparent that these instruments of policy, mandated by Congress, operate to contribute significantly to the very real distress of small farmers.

Politics Over Policy

The principal driving force for the extraordinary abuses in farm programs is electioneering politics. A typical member of the House or the Senate will often think nothing of pushing through some kind of special detail that may cost tens or hundreds of millions of dollars, simply because he believes he might get a favorable headline or two in a small newspaper back home, or because his newsletter is coming out soon and he needs some copy that demonstrates his fealty to "helping the farmer." He can count on little opposition because few congressmen want to be stigmatized as "antifarmer," and because the executive branch has a track record of eventually approving farm legislation. Usually the details are so complicated and the impact so uncertain that it is difficult or impossible to explain how much a specific proposal will cost or what its true consequences will be.[4]

There is no need for the congressional entrepreneur to wait for routine consideration of farm bills. There is always an occasion for an amendment passing out a farm goodie: maybe it is an expiring farm law of some kind; or a drought; or a real glitch in the operation of one of the programs that cries out for modification; or a drumbeat of publicity about some special problem that catches the attention of the public for just long enough to encourage the entrepreneurial politician to call for a hearing; or maybe it is a completely unrelated matter that will move a legislative vehicle. Maybe it is just the appearance of a "legislative vehicle," a "window of opportunity," or the "silly season," meaning an election year. Rarely, there will be a lobbyist who is just crafty enough to induce the system to move. And, of course, there is always the appropriations bill, in recent years fair game for any purpose.

SPECIAL INTERESTS: WHO MAKES POLICY?

While most of the momentum for all this micromanagement comes from within Congress itself—at least as it relates to the farm programs—there are other forces at work, as well. Consider the case of the continuation of government farm loans to insolvent debtors in 1987 and 1988. In this case, the players were legion. They included: militant borrowers determined to keep their assets and their loans despite real insolvency; vigorous executive branch officers intent upon inducing normal business practices into delinquent loan management; a public interest law firm; an eccentric judge who could never be satisfied; a political climate that made it possible for political entrepreneurs in the authorizing and appropriations committees of Congress to further their reputations as champions of the family farmer; and the proverbial "window of opportunity" that made it possible to reach new heights of micromanagment.

Once again, Congress forced its will, utilizing innovations in the legislative process that removed opportunities for effective input from the executive branch. Once again, the doctrine of separation of powers was weakened.

The Reagan Administration had tried earnestly during its entire tenure to manage the Farmers Home Administration (FmHA) portfolio with sound business practices, consistent with its mission of assisting family farmers. This attempt was born of the conviction that both borrowers and taxpayers are best served when borrowers are accountable for their debts to the full extent of their assets—that is, when loans are treated like loans, not like grants, and when they are serviced in a way to increase the chances for performance by the borrowers.

The administration executives responsible for FmHA were skilled and effective proponents of this approach, and vigorously pursued administrative and legislative initiatives to assure loan repayments. Their efforts were greatly complicated by the severe recession in agriculture during the period 1980-85. Other agricultural lenders dumped many of their nonperforming farm loans onto FmHA.

In 1985, Vance Clark, a highly regarded former senior vice president of the largest agricultural lender in the country, the California-based Bank of America, assumed leadership of the FmHA. He brought a new wave of vigor, conviction, and skill to the agency. Significant efforts were made to establish procedures to continue as many borrowers as possible, focusing foreclosure on those who were most insolvent, and least likely to ever return to profitability.

These efforts to introduce discipline into farming and farm lending made Congress very uncomfortable. One highly qualified candidate for the vacant under secretaryship which included responsibility for management of the FmHA, was unable to gain support for confirmation even from Republicans in the Senate because he had pointed out at a congressional hearing in Iowa that the number of farm failures was significantly less than many members of Congress were saying. The nominee was accused of "insensitivity to the plight of the farmers."

Given such dynamics, it is no surprise that Congress repeatedly provided major relief to FmHA borrowers. In the Emergency Agricultural Adjustment Act of 1984, in the Food Security Act of 1985 (the quadrennial Farm Bill), and, in a provision of the Continuing Resolution appropriations bill for fiscal year 1987, Congress required the Secretary of Agriculture to reduce the interest rate and stretch out loan terms for FmHA borrowers.

In May and June 1987, after extensive pleadings by the Farmer's Legal Action Group (FLAG), a farm advocacy group, Judge Bruce Van Sickle ruled in federal court that FmHA's procedures for beginning liquidation were unconstitutional abridgements of borrower's rights. The ruling provided detailed direction to FmHA, stipulating that it could not initiate foreclosure action against all borrowers nationwide until the court determined that the forms to be used provided expanded explanations of the borrower's options when issued foreclosure notices. For all practical purposes, the advocacy group had achieved success. No FmHA borrower needed to service his loan for the immediate future.

Stacking the Deck

About this time the House Committee on Agriculture began lengthy deliberations on difficult and complicated legislation to address the problems of the Farm Credit System, which were legion. The congressional committees did not give public notice that they would consider FmHA matters. The 1985 Farm Bill had provided every opportunity to deal with that subject. The hearings and mark-up sessions for the FCS bill were lengthy and full of their own drama, but at the end of the process there appeared in Washington the lawyers who had represented FLAG in the North Dakota Federal Court.

The FLAG lawyers found two members of the House Agriculture Committee, Timothy J. Penny (D-MN), and Tom Coleman (R-MO), who were willing to put into the Farm Credit System bill the detailed "borrowers rights" language of the latest district court ruling. Of course, the administration earnestly objected to these proposals because they were contrary to sound lending policy and because appeal was pending on Judge Van Sickle's ruling. Executive branch lawyers believed they had an excellent opportunity, if not virtual certainty, of winning the case on appeal in the 8th Circuit Court of Appeals. But with "bipartisan" support for including the FmHA language, the deck was stacked against the administration. The attorney for FLAG and his team spent virtually every day in the halls and offices of the House Agriculture Committee.

Without the introduction of a printed bill, without a hearing, with only limited opportunity for open comment by administration policy-makers during mark-up, and without significant debate by the members worthy of an amendment with a multibillion dollar impact, these provisions were added to the Farm Credit System bill, H.R. 3030, when it was reported from the Agriculture Committee. And, because the term "borrowers' rights" seemed so untouchable, no one was willing or able to try to strike the provisions during the very limited opportunity provided for floor debate under House rules. So the bill passed the House with those objectionable provisions included. (For more on House rules, see Chapter 8.)

Next the Senate Committee on Agriculture took up H.R. 3030. The Democrat majority had just been returned in the previous year's elections, partially because of their success in making Republicans accountable for the lingering recession in the upper Midwest. Two new Democrat senators from the region where FLAG was most active, Kent Conrad of North Dakota and Tom Daschle of South Dakota, joined with Senator Tom Harkin (D-IA), the prairie populist of the 1980s, to champion the language now in the House-passed bill. As in the House, the Senate did not have FmHA matters on its agenda, and held no hearings on this legislation. During the Senate subcommittee mark-up, staff members for FLAG were in perpetual presence, often operating as if they were official staff of the United States Senate, exercising privileges of access accorded to highest ranking members of the committee staff or senators' personal staffs. This is an innovation of immense importance and growing frequency.

But the Senate was not as easy a nut to crack. The ranking Republicans, Senators Richard Lugar of Indiana and Rudy Boschwitz of Minnesota, were willing to help the administration make the point that everyone, including indebted farmers, is better off if their farming operations are financially sound.

During the endless closed and confidential negotiating sessions between USDA officials and senatorial staff over a three-month period, administration operatives finally objected that outside lobbyists were gaining special advantages in a matter involving ongoing litigation to which they were a direct party. Only then were these lobbyists excluded from the meetings. However, the Democrat majority provided them desks and chairs just outside the doors of the rooms where the meetings were being held. Regularly, official Senate staffers working for the committee or for individual Senators would rush out to carry the latest development in the negotiations and return with appropriate counterproposals. FLAG remained present by virtual proxy. The whole process seemed endless. Eventually, the Senate committee reported a Farm Credit System bill which included the fundamentals of the court language.

The Coup de Grace

While all this was dragging on in the Senate, the appropriations process for Fiscal Year 1988 had stalled as well, and the infamous Continuing Resolution was working its way through the system. Not content with their success in the authorizing committee in House, nor with the progress in the Senate, FLAG left nothing to chance. They had recourse to the omnipresent Mr. Whitten, who took it upon himself to include specific language in the appropriations for the FmHA requiring that USDA provide new credit to all delinquent borrowers, so long as the payments of principal and interest for the new loan could be paid by the borrower. In short, no longer could FmHA require that payments due from previous indebtedness count as part of a borrower's financial obligations when determining whether to grant a new loan or not. Obviously, no private bank could remain in the farm lending business under such conditions.

Finally, Mr. Whitten and his committee cut funds from the FmHA administrator's office account, leaving him with insufficient staff to work out new procedures to counter this kind of micromanagement.

At the very end of the 1st Session of the 100th Congress, the Senate completed its deliberations on the Farm Credit System bill. As in the House, the greatest attention during floor consideration by a weary and eager-to-depart Senate was on the complicated and controversial provisions reorganizing the Farm Credit System. Thus, the "borrower's rights" provisions remained and were included in P.L. 100-233, "The Agricultural Credit Act of 1987," signed into law on January 6, 1988.

The executive branch found itself steamrollered by at least half a dozen different forces, all driven by and serving the intent of political entrepreneurs in Congress, and using all means and opportunities at their disposal to achieve their goals without regard to tradition, process, precedent, or good policy.

UNTANGLING THE TAR BABY

This review of some of the aspects of farm programs and activities of Congress in dealing with the programs and activities of the Department of Agriculture demonstrates that most of the drive for increasing micromanagment by Congress is internal. Its purpose is to gain a short-term political advantage over the opposition, often only in perception, so as to be perceived to be "doing things" for constituents. Unfortunately, this position is attained by destroying the structures and procedures which hold individual members of Congress accountable for policy failures. In fact, failures serve to create the occasion for subsequent actions and more apparent "service."

Brer Rabbit Congress is hopelessly tangled in the Tar Baby of micromanagement. It will take an enormous amount of discipline to get out of this predicament. Will the discipline come from within, or will it come from a resurgent executive?

Notes

1. For a rather insightful description and analysis of Mr. Whitten's career in Congress, see Alan Ehrenhalt, editor, *Politics in America: The 100th Congress*, (Washington: Congressional Quarterly Press, 1987), p. 820-823.

2. For a brief review of a comprehensive list of "pork," see Doug Bandow, *The Dirty Secrets of the 1987 Continuing Resolution* (Washington: The Heritage Foundation, Thomas A. Roe Institute for Economic Policy Studies, 1988.) For all of the details of micromanagement see the CR itself, P.L. 100-202, "A Joint Resolution Making Further Continuing Appropriations for the Fiscal Year 1988 and for Other Purposes," 450 pp.

3. An entertaining but completely accurate description of the way in which present farm programs operate in practice is found in Blake Hurst, "Farming With Uncle Sam: High Finance Comes to Rural Missouri," *Policy Review*, (Washington: The Heritage Foundation, Spring 1988).

4. A recent report by the General Accounting Office found that USDA estimates for just the "loan rate" part of farm programs, made at the time of their adoption, between 1972 and 1986, exceeded costs by $46 billion. This was an error of more than 42 percent! United States General Accounting Office, USDA's Commodity Program: The Accuracy of Budget Forecasts (Washington: Superintendent of Documents, 1988).

6. The Congressional Budget Mess

MARGARET N. DAVIS

When attention is focussed on Congress, the context today is almost always the budget. The process by which the federal budget becomes law is almost unbelievably complex, and its impacts now go far beyond just budgets. The "budget process" is increasingly the arena in which all policy questions, from foreign policy to water policy, are settled. In this chapter, Margaret Davis, an experienced Senate staff member, outlines the history of the budget process, and explains how it works today. She also suggests ways to improve the situation.

The general perception of the federal budget is that it consists of many numbers, reporting how much money the government collects in the form of taxes and how much it spends. It is common knowledge that the government is no longer able to balance its budget; it constantly spends more than it collects, thereby creating a budget deficit which drains America's economy. While this perception of the budget is correct to a point, the federal budget is much more than a double-entry ledger. The budget is both the government's major fiscal policy tool and the major policy document for determining federal priorities.

During the Reagan years, the federal budget deficit rose to the historic level of $221 billion. Federal expenditures, one-half of the deficit equation, now total more than $1 trillion, comprising one-fourth of the nation's Gross National Product (GNP). President Reagan's critics continually have blamed him for the huge budget deficits. His response was that Congress, not the president, was to blame for the budget problems. Congress, after all, appropriates the money.

Unfortunately the public does not understand the full role of Congress where the budget deficit is concerned. Members of Congress are quick to take credit for special projects in their districts, but they are just as quick to denounce any responsibility for the budget deficit. As legislators have learned the rewards of increasing the amount of federal funds flowing to their constituents, congressional dominance of the budget process has increased, at the expense of the executive branch.

This chapter argues that there is a danger in allowing Congress such dominance over the federal pursestrings, while restricting the spending discretion of the president. The president has a broader constituency than does Congress. A president who views the budget process as more than just a way to obtain federal funds for special projects and constituents will serve the nation better. Substantial reforms in the current budget process are necessary to restore a balance between the executive and legislative branches and to insure a healthy fiscal condition for this nation.

THE BUDGET PROCESS DURING
THE FIRST 185 YEARS

The Constitution of the United States contains several sections that grant Congress fiscal powers. Article I, Section 8, lists several of the financial responsibilities of Congress, beginning with: "The Congress shall have power to lay and collect taxes, duties, imposts and excises, to pay for the Debts and provide for the common Defence and general Welfare of the United States." Although the Constitution clearly places the power to tax and spend under the legislative branch of government[1], the executive branch also has constitutional responsibility for the nation's financial decision-making. The Constitution provides that money is to be drawn from the Treasury, a department that falls under the executive's administration. The president also has the power to recommend legislation to Congress and is charged with taking "care that the Laws be faithfully executed."

Executive Control over Spending

Operating under these provisions, the original budget process consisted of a single appropriations bill passed by Congress. The executive branch was left to decide how best to divide the funds among the competing government entities. Spending was allocated where the executive deemed necessary.

In time, appropriations bills became more detailed and began specifying amounts and purposes for federal funds expended. The executive branch was able to retain some control over how the funds were allocated by transferring funds among different appropriations accounts. In this way the nation's priorities, as determined by the executive, could be met through adequate funding. Another method used by early presidents to set national priorities consisted of impounding funds. Although the Constitution requires that all funds actually spent must be appropriated by Congress, it does not specify that all congressionally-appropriated funds must be spent. Throughout American history, in fact, presidents have refused to spend monies appropriated by Congress. The first was President Jefferson, who announced in 1801 that $50,000 in funds Congress had appropriated for fifteen gunboats would not be spent. A year later, again properly using his executive discretion, he decided to spend the funds on improved gunboats.

In addition to transferring and impounding funds, another funding mechanism used by the executive was to request additional funds, known as deficiency appropriations, for agencies which spent all their previously appropriated funds and could not continue to operate without additional funding. Congress routinely appropriated the deficiency funds, since refusing the funds would have resulted in many agencies being forced to close down, a prospect Congress has always found difficult to face. In these early days, the legislative branch appropriated the funds, but the executive branch dominated the spending decisions.

Congressional Attempts to Manage the Budget

After the Civil War, Congress found itself in the pleasant position of amassing budget surpluses due to large amounts of revenues flowing into the Treasury from customs tariffs. Congress quickly began spending freely, especially on such pork barrel projects as dams and other water projects. Individual legislative committees began appropriating funds, so that eventually only seven of the thirteen appropriations bills were controlled by the Appropriations Committees. Spending and revenue measures were passed independently of each other and there was no process in place to inform Congress of the total amount of funds it was spending. In addition, as long as budget surpluses continued, agencies felt free to increase their requests for deficiency funds.

This lack of a formal budget process resulted in the disappearance of budget surpluses, although the congressional appetite for spending remained healthy. In an attempt to exercise some control over free-spending Congresses, presidents vetoed some spending measures and the administrations used their transfer of funds authority to execute the president's fiscal policies. Thus, an administration was able to impose the fiscal responsibility that Congress lacked.

Congress slowly recognized its lack of fiscal discipline and began to take some actions to improve its operations. To prevent agencies from running out of funds before the end of the fiscal year, Congress passed the Antideficiency Act of 1905. This act required the apportionment of funds to the agencies throughout the year, rather than in one lump sum at the beginning of the year. In 1912, the Taft Commission on Economy and Efficiency recommended a comprehensive executive budget system under which the Congress only handles policy decisions, with the executive branch controlling budget implementation.

Finally, Congress established an executive budget system in the 1921 Budget and Accounting Act. The president was required to submit a budget, as well as supplemental funding requests, to Congress each year. Agencies were no longer allowed to seek funds directly from Congress; instead requests had to come from the president. The Bureau of the Budget, reorganized as the Office of Management and Budget in 1970, was established to provide spending and revenue estimates and make budget recommendations. All spending jurisdiction was firmly consolidated into the House and Senate Appropriations Committees. By passing this Act giving the president statutory authority over the budget, Congress acknowledged the executive branch to be more adept at establishing and overseeing national spending policy.

Friction Between the Executive and Congress

In executing its budget policy, the executive branch began to increase the amount of appropriated funds it impounded. While America was at war, President Roosevelt stated his intent to defer all federal spending on construction projects unless the projects were critical to the nation's defense. But since construction projects are the core of congressional pork barrel spending, Congress rebuffed the president's budget recommendation that the defense effort be the sole focus of government spending.

For example, in the 1941 appropriations bill for the War Department, Congress included funding for several flood control projects. The president did not veto the bill because he needed the defense appropriations for the war effort; however, he did announce that the funds for the flood control projects would not be released.

Congress began to grow so uncomfortable with the executive branch's control over the budget that attempts were made to legislatively modify the process. In 1943, for example, the Senate attached language to an appropriations measure that prohibited funds in the bill from being impounded unless Congress consented. Although this language was dropped from the bill in conference, it was an important first step taken by Congress in its effort to regain full control over spending.

The Legislative Reorganization Act of 1946 provided for Congress to consider a legislative budget. For three years in a row—1947, 1948, and 1949—Congress tried to draft a legislative budget, but was unsuccessful each year, and eventually abandoned the idea. Congress still was unable to handle fiscal responsibility. The battle between Congress and the president over the spending of appropriated funds continued to escalate.

As the 1948-49 recession deepened, President Truman thought it prudent and in the nation's best interest to reduce federal expenditures. He succeeded, as total fiscal year (FY) 1948 expenditures were only $29.8 billion, a 14 percent reduction from FY 1947, and less than one third of the amount spent in FY 1945. In fact, only once in the forty years since then has there been a reduction in federal spending from the previous year (FY 1965). In achieving his spending reductions, Truman angered Congress, particularly with respect to his impoundment of appropriated funds.

Disputes between Congress and the executive branch over whether or not the executive branch was obligated to spend funds appropriated by Congress continued throughout the Eisenhower and Kennedy Administrations. Defense spending was the focus of many of these disagreements, as Congress wanted certain weapons and vehicles that the Pentagon believed were unwarranted.

The Impoundment Battle

President Johnson was the first president who elected not to spend large amounts of funds appropriated for domestic programs. Programs from which he withheld funds included federal highway trust funds, federal housing programs, and agriculture funds. In 1967, President Johnson impounded $10.6 billion, 6.7 percent of the federal budget.

While the Democratic Congress was not satisfied with Johnson's impoundment policy, it found the situation intolerable under Republican President Nixon. President Nixon, not interested in continuing the Great Society programs of the Johnson Administration, had very different national policy goals than Congress and these differences were embodied in the budget debate.

In implementing his fiscal policies, President Nixon chose not to release funds for domestic programs which he felt were ineffective, duplicative, or unnecessary. For example, in order to prevent fiscal irresponsibility and to better implement his budget proposals, Nixon released funds only for public works projects recommended in his budget. He did not release funds for other projects added by Congress. By 1973, Nixon had impounded funds for over 100 federal programs. Since these programs served the special-interest constituents of Congress, his actions enraged members who felt their constituencies—and therefore their incumbency—were threatened. Like President Johnson before him, Nixon stated that the impoundments were necessary to fight inflation. But Congress was unwilling to accept that as justification for using the impoundment procedure to terminate such unessential but politically popular programs as low-interest loans made by the Rural Electrification Administration.

As members of Congress saw the President reducing the amount of federal funds spent on their pet projects, they began to challenge the President's authority to refuse to spend money appropriated by Congress. As previously noted, the Constitution gives Congress the right to appropriate funds, but spending the funds is an executive function since the funds are withdrawn from the Treasury. Furthermore, Nixon argued that impounding funds was within his constitutional power since he did it to attain fiscal stability for the nation.

Soaring Spending

In the meantime, federal spending had begun to soar, and Congress had begun enacting spending limitations as a way to control expenditures. The Revenue and Expenditure Control Act of 1968 included a spending ceiling for FY 1969. The ceiling proved to be ineffective, first, because so much of the budget consisted of mandatory spending that could not be limited through appropriations, and second, because Congress had exempted itself from the spending limitation. Despite the failure of the spending limitation to curb the growth in spending, Congress enacted spending ceilings for both FY 1970 and FY 1971. Again, the spending ceilings were exceeded and only served to highlight the lack of congressional discipline in fiscal matters.

When President Nixon requested a spending ceiling of $250 billion for FY 1973, Congress refused to enact one.

One factor that contributed to the unchecked growth in spending was the rise in "backdoor" spending; that is, spending outside of the normal appropriation process. The authorizing committees began to pass measures creating entitlement programs for granting loans, borrowing, and contracting authority. Backdoor spending was so prevalent that by 1974, only 45 percent of spending was controlled by the Appropriations Committees.

It was this fiscally chaotic atmosphere—constant confrontation between the executive and legislative branch over the expenditure of appropriated funds and expansion of the "uncontrollable," mandatory spending portion of the budget—that prompted the next congressional effort to reform the federal budget process. The clear purpose this time was to limit the role of the executive branch so that Congress could claim full control of the federal pursestrings.

One of the first steps was passage of a bill requiring Senate confirmation of both the director and deputy director of the Office of Management and Budget. The bill included confirmation of the two Nixon appointees already serving as OMB Director and deputy director. Arguing that the application of the bill to incumbent executive officers was a violation of the separation of powers, Nixon vetoed the measure. A modified version exempting the incumbents passed Congress, was signed by Nixon, and remains the current law.

Work on a new budget process for Congress began in earnest in the fall of 1972 with the creation of the Joint Study Committee on Budget Control. From the many proposals for budget reform issued by the Committee emerged the Congressional Budget and Impoundment Control Act of 1974. Since amended, it remains the governing law on the federal budget process.

FEDERAL BUDGETING UNDER THE CONGRESSIONAL BUDGET ACT

The Budget Act was written to increase the spending power of Congress and to reduce the influence of the executive branch over fiscal matters. In the words of the conference committee members who wrote the Act, its purpose was to:

> assure congressional budget control; provide for the congressional determination of the appropriate level of Federal revenues and expenditures; provide a system of impoundment control; establish national budget priorities; and provide for furnishing information to Congress by the executive branch.[2]

In practice, the Act has allowed Congress to dominate the budget process. Since passage of the Act in 1974, only once has the executive branch successfully controlled the budget debate and spending priorities (President Reagan's first budget in 1981 for FY 1982). In every other year, Congress has asserted its spending preferences over the administration.

The first nine titles of the Act comprise what is known as "The Budget Act." They created House and Senate Budget Committees which were given the responsibility of crafting the Congressional Budget Resolutions. The House Ways and Means Committee and the Senate Finance Committee retained jurisdiction over revenue measures and the Appropriations Committees retained full appropriations duties. The Congressional Budget Resolution was to set ceilings on the public debt, outlays, and new budget authority, and set a floor on revenues. The parameters of the budget were to be enforced through procedural points of order. The Congressional Budget Office (CBO) was established to provide economic and budget data to Congress. A timetable was devised for each step of the budget process and all future permanent appropriations were required to come from the appropriations committees in order to control backdoor spending.

Controlling Impoundment: Deferrals and Rescissions

Title X of the Act contains impoundment provisions and was the original focus of most of Congress when the 1974 Act was enacted. Two types of impoundment were defined: deferrals, which were to delay spending of funds; and rescissions, which were cancellations of spending authority. The purpose of this title was to prevent a future administration from executing its policy goals when those goals conflicted with the spending wishes of Congress. The administration must now inform Congress of all intended deferrals and rescissions. Unless Congress fully rejects a proposed deferral, the deferral of funds occurs. Congress must agree to a rescission within 45 days, and if it does not, the administration must release the funds.

The impoundment title has been successful for Congress. It is nearly impossible for funds to be rescinded, given that Congressional action in both chambers must take place—in a short time frame—to approve a rescission. Getting Congress to take action is always more difficult than retaining the status quo. In addition, Congress tends not to eliminate funding for a program once that program has begun.

In FY 1975, the first year that the impoundment provisions were in place, federal spending on nondefense discretionary programs—the traditional pork barrel part of the budget which funds grants and construction projects—grew by an astonishing 26.4 percent from the previous year. Prior to removal of the president's impoundment authority, Richard Nixon had been able, during the 1969-74 period, to hold the growth in domestic discretionary spending to an average of only 7.3 percent per year.

During his administration, even though operating under the impoundment control provisions, President Ford continued to try to control inflation and government spending by proposing to defer and rescind funds. Of the $7.4 billion in rescissions proposed by Ford for FYs 1975-77, Congress approved only 7 percent. Because it takes affirmative action by Congress to overturn deferrals, Congress allowed 289 of the 330 proposed deferrals to stand. But when funding for favored projects was slated for deferral, such as Ford's request to defer highway construction grants, Congress acted quickly to reject the proposal. Rescission requests made by President Carter fared slightly better in Congress. Congress agreed to 41 percent of Carter's proposed rescissions, totaling $2.6 billion in savings. Only 18 percent of Carter's proposed deferrals were rejected, as opposed to the 24 percent rejected under Ford.

Despite the recent lamenting by Congress on the size of the budget deficit, President Reagan's rescission and deferral requests have met strong opposition from Congress. During the first year of the Reagan Administration, the very first year in which he was able to dominate the budget process, Congress accepted an amazing 79 percent of the Administration's proposed rescissions and rejected only 9.6 percent of his recommended deferrals. Unfortunately, this success rate has not continued throughout the Reagan years. In FY 1982, Congress agreed to rescind $4.4 billion of the $7.9 billion requested by Reagan; but in FY 1983, Congress refused to accept any of them. In fact the acceptance rate for rescissions for the FY 1982-87 period was 17 percent, resulting in a spending reductions of only $4.8 billion. The president had sought to save $27.9 billion through rescissions during the six-year period.

This experience has shown that one of the main objectives of the 1974 Budget Act has been accomplished. Congress has indeed been able to control the impoundment of funds. The president is no longer able to reduce unilaterally the expenditure of appropriated funds. The Congress has put such a brake on the impoundment process that in FY 1986 when the president felt it in the nation's interest to rescind more than $10 billion, Congress only agreed to rescind $143 million. Congress's reluctance to agree to the president's rescission requests has severely limited the executive's ability to impose fiscal discipline.

Spending and Deficit Growth Under the Budget Act

While the initial focus on the 1974 Budget Act may have been on impoundment, now the requirements of the Budget Act titles dominate the budget debates between the executive and legislative branches. And while the Budget Act may have given more control to the Congress in setting national priorities and aggregate budget totals, the results have not been good for the nation.

Placing the major responsibility for spending decisions in congressional hands has resulted in total federal spending amounting to an average of 22.7 percent of Gross National Product in the eleven year period under the Act (FY 1977-87). This compares to the spending level averaging only 19.4 percent of GNP in the eleven years prior to the Act's passage (FY 1964-74). The growth rate in federal spending also has increased.

From FY 1964 to FY 1974, the growth in federal spending averaged 8.5 percent per year. After implementation of the Budget Act, spending has grown at average rate of 9.6 percent per year. The effect of congressional budgeting on the deficit mirrors the spending growth pattern. The deficit has averaged 3.8 percent of GNP during the last eleven fiscal years. In the period before congressional dominance of the budget (FY 1964-74), however, the deficit averaged less than 1.1 percent of GNP. In fact, in FY 1969, the country actually ran a budget surplus, a feat impossible while Congress has controlled the budget process.

CONGRESSIONAL DOMINANCE OF THE BUDGET PROCESS

Congressional dominance of the budget process has enabled Congress to substantially reorder national priorities. In the last eleven years that the executive branch dominated the budget process, the average national defense spending accounted for 7.8 percent of GNP and non-defense discretionary spending averaged only 4.8 percent of GNP. Congress has altered that ratio: in the years after passage of the Budget Act, defense spending declined to an average 5.6 percent of GNP while nondefense grew to an average 5.0 percent of GNP. Thus Congress has been successful in altering budget priorities by increasing the emphasis on nondefense spending at the expense of defense spending.

Most nondefense spending is not "discretionary" but consists of entitlements and other required government benefits. Since passage of the Budget Act, this type of nondefense spending has grown enormously. Prior to the Act, uncontrollable spending absorbed 6.7 percent of GNP; during the last eleven years it has averaged 10.7 percent of GNP. This last result is alarming for those who believe that government spending should be used to promote a program of growth and opportunity rather than to create a nation dependent on government benefits.

These results are very disappointing but not surprising. Responsible budgeting calls for Congress to make choices between two competing goals. On one hand, the deficit must be reduced through either spending reductions or increased taxes. On the other hand, serving the constituents and enhancing reelection prospects is made easier by increasing federal spending in the district and lowering taxes. Congress quite naturally has continued to follow policies that enhance incumbency, even at the expense of the national interest.

Removing the Executive from the Budget Process

During the first years of the congressional budget process, when President Ford was trying to restore confidence in the executive branch after the Watergate experience, Congress used the Act to assert its authority over the budget. The new Budget Committee chairman pressured members to work within the process. The FY 1976 budget was the first under the Act although the Act was not mandatory until the FY 1977 budget cycle. Congress adopted a resolution which only contained aggregate levels for spending, revenues, and a deficit, and went on record for the first time supporting a deficit of $74 billion, $22 billion more than the budget submitted by Ford. The congressional budget resolution also contained higher spending and revenue levels than the president recommended. This result would become the norm in future years.

The fiscal year 1977 budget, developed during calendar year 1976, was President Ford's last and the first budget created by Congress under full implementation of the Budget Act. Congress used the president's budget as a starting point for drafting its own spending blueprint. In the end, the policies were vastly different from those the president recommended. Congress chose to fund a higher level of spending and to implement fewer tax reductions than the president desired. With regard to spending, Congress did agree to fund all but $300 million of the $101.1 billion the president requested for defense. But rather than impose tax cuts to stimulate the economy, Congress voted for increased spending on jobs programs and other domestic programs. Congress was successful in adhering to the timetable it had set for itself on the budget, and all 13 individual appropriations bills were enacted prior to the beginning of the fiscal year for the first time since 1948.

There was much congressional praise for the new budget process based on the FY 1977 experience. The executive branch had basically been removed from budget discussions. The budget was claimed to be the budget of Congress rather than of the president. After Carter assumed office, Congress initially demonstrated a willingness to work with the new Democratic president on budget policies. Negotiations between the executive branch and Congress took place as they tried to work together on an economic stimulus package.

Ignoring Carter

While the Budget Act called for a first budget resolution that set budget targets and a second resolution that set binding ceilings, after Carter proposed a two-year economic stimulus package, Congress tried to accommodate the president by passing a third budget resolution. Then Carter withdrew his tax rebate plan which had been the cornerstone of the stimulus package. This action by the executive—sudden withdrawal at a late date of a key element of the budget—angered congressional budget leaders who felt they had gone out of their way to work with the president. A showdown later occurred between the Congress and Carter over the inclusion of several special provisions in the public works appropriations bill. While Congress was unable to pass all appropriations bills before the fiscal year began, it did pass all bills prior to adjournment, avoiding the need for a full-year continuing resolution.

The disorganized and ineffective Carter Administration caused problems with Congress that extended to the budget process. Congress consistently passed budget resolutions containing less domestic spending, higher defense spending, lower tax cuts, and smaller deficits than those proposed by Carter. The president was a minor player in the budget debate; the most heated disputes were between the two chambers. In the FY 1979 budget, for example, the Senate voted for no new local public works projects while the House supported a $2 billion public works program. After reaching an impasse on this issue in conference, the full Senate rejected the new public works program. Since the House insisted on funding for the program, "smoke and mirrors" were used in the final budget agreement that allowed both sides to claim a victory. The use of such "phony budgeting" would increase as Congress became more sophisticated in the budget arena.

Another example of Congress ignoring Carter's budget recommendations was the insistence by Congress on providing much more for defense than requested. The Senate led the charge for higher defense spending in order to implement the SALT II Treaty. For FY 1980, the Congressional Budget Resolution called for $4.1 billion more in defense than the Carter request; for FY 1981, defense spending approved by Congress was $12.1 billion higher than recommended by the president.

Several changes were made to the congressional budget process during the Carter years. Instead of a one-year budget resolution, Congress began adopting budgets for three years. While the outyear projections were a valuable tool for estimating future fiscal situations, there were no mechanisms in place to enforce the outyear spending and revenue assumptions. The first year of the budget resolution remained the operative one. Of greater importance was the implementation of the reconciliation process in 1980 for the FY 1981 budget. Reconciliation instructions in the budget resolution direct the authorizing committees to make changes needed in order to comply with the spending guidelines of the budget resolution. The FY 1981 budget resolution called for the authorizing committees to reduce the deficit by $10.6 billion. The FY 1981 reconciliation bill, containing all of the measures written by the authorizing committees, achieved savings of $8.2 billion by increasing revenues by $3.6 billion and lowering spending by $4.6 billion.

Reagan Asserts Leadership

The reconciliation process became a very effective tool for deficit reduction under the Reagan Administration. During the first year of the fiscally conservative Republican administration, the congressional budget process would be dominated by the executive branch for the one and only time. The Senate was controlled by Republicans for the first time in a quarter of a century, which made negotiations between the White House and the Senate easy, as the Senate Republicans were eager to accommodate the president who had helped them regain majority status. In order to succeed in negotiations with the House, the administration worked not only with the House Republicans, but also with a number of conservative Democrats who shared the Republicans' concerns about the fiscal state of the nation.

President Reagan submitted his FY 1982 budget in March of 1981, two months after Carter had issued his proposal. The Reagan budget was a dramatic departure from the Carter proposals, calling for large tax reductions, increased defense expenditures, lower spending growth in domestic discretionary programs, and reforms of several entitlement programs.

The budget resolution was a major victory for the new administration and demonstrated that a strong, assertive president, backed by an election mandate, could exert his budget priorities on Congress, even within the restrictive Budget Act process.

The new administration also proved to be effective in getting the budget resolution implemented, largely through an extended use of the reconciliation procedure begun the previous year. By placing all the spending reductions in one measure, the bill had a better chance of passage since the total savings were larger and members could justify spending reductions in their favored programs since spending on other programs was also being lowered. The budget resolution called for the authorizing committees to make programmatic changes that would reduce spending in FY 1982 by $36 billion, slightly less than the $41 billion in reductions that Reagan had requested. The Budget Committees agreed with the White House that one single reconciliation bill would be the vehicle for the entire spending package. An additional indicator of the influence Reagan had on budget actions was the administration's success in getting Congress to pass a revolutionary tax-reduction plan, lowering FY 1982 taxes by $37.7 billion.

Congress Closes the Door

But the administration's success in dominating the budget process was short-lived. As inflation remained high and projections showed the deficit growing, the president requested an additional deficit reduction package of $13 billion in savings and $3 billion in increased revenues. Congress refused to take any action on the proposals. The administration then tried to control spending through the individual appropriations measures. As FY 1982 began, not one of the 13 appropriations bills had been enacted, so a continuing appropriations measure was enacted to fund the government through November 20. Congress passed a full-year continuing resolution on November 19 for the 12 appropriations bills that had not been enacted by then. Claiming that the spending level was too high, the president vetoed the spending bill and for the first time in history, the entire government was forced to shut down due to lack of funds. This action forced Congress to negotiate with the White House. On December 11, Congress passed a full year continuing resolution encompassing ten of the individual appropriations bills and saving $4 billion.

The appropriations showdown between the executive and legislative branch over funding levels would continue throughout the Reagan Administration. Unable in any future years to enlist congressional support for the president's fiscal policies, the administration turned to the appropriations process as the only viable option for influencing spending decisions. In all future budget resolutions, Congress opted for lower defense spending, higher taxes and higher nondefense spending than supported by the president. The president's budget was thereafter regularly pronounced "dead on arrival" when it was received by Congress, and few of the president's recommended budget proposals were seriously considered by Congress. The president became frustrated as he signed tax increase bills accompanied by congressional promises of spending reductions which never materialized.

Despite the deficit reduction measures enacted for FY 1982, the deficit rose to $128 billion. By FY 1983, the deficit had soared to more than $200 billion. Budget discussions were no longer about economic policies and national priorities but instead focused on the deficit and how best to reduce it. A great rift developed between Congress and the president as Reagan insisted that spending reductions, rather than the tax increases Congress recommended, should be used to lower the deficit.

The disagreement led to the congressional budget process collapsing.

In 1984, negotiations between the administration and Congress on the FY 1985 budget failed to produce an agreement, and Congress ignored its own budget procedure. In a reverse of the process, Congress enacted a deficit reduction measure prior to adopting the congressional budget resolution which is supposed to set the spending and tax goals. Appropriations bills were passed prior to the adoption of the budget resolution by routinely waiving the requirement prohibiting such action. In fact, the budget resolution was not adopted until the first day of the new fiscal year.

Attempts at Reform

In 1985, with the budget process no longer respected, with deficits continuing at the $200 billion level, with Congress and the administration at odds with one another over the budget priorities, and with the federal debt level reaching an unprecedented $2 trillion, Congress was forced to admit its lack of fiscal discipline. It reacted by enacting the Balanced Budget and Emergency Deficit Control Act (known as Gramm-Rudman-Hollings), a revolutionary law mandating that Congress gradually reduce the deficit to achieve a balanced budget in five years. The legislation contained severe consequences—automatic across-the-board spending reductions—that occur if Congress fails to meet the deficit targets.

The automatic spending reduction process known as sequestration, which is the unique feature of Gramm-Rudman-Hollings, was automatic because the sequester report—which estimates whether the deficit target will be met and if not, by how much spending must be reduced—is prepared jointly by the Office of Management and Budget (OMB) and the Congressional Budget Office (CBO), and then sent to the Comptroller General who issues his report to the president. The president then issues the sequester order, if the Comptroller General's report indicates the deficit target was missed. If Congress has not met the deficit targets, then this automatic sequester process begins and spending cuts are made by formula with no influence by Congress.

The sequestration procedure was challenged, and in July 1986, the Supreme Court ruled that the role of the Comptroller General in the sequester process was unconstitutional. Gramm-Rudman-Hollings, however, contained a backup provision requiring Congress to send a resolution to the president to issue the sequester order. This backup sequester process was not thought to be very effective since it required Congress to approve the spending reductions. It was thought nearly impossible for Congress to pass such a resolution, and indeed the experience in 1986 proved it to be true: the Senate defeated the sequester resolution and the House never took it up. The Senate preferred reinstituting an automatic process in order to force Congress to reduce the deficit, and in 1986 adopted legislation giving the role of the Comptroller General to the Director of the OMB. In 1987, a version of this legislation, reconstituting Gramm-Rudman-Hollings (often called Gramm-Rudman-Hollings II) was enacted and remains in force today.

A Democrat Senate: New Heights of Acrimony

When the Democrats regained control of the Senate following the 1986 elections, partisan battles between Congress and the administration over how to reduce the deficit became commonplace. The fracture between Congress and President Reagan reached its peak during the fall of 1987 as Congress was trying to complete budget action for fiscal year 1988. The fiscal year had begun. No individual appropriations measures had been sent to the president, nor any agreement on a reconciliation measure that would reduce the deficit sufficiently to comply with the requirements of the recently reconstituted Gramm-Rudman-Hollings Act. The government was operating under a continuing resolution funding all programs. On October 20, the president had issued an initial sequester order for FY 1987 based on the OMB report. If no further action were taken by Congress, on November 20 enough spending authority would be permanently canceled to lead to a reduction in outlays of $23 billion. That translated into an across-the-board reduction of 10.5 percent in defense programs and 8.5 percent in nondefense programs.

The president had indicated that the reconciliation bill that had passed the House and the one being prepared by the Senate were unacceptable to him, due to the $11.5 billion increase in taxes contained in the measures. Additionally, he was prepared to veto the appropriations measures that had been passed by Congress, as they were all spending more money on domestic discretionary programs than he had requested. The president's advisers had indicated to Congress that the president found the sequester a more acceptable way to comply with the deficit reduction mandate of Gramm-Rudman-Hollings than the reconciliation and appropriations bills as Congress had prepared them. Facing the difficult choice between the president vetoing Congressional budget implementation bills and allowing the sequester to stand, or revising its budget measures, Congress found itself paralyzed. Many Democrats felt the president was only bluffing; they did not believe he would be willing to accept a $11.5 billion cut in the FY 1988 defense budget. However, other members of Congress were unwilling to take that risk.

The Budget Summit

On October 19, 1987, the United States stock market experienced its largest one-day decline. The existing budget chaos could only have served to keep the market from recovering. The market decline produced enough concern in both the White House and Congress that the president announced he was willing to have his top economic advisors meet with the Congressional leadership to resolve the budget dilemma and to reach an agreement on how to meet the deficit target to avoid a permanent sequester.

The summit meetings began, but little appeared to be achieved each day, as Congress insisted on tax increases to help reduce the deficit while the White House leadership preferred reductions in social programs and entitlement growth. Finally, on November 20, the day the final sequester order went into effect, the budget summit members reached an agreement. For the fourth time in his seven-year tenure in office, President Reagan was forced to accept congressional demands that he raise taxes. He also agreed to a much smaller increase in defense spending than he had sought; in fact, under the agreement nondefense discretionary spending would grow at three times the rate of defense spending.

The budget summit was unique: It contained spending ceilings for the major categories of defense, international affairs, and nondefense discretionary spending for both FY 1988 and FY 1989. The revenue increases and entitlement savings for both years were to be enacted in the 1987 legislation. Participants hoped that this two-year agreement would eliminate any similar budget crisis the next year, as well as send a signal to the markets that the deficit would be reduced in both years to meet the requirements of Gramm-Rudman-Hollings. But even after the agreement was reached, there was difficulty reaching a consensus on how to implement the summit plan. There was little fiscal stability, as the country had been operating on short-term continuing resolutions at FY 1987 levels since October 1 and funding had been withheld from agencies since November 20 in compliance with the sequester order.

The Executive's Choice: All or Nothing

On December 22, Congress passed both the reconciliation bill and a continuing resolution for FY 1988 and adjourned for the Christmas recess. The president had no choice but to sign these two mammoth pieces of legislation, passed in the early morning hours. For the second year in a row, the entire funding for the government for the fiscal year was contained in one appropriations bill. Unfortunately, unlike George Washington, who also received such a bill, Reagan had no choice on how to allocate the funds within the government. While he had agreed to the aggregate totals for defense, international affairs, and domestic spending, he was forced to accept Congress's decision on how to divide appropriated funds within each of those categories. The president had once again been placed in an all-or-nothing position by Congress.

After having its own budget process in place for eleven years, Congress has failed to control its spending appetite. The delays in passing appropriations bills prior to the beginning of the fiscal year are as bad as before the Budget Act was enacted. While Gramm-Rudman-Hollings has forced Congress to gradually reduce the deficit, it has created more heated debates on how the deficit should be lowered. The clashes between the administration and Congress have escalated, as Congress continues to force its spending policies on the president.

Appointing a New Branch of Government

As if in recognition of its own inability to handle fiscal responsibility, Congress included a provision in the Omnibus Budget Reconciliation Act of 1987 creating the National Economic Commission. The creation of this Commission by Congress is significant. Congress has not only decided that it does not want the executive branch to have the authority to execute budget policy as it best sees fit, but has now admitted that it is not able to meet the budget goals it has imposed on itself. Instead, Congress has established a Commission to decide budget priorities and deficit reduction measures. To be sure, Congress can ignore any and all of the proposals issued by the Commission; but more likely Congress will implement the proposals and let the Commission receive all of the criticisms from constituencies affected by the deficit reduction measures that are implemented.

The Commission's recommendations may make the FY 1990 budget debates less contentious, although Congress and the new president may have disagreements about which, if any, of the Commission's proposals should be implemented. In the past, Congress has shown a willingness to cooperate most with the White House during the first year under a new administration, so the Commission's report may facilitate the process as it gives both branches a common frame of reference. However, the creation of such a commission is definitely not a panacea for the nation's budget woes. A branch of government already exists that is to make such decisions on national spending priorities. The executive branch wants to promote economic prosperity for the country, and implementing fiscal policy through the federal budget is one way to insure economic security. Congress should work with the executive branch, rather than thwart or confront it, to attain sound fiscal goals. Congress should not involve an unelected third party in a role easily filled by the president.

REFORMS NEEDED TO IMPROVE
THE PROCESS

While the current budget process may allow Congress to dominate the budget debate in a way not experienced during the first 185 years of this government, it does not serve the nation as well as the process that allowed for more influence from the executive branch. Congress has consistently demonstrated its unwillingness to make the hard decisions necessary to control the growth in federal spending. There are several reforms to the process that, if implemented, would allow for a more balanced relationship between the legislative and executive branches. Such reforms would also increase the possibility that the nation could be restored to a fiscally sound position. The following reforms are designed to create a new, sound fiscal policy by restoring balance and discipline to the budget process.

Enact a Balanced Budget Amendment

One of the most discussed measures for restoring the fiscal strength of this nation is the enactment of a constitutional amendment to balance the budget. There have been several votes in Congress on such an amendment. The Senate has passed the amendment, but the House has never garnered the two-thirds vote required to pass a constitutional amendment calling for a balanced budget even though 32 of the 34 states required to do so, have called for a constitutional convention on such an amendment.

While a balanced budget amendment is very important to ensure responsible budgeting, it may lead to more heated confrontations between the executive and legislative branches over how best to achieve the balanced budget goals each year. The experience under the Gramm-Rudman-Hollings law has shown this to be true. Faced with a known deficit target, Congress has shown a preference to enact tax increases to boost (or at least retain) the current level of spending, while the president has preferred reducing spending to correspond with the current revenue level. The Gramm-Rudman-Hollings limitation on the size of the deficit, however, does force the executive and Congress to hammer out an agreement to comply with the law. This would also happen under a balanced budget amendment, although if some of the reforms listed below were implemented, a balanced budget could be achieved by the executive alone.

At a minimum, the current structure of Gramm-Rudman-Hollings should be retained and complied with by Congress. This will insure a balanced budget by FY 1993. After the experience of successfully reducing the deficit for seven years in order to achieve that final goal of Gramm-Rudman-Hollings, perhaps Congress can continue to discipline itself and not return to its old habit of expanding entitlement programs, increasing federal spending, and amassing a huge budget deficit. Such an outcome is unlikely, however, which is why a balanced budget amendment is imperative.

Grant Line Item Veto Authority

The best way to restore the role of the executive branch in the budget process is to give the president authority to veto a specific line item in any appropriations measure. A modification of this would be to allow the president not only to veto or accept a line item, but to have the alternative of writing a lower level of funding for the line item. This latter method is often called the "item reduction" veto. Forty-three state governors currently hold some form of item veto authority.

The line item veto would allow the executive to strike funds for programs deemed by the administration not to be in the best interest of the nation. Such programs can be found in both the defense and domestic accounts.

A line item veto authority would reduce the need for continuing resolutions and congressional-presidential showdowns over appropriations bills. Armed with item veto authority, for example, President Carter could have merely vetoed funding for the six water projects he found objectionable in the FY 1979 Public Works appropriations measure, rather than vetoing the entire bill. As a result of the showdown over the projects, the public works funding was bottled up in a continuing resolution for the entire fiscal year. The line item veto would give the president more bargaining power on spending measures since he could threaten to veto the particular item in dispute between the two branches.

The line item veto would not give authority to the president to alter the budget priorities set by the Congress in its spending measures since the veto can only be used to withhold funds (or possibly lower funding for) an item. It cannot be used to increase spending on a program. Thus, the debate between national defense spending and domestic spending would still exist. Other process reforms would be necessary to increase the role of the president in influencing the outcome of that debate.

Clearly, the line item veto would be most effective if it were enacted in conjunction with a deficit limit measure such as the Balanced Budget Amendment. In that case, vetoing items would be justified by the need to comply with the deficit limit, thereby giving the president the ability to decide which programs need to be reduced in order to comply with the law. If Congress were to enact measures spending more than allowed under the limit, the president would have full discretion to use the line item veto authority. The result would be funding for the year that more closely approximated his own budget recommendations.

Enhance the Rescission Process

As the fiscal year progresses, the executive branch is in the best position to determine which agencies need the full funding appropriated to them. In addition, changing national conditions between the time the budget was implemented and a later point in the year may warrant the cancellation of a program or agency. When this occurs, the administration proposes to Congress that the funds be rescinded. The rescission proposals are referred to the appropriate committee and generally are never heard from again. In FY 1985, Congress refused to accept 148 proposed rescissions.

Some enhanced rescission proposals include making the rescission process similar to the deferral process, whereby the rescission is effective unless Congress adopts a measure rejecting the rescission; other proposals consist of placing legislation accepting rescissions on a "fast track." Under the enhanced rescission process, the administration would be assured a floor vote on the proposed rescission which reflects his spending policies. Knowing of the floor vote, the president would be in a position to discuss the proposal with members of Congress and fully debate the merits of the rescission. Members of Congress would have to state publicly whether or not they favored a certain level of funding for a specific program which the president had deemed unnecessary. Enhanced rescission authority would assure the president a debate on programs often not identified in large appropriations bills and that may not have support outside of the leadership or the appropriations committee. For example, FY 1988 funding was placed in a single appropriations bill presented to Congress after 9:00 P.M. on the night that the current continuing resolution funding expired. Given this timing, legislators were forced to vote on the measure without knowing the details in the bill. The president also was compelled to sign the mammoth bill in order to avoid shutting down the government due to lack of funds. After the bill was passed into law, it was found that several special interest projects were funded which the president believed were unwarranted given the need to comply with the Gramm-Rudman-Hollings law. If enhanced rescission were in place, and the funding for these projects were proposed to be rescinded, the issue of funding of special projects would be brought before the Congress where a majority would be difficult to muster. The burden would then be on Congress to reject the savings proposed by the president.

Like the item veto, enhanced rescission would not alter congressional priorities. If the majority of Congress indicated that funds proposed to be rescinded should be spent, then the rescission would be defeated and the president would release the funds. He still would not be able to increase the funding for any program above the level appropriated by Congress. However, enhanced rescission could reduce spending by increasing the acceptance rate of rescission proposals.

Require Separate Enrollment of Any Full-Year Continuing Resolution

In recent years, Congress has engaged in the practice of sending the president a "take-it-or-leave-it" package on government funding. While historically there has been a continuing resolution for the entire year covering only a few of the individual appropriations measures that failed to be enacted, the appropriations process has become so protracted that for both FY 1987 and FY 1988, the president was presented with one full-year continuing resolution which contained funding for all 13 individual appropriations measures. With no item-veto authority, the president was placed in the position of either vetoing the bill and shutting down the entire government, or signing the bill which contained funding levels for some agencies that he agreed with and funding levels for others with which he strongly disagreed.

No president should be placed in such a position by Congress. In fact, in his 1988 State of the Union address, President Reagan showed the entire nation the massive continuing resolution he had recently signed and vowed never to sign another one. If Congress is unable to pass the 13 individual appropriations measures, then at a minimum, the continuing resolution should be enrolled as separate appropriations measures corresponding to the regularly identified 13 bills. Under a separate enrollment procedure, the president would in essence receive 13 individual appropriations measures each year. He could then sign those he considers acceptable, while vetoing those with funding levels inconsistent with national needs. The president's authority in the budget process would be enhanced because spending he supports could no longer be held hostage to spending he finds unacceptable.

Enforce Budget Resolution Allocations

Under the current budget procedures, the amounts agreed to in the congressional budget resolution for defense and nondefense spending are rearranged during the appropriations process. Because defense spending is the largest single item in the budget, the appropriations committee generally transfers funds out of defense accounts in order to increase funds in nondefense accounts. In the FY 1983-87 period, for example, $27 billion in funds recommended by the budget resolution for defense was shifted by the Appropriations Committees out of defense and into domestic programs. An enforcement mechanism is needed to ensure that after the administration and Congress have arrived at a budget agreement on defense and nondefense spending, the appropriators do not destroy that agreement by reallocating funds.

The budget summit agreement reached in 1987 for fiscal years 1988 and 1989 recognized this problem. The summit agreement set specific spending amounts for defense, international affairs and nondefense discretionary spending for both years. In the reconciliation measure passed in 1987 to enact the legislative changes required by the summit agreement, language was included stating the specific ceilings for each category for FY 1989 *and*, as an enforcement mechanism, making it out of order to consider any appropriations measure which did not adhere to the ceilings. While points of order are routinely waived in the House, it would take a super-majority of 60 votes to waive this enforcement measure in the Senate. The enforcement mechanism has been effective, as all discussions of spending for FY 1989 have retained the spending level for defense. Instead, the FY 1989 budget debate has focused on how to allocate the pool of funds provided for nondefense spending.

A permanent enforcement mechanism needs to be in place to ensure a similar outcome in future years. The budget resolution contains an estimate of allocations for spending for each of the committees. The Appropriations Committee then makes its own suballocation for each of its subcommittees. To enforce the defense and nondefense spending levels contained in the budget resolution, the budget resolution must also contain binding suballocations to the Appropriations Committee for defense and nondefense spending. A point of order, similar to the one in place for FY 1989, should be instituted to ensure that the nondefense spending allocation is not exceeded. This reform will assure that once a compromise between the executive and legislative branch is reached, there is no danger of the agreement being breached through a lowering of defense spending in the appropriations process.

Require a Binding Joint Budget Resolution

Under the Budget Act, the president submits his budget recommendation to Congress, and then Congress prepares its own budget. The congressional budget resolution is a concurrent resolution, meaning that it is adopted by each house but is not signed by the president and therefore has no force of law. As President Reagan once noted: "It's called the president's budget, and yet there's nothing binding in it. It is submitted to the Congress and they don't even have to consider it."[3] A positive reform is needed to reestablish a balance between the legislative and executive branches. One solution is to convert the congressional budget resolution into a joint resolution which would require the president's signature (or a veto override) for enactment.

This reform would assure executive branch participation in discussions on spending priorities and policies. While in the past the administration has been consulted on the budget, and in some years, such as 1981, has strongly influenced the budget outcome, there are no incentives for Congress to cooperate with the executive branch since the president has no formal role in the budget process other than submitting his budget.

By elevating the budget resolution from the status of concurrent resolution to the status of enforceable law (requiring the president's signature prior to enactment), disputes on spending priorities would be resolved much earlier in the process. The president would have the opportunity to fully express his views on the budget. He would not have to wait until the appropriations process to begin debate on spending levels. He would also be able to affect the outcome of the budget process since his approval would be necessary for the budget resolution to become effective.

Eliminate the "Baseline" Concept for Budget Comparisons

Congress has been able to control the budget debate by controlling the language used to describe budget actions. In particular, it has successfully redefined what constitutes a "spending cut." Congress has developed a method of making budget comparisons which allows an actual increase in spending to be classified as a "cut." This method should be abandoned and a new process implemented so that when Congress and the president refer to a reduction in spending, it means the same as a reduction in

BASELINE BS

spending for an individual or business. That is, it means spending less than was spent in the previous time period.

The Budget Act required the president's budget report to contain not only a budget plan for the upcoming year, but also a "current services" budget, which is defined as an estimate of spending and revenues under current policy, including inflation, changing demographics, and program growth contained in past congressional budgets. The CBO produces a similar projection known as the "baseline." Demographic changes usually mean that more people are entitled to government benefits. The result: spending on entitlement programs invariably is increased under the CBO baseline projections. Inflation built into all programs also increases spending outlays under the baseline concept. In fact, baseline spending projections are always higher than the previous year's actual spending levels.

In the early years under the Budget Act, the congressional budget resolution was derived by starting with the president's budget and then changing it. All discussions were couched in terms of changes made by Congress to the president's budget. The Senate budget resolution for FY 1979, for example, was said to increase Carter's defense spending by $1.4 billion. By the end of the Carter years, Congress used the baseline prepared by CBO as the basis for comparing all budget proposals. This diminished the role of the executive branch removing the president's budget from the centerpiece of congressional budget debates.

The reason for the popularity of the baseline estimates is easy to understand. By making all budget comparisons relative to an inflated baseline, Congress can take credit for "cuts" when in reality spending is still growing, but by less than it had been. When the public considers a spending reduction, it thinks in terms of reducing spending from the prior year. But under the baseline comparison concept, a spending reduction means spending less than Congress *would like to spend*. The 1987 budget summit agreement, forged in a crisis atmosphere and designed to restore confidence in America's markets, claimed to be reducing spending in FY 1988 by $19.2 billion. In reality, the budget summit agreement allowed spending in FY 1988 to increase by $51.8 billion from the FY 1987 level.

Congress also uses the baseline projections to discredit the president's budget proposals. By comparing the president's budget to high baseline spending, Reagan's proposals were described as deep budget cuts even though funding increased from the previous year.

Eliminating the baseline for budget comparisons could increase the executive's ability to expose to the public exactly how much *Congress* is spending. An end to the baseline would eliminate a bias toward increased spending in the budget process. Voters would probably not support the budget summit agreement if they knew that it called for a $11 billion increase in taxes so that spending could grow by more than $50 billion. Without the baseline concept, Congress would no longer be able to claim "savings" for actions that actually only slow the growth of spending.

RESTORING THE EXECUTIVE

This chapter has shown how the current budget process has evolved into a procedure which promotes confrontation rather than negotiation between the executive and legislative branches. The Congress largely dominates budget decisions, leading to higher spending and larger deficits than in the period preceding the enactment of the Congressional Budget Act.

The short-term gains to legislators from implementing new spending programs and increasing benefits under existing programs are very concrete and centralized while the long-term benefits that accrue from low deficits are more difficult to measure. This creates an institutional bias in the system toward higher spending by Congress. The president, who serves the broader constituency of the nation as a whole and who has a longer term than members of the House of Representatives, generally has a different perspective than Congress. As such, he has valuable insight on budget priorities which should be incorporated into decisions on the spending of federal funds. Reforms should be enacted to increase the role of the executive branch in the budget process and to take advantage of the different perspectives the executive and legislative branches have on the fiscal policy role of the federal budget.

The reforms proposed above would all serve to restore an effective and constitutional balance between Congress and the White House on budget priorities. They could also stem the inherent congressional tendency to overspend. Unfortunately, there is little chance of these reforms being enacted, with the possible exception of the proposal for separate enrollment of full-year appropriations measures. Different versions of the reforms have been introduced in Congress, but none have been successful. During the debate on Gramm-Rudman-Hollings II, thirteen budget process reforms were adopted by the Senate. All of the provisions, however, except those that applied only to the Senate, were deleted in the conference with the House. Future administrations need to continue to ask for budget process reforms such as those outlined above, but without an aggressive campaign by the administration to educate the public, the congressional budget process will not substantively be reformed.

Notes

1. See Article 1, Sections 8 and 9, of the U.S. Constitution.

2. U.S. Congress, Senate Conference Committee, *Conference Report to Accompany S.1541*, June 12, 1974, S.Rept. 93-924, p.49.

3. As quoted by John Herbers, "President Denounces Budget Process," *New York Times*, May 29, 1982.

7. The House Dynasty: A Public Choice Analysis

MARK CRAIN

In this chapter, economist Mark Crain applies Public Choice theory to one of the most important institutions of the House of Representatives: the committees. Although committee chairmanships are less under control of the House leadership than in former years, the actual membership on certain more desirable committees is still controlled by the Speaker. Professor Crain shows how this power to reward has been used by the Speaker to influence individual members on policy issues.

The source of the resurgence of congressional power during the Reagan era is the focus of this chapter. That Congress has increased its influence is in no way universally accepted. To the contrary, we hear much about the breakdown in congressional discipline and how members of the U.S. House and Senate no longer represent a cohesive force, or are any match for either the executive and judicial branches. But quite the opposite is true. The question addressed in this chapter is *how* this shift came about. What were the institutional sources for the resurgence of Congress?

The thesis is that the leadership in Congress—especially the House leadership—has used the committee system effectively to control the national political agenda. The nature of the rules of House procedure has allowed the Democrats, as the majority party in Congress, to seize control of national lawmaking through hardball tactics and astute use of the institutional rules. The emphasis of the chapter will strike some readers as strange; namely its focus on the *internal* rules of Congress. There are a couple of reasons for this emphasis; the main one is that in the U.S. Congress, most things happen in, or because of, the committee system. (The same can be said for state legislatures, where committees are a ubiquitous feature.) Yet the main function of the committee system in U.S. legislatures has been ignored almost totally. They are *controls.* More than any other device, the committee system allows the majority party in the legislature to dominate national politics.

The second reason for emphasizing the institutional rules of Congress is force of habit. One of the most important lessons of the public choice approach is that institutions matter. What this means is that the behavior of politicians, like behavior in other contexts, is shaped by the rewards and costs of alternative choices. Rewards and costs, in turn, are defined by the rules and institutions that govern an organization. For example, institutions are central to understanding the source of differences in congressional versus presidential policy goals. It is extraordinary that in 1984 Congress faced the same voters the President did, yet following the elections Congress and the President responded to these voters quite differently. How can these two branches of government respond to the same electoral signals in such radically different ways? The public choice tradition teaches us how to approach such apparent paradoxes in politics.

THE PUBLIC CHOICE EXPLANATION

According to many Washington pundits, the decline in the Reagan presidency began with a fluff-filled and feel-good reelection campaign in 1984. Lacking in substantive issues, the reelection victory for the President was hollow. Never mind the overwhelming electoral margin that returned the incumbent to the White House, there was no real mandate to move forward on major policy fronts.

The story continues with Iran-Contra hearings, stock market convulsions, budget summits, Supreme Court nominations, Panama, and so on. The gist is: through a series of crippling mistakes the Reagan presidency transformed itself into a spent force. And underlying this train of thought is that declining presidential influence grew out of internal mismanagement.

We might generically label this reasoning the "self-inflicted wounds" thesis. And what lesson are we to draw from this thesis? Simple: the balance of national political power between the respective branches can be restored if only the electorate will choose to put strong and competent leaders in control of the White House.

Before the typesetting begins on the history books, we should consider a competing explanation of the shifts in national influence. For the media, it is mostly too late. The self-inflicted wounds thesis—well-polished and easily stylized to anecdotes—makes good popular press. But the imbalance between the executive branch and the legislative branch can be understood better by examining the rise of the latter, not the decline of the former. As the political power of the Democrats in Congress became more glaring between 1981 and 1988, the illusion was created that presidential power during the Reagan years faded "on its own." It is this illusion, fueled by anecdotes, that has become the common wisdom.

The Congressional Turnabout

On the Senate side, the big change came abruptly with the 1986 elections. In that year, when the Democrats regained the majority, and took control of the committee system. This meant that all committee chairmanships, staffs, budgets, and so forth, switched from Republican to Democrat control. For the first time, Ronald Reagan in 1987 submitted a budget and other legislative proposals to a Congress with the Democrats in control of both houses.

The effect of the party reversal in the Senate should not be underestimated. Neither should it be overestimated, which is more often the case. The congressional resurgence began much earlier, during the first Reagan term, and on the other side of

Capitol Hill. In the House, the rise of the Democrat Party, which was much more subtle, effectively blocked many of the Reagan initiatives. This will be the main focus of this chapter. The Democrat House leadership launched the ascent in 1982 using the rules of the committee system with dedication. Their strategy has been extremely effective. Over the course of the Reagan presidency, support among House Democrats for administration-backed legislation was nipped in the bud. Congressional voting records illustrate this abrupt shift in House support for Reagan-backed legislation. House Democrats changed their colors, and the question is, "Why?"

In 1981, the "average" House Democrat supported President Reagan's positions nearly half the time on roll call votes. By 1986 support among House Democrats for Reagan initiatives had been cut in half. Can we attribute this chameleon-like change in House Democrats to a weakened presidency? If not, what accounts for this congressional turnabout?

Off-hand, we recall the early role of the Boll Weevils—conservative Southern Democrats. Did the breakdown of the coalition of Boll Weevils and Republicans damage the Reagan Administration's congressional base? Undoubtedly this was a factor but, as the analysis of voting behavior later in this chapter will show, it was not a predominant factor. In fact, presidential support among the Boll Weevils changed very little between 1981 and 1986. And as far as different geographic regions of the country are concerned, there is really no significant difference in the changes among Democrats.

A distinct pattern to the changes in congressional support for Reagan initiatives does emerge from congressional voting data, however. This pattern reveals much about the muscle of the majority party leadership in the House. In effect, the notion that parties and party leaders no longer wield much influence over House members is misguided. Parties use the committee assignment process as both carrot and stick to control the voting behavior of their members.

The remaining sections of this chapter will provide the explanation for the turnabout. First we will examine the organization of congressional activity from a public choice perspective. Our approach focuses on the role played by the rules and institutions that constitute the legislative process. The rules are emphasized because they shape the incentives of the relevant actors within the process. The leadership is provided with specific rights to set rewards and punishments, and these provide a direct mechanism to influence the outcomes of the process. A bit of institutional background is also provided about the federal legislative process generally, and the House committee system specifically. The purpose of the committee system as a mechanism for maintaining control will be emphasized.

Next, this chapter will develop empirical evidence to support our thesis, using congressional roll call voting data.[1] Specifically, we will show how the model of congressional control developed below predicts where the leadership should be most effective in influencing the voting behavior of party members. This prediction explains changes in presidential support among Democrat House members. This is really the point where Congress and the president come face to face over which branch will have its say over policy.

Finally, this chapter will conclude wiith a discussion of current proposals for reforming the legislative process.

CONGRESSIONAL COMMITTEES AS LOYALTY FILTERS

The theory behind the "committees-as-controls" idea is called signaling, or filtering. Developed by such scholars as Michael Spence, Albert Hirschmann, George Akerlof, and Joseph Stiglitz, signaling theory is one of the most significant contributions to economics in the postwar years.[2]

It is said that Spence's work launched a thousand articles, but none has yet applied the theory to the organization of legislatures. The congressional committee system is a near-perfect example of the theory in practice. What the theory is about, in a nutshell, is how institutions—*rules*—are used to obtain information.

When a congressman is first elected, what does the party leadership know about him? Not much, for the most part. Party leaders seldom dwell on nonincumbents, and with good reason.

The rules of the organization—in this case the *Constitution*— gives the right to elect representatives to the voters and not to party leaders. If party leaders could choose their new members, Congress would be a very different organization. But since they cannot, they have little incentive to find out about party members until after election day.

But what happens once new members are elected? The leaders need to know if they can count on a member for his support when they need it. If a member cannot be counted on, the party leaders have a good system for damage control. The leadership uses the committee system to (1) determine how loyal party members are, and (2) prevent less loyal members from becoming involved in major policies.

Committees as Farm Teams: An Analogy to Baseball

The organization of professional baseball is a useful analogy for the congressional committee system. In baseball there are two levels, a minor one and a major one. Minor league teams are farm clubs for the major league teams. This organizational structure is a quality control mechanism. The quality of a player is determined in the minor leagues, so that the team avoids making mistakes where they would hurt the most—in the major leagues.

The congressional committee system, like professional baseball, has minor committees and major committees. The United States House also has an "all star" league of committees that are designated "exclusive committees." Exclusive committees, as the name implies, are the most powerful: Appropriations, Rules, and Ways and Means. Congressmen must first prove themselves on the minor committees and give party leaders an opportunity to get to know them better—by watching their voting habits for example—before having a shot at the major or all star committees.

Of course, not all members can vote the way their leadership would like them to vote. If they did, they might not be around in the next Congress because constituents would vote them out of office. And, for those members who are "disloyal" to the party leadership, the chance of moving up onto an exclusive committee is remote. The tendency is thus to filter out those members who are unable to toe the party line. Such members wind up their congressional careers as chairmen (or high ranking members) of the minor committees. In effect, the congressmen who are less able to support the party leaders are inhibited from reaching positions of prominence.

But this gets well ahead of the story. Some institutional background about the committee system as a filtering mechanism is needed.

Damage Control and Congressional Committee Assignments

Making a committee assignment in Congress is risky business. In a standard business firm, the analogous decision would be a risky, long-term investment. The party's choice about who to put on what committee is exactly this same type of long-term, high-stakes decision. Once assigned to a committee, party members remain there virtually as long as they desire, typically rising up the committee leadership ladder as quickly as the seniority system permits.

There are spectacular exceptions, of course. In 1983 then-Democratic Congressman Phil Gramm was stripped of his assignment on the Budget Committee, which provoked him into switching parties. (The party switch came after Gramm resigned from the House and was reelected in a special election.) These events are rare exceptions; once a member is assigned, he is not likely to be removed from a committee against his will. The point is that committee assignments have lasting, multiple-term consequences, affecting the flow of policies from committees for years to come.

The Rules for House Committee Assignments

Committee assignments in the House are accomplished in two stages. First, the total number of committee slots that each party will receive is agreed upon by the Democrat and Republican leaders.[3] Second, the party leaders independently decide which of their members will be nominated to fill each slot. Democrat committee assignments in the House are recommended by the Policy and Steering Committee and Republican assignments by the Executive Committee of the Committee on Committees. The recommendations must be approved by majority vote in the full party caucuses and, finally, approved on the House floor.[4] The most important exception to this assignment process is that Democrats on the Rules committee are appointed by (and serve at the pleasure of) the Speaker of the House.

The party ratios vary for each House committee, and they are seldom equal to the ratio that exists between the two political parties in the full chamber. Table 1 lists the party ratios on standing committees in the U.S. House in the 100th Congress (1987-88). It shows, for example, that the Democrats controlled 69 percent of the seats on the Rules Committee, while they controlled only 59 percent of the seats in the full House.

There is no predetermined rule for committee sizes or ratios, so party leaders have total discretion to set these parameters. This is crucial to the overall applicability of the filtering theory to the committee system because without this discretion the party would have to fill all vacancies. As it is, if the pool of potential members contains no one of the leadership's liking, the vacant seat can be eliminated. Similarly, if an unusually large crop of freshmen legislators are elected at one time, the less important ("minor") committees can be expanded to accommodate the sudden influx of unknown members.

Another aspect of House committees that conforms to the filtering model is the variation in their influence. Take the example of international trade: The House Foreign Affairs Committee loses jurisdiction over trade bills to the Ways and Means Committee. Members who desire to be principal players on trade policy would therefore need to be assigned to Ways and Means, not Foreign Affairs. In other words, the differences between the committees are much more than nominal or simply to allow members to specialize in legislative subjects. The basis for distinction resides in the *importance* of the issues over which each committee has oversight.

In 1974 the House revised certain procedural rules regarding committee assignments. Reforms enacted in that year required all members to be assigned to at least one major committee, and to no more than two major committees. Therefore, members assigned to an exclusive committee cannot serve on any other standing committee.

Table 1 lists the designations that the House has given to its standing committees: there are three "exclusive," eight "major," and eleven "minor" committees. Naturally, the party leaders want to entrust to the more loyal party members the committee positions which have more responsibility. Party members who exhibit the least loyalty to the leadership's policies will be the most isolated from key positions of power. The tendency of the leaders to use caution in making committee assignments to the key posts is understandable, given the long-term nature of this commitment.

Filtering for Loyalty

Against this institutional background concerning the nature of the problem facing party leaders, the role of the committee system as a filtering mechanism is easily recognized. The committee system identifies and sorts party members on the basis of loyalty to the leaders' policy positions. Some committees are functionally equivalent to observation tanks or farm teams in the baseball analogy; the qualities of party members are discovered in the less important committees.

Newly elected party members differ widely in many respects, but from the leadership's standpoint, these mainly boil down to questions of "loyalty"—that is, whether a member can support the leadership's policy objectives. This means that the leaders need a mechanism to discover this information for themselves.

Contrast this institutional arrangement with that of a standard business firm. Managers (or owners) make the hiring decisions, which gives them ample incentive to discover how an applicant is likely to pan out before a hiring decision is made. Party leaders have little incentive to behave similarly since they are not part of the initial "hiring" process. After a new party member is elected, however, the leadership has considerable interest in discovering information about him.

Unlike the conventional view of committees (which will be characterized more completely below), this filtering theory suggests that unimportant committees will be an essential compo-

Table 1 Standing Committee Ratios, Sizes, And Designations—U.S. House 100th Congress

Committee Name	Democratic Members	Percent of Total seats	Republican Members	Committee Designation
Agriculture	26	(60.5)	17	M
Appropriations	35	(61.4)	22	E
Armed Services	31	(60.8)	20	M
Banking	30	(60.0)	20	M
Budget	31	(60.0)	14	N-M
District of Columbia	7	(63.6)	4	N-M
Education & Labor	21	(61.8)	13	M
Energy & Commerce	25	(59.5)	17	M
Foreign Affairs	25	(59.5)	17	M
Govt. Operations	24	(61.5)	15	N-M
House Administration	12	(63.2)	7	N-M
Int. & Insular Affairs	23	(62.2)	14	N-M

Committee Name	Democratic Members	Percent of Total seats	Republican Members	Committee Designation
Judiciary	21	(60.0)	14	M
Merchnt Marine & Fishries	25	(59.5)	17	N-M
& Civil Service	13	(61.9)	8	N-M
Public Wrks.& Trans.	30	(60.0)	20	M
Rules	9	(69.2)	4	E
Science & Tech.	27	60.0)	18	N-M
Small Business	27	(61.4)	17	N-M
Standards of Official Conduct	6	(50.0)	6	N-M
Veteran's Affairs	21	(61.8)	13	N-M
Ways & Means	23	(63.9)	13	E
TOTALS	482	(60.88)	310	

*In the full House there are 258 Democrats—(59.3%) and 177 Republicans.
M=Major;
E=Exclusive;
N-M=Non-Major;

nent of the system. Members assigned to these will have little part in substantive policy decisions. But, while being held in these observation tanks, the new members are sorted according to their conformity characteristics. Thus, before a long term commitment is made to place a member on a substantive committee, the leaders have an opportunity to obtain much more information about each member.

The Voting Record as a Signal of Loyalty to the Leadership

In order to reduce the uncertainty associated with making a committee assignment, party leaders look for signs that identify the loyalty qualities of party members. The voting record of a member is one of the most important signs in this regard. Of course there are others, such as bills sponsored and cosponsored, but the voting records are good signals of support for the leadership's policy goals.

A congressman's voting record acts as a form of implicit guarantee about his ability to support the leadership's positions "publicly," while continuing to get reelected. Obviously, some party members do not have this ability, because voting in accord with the leadership would put them at odds with the voters back home. This tension between voting the district versus voting the party line is present to a greater or lesser extent in every member; that is, this is not strictly an all-or-none situation. The less these two constituencies are in conflict, the easier it is for the congressman to make up his mind about his final voting choices.

Another way of thinking about this dual nature of a congressman's voting calculus—although it abstracts somewhat from the complexity of the real world—is to imagine the characteristics of the constituents in the home district of "the" party leader. How closely does the district of a party member resemble the leader's district? If they are virtually identical, then a vote for the folks back home will totally please the leader. If the member's district looks nothing like his leader's district, he has a real problem. By keeping the voters happy, he will surely displease the leader.

The Conventional View of Congressional Committees: Specialized Subjects and Jurisdictions

The function of the committee as a source of control for the legislative leadership has not been generally stressed by scholars. Nonetheless, committees are a major means by which the leadership controls legislative outcomes. In the conventional view (e.g., of Shepsle, Weingast, Moran, and others) congressional committee assignments are depicted as a voluntary process. Each member simply chooses whichever committee best suits his constituency. The shortcoming of the conventional view is that it ignores institutional reality. It asserts that the purpose of legislative committees is to allow members to specialize in particular subject areas of public policy.[5]

A statement reflective of this reasoning is as follows:

> ... [T]he committee system enforces the following trade: each legislator gives up some influence over many areas of policy in return for a much greater influence over the one that, for him, counts the most. Thus, we find that representatives from farming districts dominate Agriculture committees and oversee the provision of benefits to their farm constituents. Members from urban districts dominate banking, urban, and welfare committees overseeing an array of programs that provide benefits to a host of urban constituents. And members from western states dominate interior and public lands committees that provide benefits to their constituents.[6]

According to this thinking, committee assignments are simply the result of a self-selection process; members choose committees based on the issues closest to their constituents' interests. The specialized subjects and jurisdictions of committees thus allow members to find legislative niches closely suited to their own ends. The "farmers-on-farm-committees" theory—although not totally without merit—obscures the primary function of legislative committees, namely the sorting, or loyalty filtering, of members within each political party.

Each congressman necessarily responds to the interests of his constituents, but this does not mean that his committee assignments will be improved by heeding their interests. To the contrary, if by voting with his constituency a congressman must buck his party leaders' desires, he may assure himself of not obtaining a preferred committee assignment. Indeed, how many members can simply *choose* to be on the House Ways and Means Committee? This, of course, is beyond the realm of hope for all but a few House members.

If a congressman wants to obtain a prized committee assignment, it typically requires years of signaling to his party leaders that he is "one of them." Evidence of such conformity is important to the leadership because it ensures that their positions on the most significant issues will be enacted where it counts the the most: at the committee stage of the legislative process. By choosing a voting pattern that conforms to the leaders' positions, a congressman is signaling his ability to serve on key committees.

In the filtering model of the committee assignment process, there is incentive to select a voting record that signals more conformity to the leadership, because it will result in a more influential committee assignment. This choice by a congressman is constrained by the fact that his voting record is public, and therefore, will have an impact on the behavior of voters and interest groups. The desire to get reelected will prevent some members from conforming to the leaders' legislative initiatives. Those who must be disloyal will, for the most part, be frozen out of the main policy debates because they will not be selected for the superior committee assignments.

How The Congressional Committee System Distorts Representative Government

It is not hard to understand why congressmen get caught up in this signaling behavior. From their individual standpoints, the obvious thing to do is get ahead in Congress. While it may be totally rational for each individual congressman to go along with the leadership in his votes, this creates a serious distortion. The root of the distortion is that congressmen "overinvest" in developing their reputations for loyalty. Because each member is trying to outconform his party peers in the competition for a plum committee assignment, the voting pattern begins to escalate out of control.

In the jargon of economics, the technical term for this problem is an "externality." This externality exists because there is no incentive for an individual congressman to take into consideration the effects of his voting actions on other members. While this may sound like a difficult concept to grasp, it is not. Consider the following analogy to education and the job market, a setting in which this externality problem is more familiar.[7]

One of the major—but perhaps unintended—functions of "an education" is to signal to employers certain information about the qualities of potential employees. This is particularly important because it is otherwise quite costly for employers to obtain this information. Education provides employers a means by which individuals of differing talents can be distinguished. Knowing that firms tend to base job offers on educational achievements, the result naturally is for individuals seeking jobs to get a degree. That is, the job hunter responds by signaling his productivity level by getting an education.

The externality problem comes in because individuals have an incentive to spend "too much" time in school. "Too much" means more than would be necessary from a productivity standpoint, if an individual's talents were known by some other means. As each individual spends more time in school, trying to signal employers, the level of education needed by more productive individuals is raised. Of course, no one individual has any reason to take this spillover effect into account when selecting the amount of education that is best for himself. But the spillover effect means that more talented individuals need even more education, if they are to signal their greater talents to employers, and so on. The end result of this signaling/self-selection process is that individuals tend to overinvest in education.

Returning from this analogy to the case of congressmen and their voting records, the overinvestment is in terms of party loyalty. As each competes to impress the leadership with his record, the standards for loyalty are raised for everyone in the party. Now, the more loyal members must vote even more in line with the leaders if they hope to have a chance to distinguish their greater loyalty. The upshot of this is that the rules and organizational principles that are used within the Congress create a bias that moves the institution too far toward the policy desires of the party leaders, and away from representative democracy.

The Filtering Theory in Summary

The authority to set the number of committee positions and party ratios and to make committee assignments is an extraordinarily powerful mechanism. The Democratic congressional leadership has used this authority astutely during the Reagan presidency to control major legislative initiatives.

The assignment power is used to open slots on more important committees for the party members who have stood most definitively behind the leadership's positions. And the reverse also holds true; the assignment power has been used by the leadership to close positions on important committees for members who did not stand firmly behind them.

The result of using voting records as a signal of party loyalty has been to skew policies in the direction of the congressional leaders. Given the rules of the game, it is only natural for each member to heed the policy preferences of the leaders in the competition to secure a significant committee post. The problem is that it escalates the standard by which members are judged by the leaders when the good slots are handed out. Those party members who cannot measure up to this standard of loyalty set by their peers can be kept off the key committees. This means, of course, that they are frozen out of major policy decisions which, for the most part, are determined at the committee stage.

EMPIRICAL EVIDENCE OF THE FILTERING PRACTICE DURING THE REAGAN ERA

The filtering theory of the committee system suggests that party members who conform in their voting habits to the party leadership will tend to wind up on the most influential committees. Committee assignments, controlled by the leaders, are a form of currency used to reward conformity and to punish the most errant of the members. In its bluntest form, the leadership can remove a member from a committee, although action that drastic is exceptional, as discussed above. In its sharpest form, the leadership selectively finesses into the exclusive spots members who conform most closely to the party line.

This effect can be illustrated with several types of empirical evidence. First, we consider the Congressional Quarterly (CQ) roll call voting data. Each year since 1953, CQ has published a voting study that tries to determine how often members voted the way the president wanted on legislative roll call votes. In 1986, for example, the average House Republican supported the president's position two-thirds of the time. In 1981, the first Reagan year, the average presidential support among House Republicans was almost exactly this same percentage, two-thirds. House Republicans maintained virtually the same level of support over the entire Reagan presidency.

But what about House Democrats? In 1981, an average Democrat supported the President's position on almost half the roll call votes. By 1986 this support had fallen by 50 percent.

The tightening of the House Democrat leadership's grip during this period of the Reagan presidency was a patient, and very effective strategy. The Democrats who sit on the exclusive House committees—Appropriations, Rules, and Ways and Means—have been the biggest chameleons when it comes to presidential support. Why? Because the Democrat leaders used their control over the assignment process to lever their party's members away from supporting President Reagan's agenda.

This effect can be illustrated once again using the CQ voting data. Suppose all House Democrats are ranked according to how much each has *changed* with respect to presidential support between 1981 and 1986 (the last year the Republicans controlled the Senate). Within this ranking, we can locate the "median" Democrat change—the point at which just as many changed more than the median versus less than the median. In other words, this is simply a technique to identify a frame of reference from which we can assess individual member changes. This ranking, divided at the median, can be classified into two groups, a "high change" group versus a "low change" group.

We find that two out of three of the Democrats on the exclusive committees fall into the high-change half of their party. Conversely, those Democrats who are in the low-change group are not likely to be on an exclusive committee. In short, those Democrats who continued to support the president over the years were prevented by their leaders from entering the exclusive committee ranks.

Table 2 Presidential Support Scores: U.S. House Fiscal Policy Committees (100th Congress, 1987-88)[a]

Committee (Number of Democratic Members)	Average[b] Presidential Support Score Among Committee Democrats	Average Presidential Support Score Among Committee & Subcommittee Chairmen	% of Committee Democrats with Lower Presidential Support Score Than Average House Democrat	% of Committee Democrats with Lower Presidential Support Score Than Their Respective State Delegations
Appropriations (35)	24% (8)	25% (9)	63%	66%
Budget (21)	22% (10)	18% (4)	75%	68%
Rules (9)	21% (6)	24% (7)	67%	89%
Steering & Policy (31)	22%(6)	20%[c] (3)	67%	74%
Ways & Means (23)	23% (8)	23% (9)	71%	64%
Combined-Fiscal Policy Committees (90)[d]	23% (8)	22% (8)	66%	67%

[a]Data source: *Congressional Quarterly Weekly Report*, Oct. 25, 1986.
[b]Averages are means. Standard deviations are listed in parentheses below respective mean values.
[c]Average for Chairman, Vice-Chairman, and 2nd Vice-Chairman.
[d]In total, there are 119 Democratic slots on the five committees shown. Twenty-nine Congressmen hold two of these slots, and, hence, are not double-counted in the "combined" count.

Presidential Support on the Fiscal Policy Committees

A second type of evidence of the way the committee system has disrupted presidential influence is presented in Table 2. The basic question in this case is whether congressmen assigned to the fiscal policy committees have different voting habits from other members. (The fiscal policy committees include the three exclusive committees, the Budget Committee, and the Policy and Steering Committee.) In other words, can we reject the claim that there is no difference between congressmen who are on the fiscal committees versus those who are not?

First, consider the Appropriations Committee data in Table 2. Thirty-five Democrats serve on this committee and, reading across the top row, the average Appropriations Committee Democrat supported the president's position 24 percent of the time. The average Appropriations Committee subcommittee chairman (there are 13) voted with the president 25 percent of the time. Next, of these 35 Democrat committee members, 63 percent were less supportive of the President than the average Democrat from their respective states.

Consider for example, Chairman Whitten from Mississippi, whose CQ presidential support score was 34 percent. The average Democratic congressman from Mississippi has a presidential support score of 38 percent. (The average score for all House Democrats in 1986 was 25 percent.) So, while Chairman Whitten is more supportive than the overall House average (one benchmark), he is less supportive than the typical Democrat from his home state (a second benchmark). These same scores and comparisons are provided for each of the fiscal policy committees in the House. The last row presents the results for all the fiscal committees combined.

What do the results in Table 2 indicate? If the fiscal policy committees contained members who were truly representative of House Democrats as a whole, we would expect the last two columns of Table 2 to read "50 percent." That is, if Democrats were assigned randomly—nonideologically—about half would be more and half would be less supportive of the president than the benchmark groups. Instead, in the fiscal policy committees, we find the *less* supportive group on the fiscal committees about twice as often as the more supportive group. Two-thirds of the

Democrats on the House fiscal committees are less supportive of the president's policies than other Democrats from their home states. The congressional deck was stacked against presidential fiscal policy intitiatives through the committee assignment process.

CONSTRUCTING PROPOSALS TO REFORM THE COMMITTEE ASSIGNMENT PROCESS

The analysis points out a specific target for reform: the power of legislative party leaders to open and shut positions on committees every two years—a source of a bias in voting patterns. If this arbitrary power is to be curbed, it will have to be replaced with a nondiscretionary rule for committee assignments. It might be worth noting that the much-maligned seniority system (which is still in use in the Senate for all committee assignments, including the most desirable ones), was such a nondiscretionary method.

Some proposals have been put forward to specify rules for proportional representation of parties on committees. Indeed, legislation of this type has been introduced into the U.S. House. Proportional representation on committees, however, would not eliminate the problem of voting bias that is stressed in this paper. Even under a system of strict proportional representation, party leaders could maintain substantial discretion, and thus their power to influence voting behavior, by their power to expand or contract the total committee size.

To achieve a sixty percent majority for example, a committee could have twelve Democrats and eight Republicans, or nine Democrats and six Republicans. Thus, a rule of proportional representation would not prevent deviating members of a given party from being excluded by their leaders from key committees.

The main object of any reform measure should be to protect the untrammeled opportunity of any member to serve on an important committee. In this case, public choice theory demonstrates that the number of positions for each party must be outside the control of the party leaders in each new legislative term. In other words, any proposal for reforming committee ratios needs to specify a formula for determining total committee sizes as well. Otherwise, it will not be true reform, and the leaders' hegemony over other members will continue, along with their disproportionate influence over policy outcomes in the House.

Notes

1. The raw data on Presidential support on roll call votes are from *Congressional Quarterly Weekly Report*, various issues. In the section on empirical evidence below, a more thorough discussion of the data sources and methods is provided. Note that "average" here refers to the mean value for all House Democrats.

2. For the seminal paper in the theory of signaling, see Michael A. Spence, "Job Market Signaling," *Quarterly Journal of Economics*, (May 1973) pp. 356-374. See also Joseph Stiglitz, "The Theory of Screening, Education and The Distribution of Income," *The American Economic Review*, (June 1975) pp. 283-300; George Akerlof, "Loyalty Filters," *The American Economic Review*, (March 1983), pp. 54-65; and Albert Hirschman, *Exit, Voice, and Loyalty*, (Harvard Univ. Press, Cambridge, MA, 1970).

3. An exception is the House Committee on Standards of Official Conduct (formerly known as the Ethics Committee). It has an equal number of minority and majority members as dictated by Rule X, clause 6 (A) (2) of the *Rules of the House*. Another exception is that members of the House Budget committee may serve a maximum of three consecutive terms.

4. Again, there are exceptions. Two slots on the Budget Committee are reserved for members of the Appropriations Committee and two for members of Ways and Means.

5. For examples of recent work articulating this view, see: Kenneth A. Shepsle, *The Giant Jigsaw Puzzle: Democratic Committee Assignments in the Modern House* (Chicago: University of Chicago Press, 1978); Barry R. Weingast and Michael J. Moran, "Bureaucratic Discretion or Congressional Control? Regulatory Policy Making by the Federal Trade Commission," *Journal of Political Economy*, Vol. 91, No. 5, 1983, pp. 765-800.

6. Weingast and Moran, ibid.

7. This particular application of the externality problem associated with signaling is taken from John G. Riley, "Testing the Educational Screening Hypothesis," *Journal of Political Economy*, (Vol. 87, No. 5 Part 2, 1979) pp. 227-252.

8. Using the Rules for Abuse

CLIFFORD BARNHART

The people were said to rule in the House of Representatives of the United States. As the author of this chapter shows, the representative character of the House is rapidly being lost. Through a combination of rules changes, use of perquisites, and manipulation of congressional districts, the members of Congress have succeeded in diluting the power of the voters to influence the course of government. The remedy is not, as many argue, changes in the mechanics of Congress, though some of these would help, but in moving policy differences out from behind the procedural curtain of Congress and into the light of political campaigns.

Consider the following complaints:

• After the stock market plunge of October 1987, Congress and the administration worked mightily to "save the economy," finally producing a two-year deficit reduction package of only $76 billion.

• Congress exhausted itself in 1987 by putting through a $600 billion continuing resolution to fund the whole government. It was later discovered to be filled with pet projects of individual congressmen—one provision even settling a personal score for a senator.

• Some members allege that today, the system of checks and balances is too slow to meet the demanding pace of modern life.

• Senators fume over nongermane amendments which they complain hold up the business of the Senate.

• Critics are frustrated at the inability of the Congress to face up to the "need" for taxes.

We are often treated to such lists of problems as proof that the institution of Congress is failing. Congress seems unable to handle all of the problems of the modern age.

While overhaul may be necessary and even useful, the problem with Congress is not structure, procedure, or even age. The main problem with Congress is the people in it. The House of Representatives and the Senate are very human institutions. Much of the work is done through friendships, political rivalries, and sometimes strange alliances. But they function as rapidly or as slowly, as effectively or as poorly, or in as fair or as biased a manner as the people in them want them to function.

Contrary to what some have alleged, it is not the system that has run roughshod over the members. Whenever the system has been revised or altered, it has been done by a leadership that wanted to achieve a particular goal. Any changes were the result of a conscious decision made in the name of the majority and designed to achieve a purpose.

For one to understand why the common wisdom about the problems of Congress today is wrong, a review of recent history is necessary. The purpose of this chapter will be to provide a review of some of the changes in rules and structure that have taken place over the last 30 years. It will also examine how they have been combined with a philosophical revolution in both parties which has created the atmosphere in which Congress deals with issues today.

THE DAYS OF "CONSENSUS POLITICS"

Some critics fondly recall days as recent as the 1950s, when making Congress work was a simple matter. President Dwight D. Eisenhower would call Speaker of the House Sam Rayburn and Senate Majority Leader Lyndon B. Johnson to the White House. The three of them would arrive at a compromise and safely assume that each could carry out his part of the bargain. While it was never quite that cut and dried, this schematic description is not inaccurate.

Those who long for a return to those days of yesteryear should not forget what happened to change that system. It was not some alien force that altered it, but a deliberate effort carried out by political leaders in Congress, over almost a generation.

This is probably seen most clearly in the actions taken in the House of Representatives. In the late 1950s, a group of younger liberal Democrats banded together to form the Democratic Study Group. Their hope was to pool their resources in order to fight the entrenched rural, southern Democrat leadership that controlled the committees. Procedurally they opposed the seniority system, but the substantive issue that focused their attention was the civil rights struggle.

The civil rights logjam was broken by an agreement between President John Kennedy and Speaker Sam Rayburn, under pressure from the Democratic Study Group, to pack the Rules Committee, which had until that time been the roadblock to progress on civil rights issues. In the House, the Rules Committee exercises life or death control over bills reported from substantive committees. Ordinarily, major legislation cannot go to the floor without a "rule." If the Rules Committee declines to grant a rule, no consideration is possible.

Their success with the Rules Committee, however, did not stop the efforts of the Democratic Study Group to modify the seniority system. The effort for "reform" broadened beyond the seniority system to include committee jurisdiction and House rules changes. But the focus of those Democrat reformers was always most sharply targeted on the power and influence represented by the seniority system.

It was not until the mid 1970s that the revolution was completed. When the large, liberal, Watergate election class joined the Democratic Caucus in 1975, direct caucus election of committee and subcommittee chairmen was accomplished. But this was far from an altruistic crusade, as is seen by the predictable result: the diffusion of power to a greater number of younger members. In other words, younger members destroyed the seniority system in order to acquire a share of power immediately.

This first step toward power for younger members was followed by an increase in the number of subcommittees and by an explosion of committee staff and committee spending. Between 1974 and 1985, the number of committees increased by 14 percent and the number of subcommittees increased by 23 percent. Staff increases were a much larger 124 percent. It became commonplace in the House that if you forgot a Democrat member's name, you could safely call him Mr. Chairman, because he was sure to be chairman of something.

Two other revolutions occured simultaneously with this diffusion of power which helped define the new power structure in the Congress. The first was the application of new technology. With computers, word processors, and other technological advances, it became possible for elected officials to communicate personally with more people than ever before. This paper explosion, combined with an increase in office account allowances and the use of the free mailing privilege, has made it possible for each and every member to build his own constituency issue by issue. Now any group list can be programmed into the computer and a personal letter, signed by a signature machine and stuffed by employees of the House, can be sent to as large or small a group as desired. A member can even print off lists of constituents who have contacted him, and then go door to door with a list of constituents' problems that he has helped to solve.

Clearly, "servicing" the constituent has reached a new level of efficiency. No wonder newly elected members are told by their party leaders that their first two years in office should be spent only on building constituent relations; the effort pays off handsomely. Over 90 percent of congressmen are reelected every two years.

The second change which took place was the increased ability of members to establish their own political base, independent of the party structure. To a great degree this comes from the success that both Democrats and Republicans have had in winning personal, not party, victories in previously solid districts. For example: Democrats Tom Downey, Bob Edgar, and Howard Wolpe all won House victories in previously solid Republican districts that continue to support Republicans in statewide and national contests. Likewise such Republicans as Dan Quayle of Indiana and Newt Gingrich of Georgia won personal victories over Democrats, running well ahead of their parties. Such victories are won through a carefully fashioned personal coalition, held together with constant attention to details. The result is a weaker party hold on elected representatives, but a stronger district and constituent influence when mobilized on issues.

THE NEW DYNAMICS

To finally understand the changes which have taken place between the 1950s and today, two other factors must be examined: the increasing liberalization of the Democrat Party (particularly in Congress), and the arrogance spawned by the permanent majority status of the Democrats in the House of Representatives.

The historic New Deal coalition of FDR was a delicate balance of liberal to moderate and even some conservative groups who were attracted by different parts of the Roosevelt agenda and who were willing to accommodate some differences in order to achieve success on each one's pet issue. As long as there was a respect for the right of the other members of the coalition to work for their goals with some mutual aid, the coalition held up. But in the late 1960s and 1970s this mutual respect broke down. There was a fundamental difference among the members of the coalition in their view of the international responsibilities of the United States, basic human values, and the degree and aggressiveness of government control over the lives of the people. While those divisions were exacerbated by the Vietnam War and the feminist and other special-interest movements, they were not caused by them.

Events worked to further divide the Democrat coalition. Examples include the uprising at the Democratic Convention in 1968, Woodstock, Kent State, the peace marches on Washington, and the rise of the drug culture. George McGovern won the nomination in 1972 and became the symbol of the divisions in the Democratic Party. The creeping extension of government control, the alternative culture and values, and the belief that the United States was the cause of world problems are at the heart of the Democrat philosophy that has dominated in the party throughout the 1970s and now in the 1980s.

George McGovern was defeated by a landslide, but he left a powerful legacy in the Democrat Party. The very liberal group of Democrats elected to the House and Senate in 1974 were almost totally in accord with the philosophy of the McGovern candidacy. The result was an elected Democrat group that was far to the left of the historic FDR coalition. While they have been reelected as individuals, their leadership has left the Democratic Party coalition in a shambles on the national level.

Power Corrupts

The second factor giving definition to the current Congress, especially in the House, is the arrogant use of power. Certainly in the House the belief that the Democrats hold a permanent majority adds to their arrogance.

For example, in 1974 a reorganization resolution passed the House of Representatives eliminating proxy voting in committee. Just a few months later the Democratic Caucus changed the House rules to allow proxy voting in committees. The same reorganization resolution stipulated that one-third of the investigatory staff should be controlled by the minority. Again, in early 1975, the Democratic Caucus abolished this minority protection.

Every two years thereafter, like clockwork, the Democratic Caucus changed the rules to restrict opportunities for the minority to participate in the formulation of new laws. In 1977 the number of members required for a quorum in committee, where most legislation is written, was reduced to one-third of the members on the committee. In 1979 the majority caucus increased by 25 percent the number of members needed to call for a vote on the House floor.

The Reagan landslide of 1980 set the Democratic rule-makers on their heels. Their response was to cheat the Republicans out of the proportional number of seats they deserved on the committees. On full committees Republicans were denied 31 seats they deserved and on sub-committees 81 seats were denied the minority.

The fireworks in 1983 were mostly internecine as the Democrats attacked then-Democrat Congressman Phil Gramm and the "Boll Weevils", as discussed below. But one particularly egregious rule change that year made it very difficult for members to offer amendments to appropriations bills limiting the use of funds. The effect was to make it more difficult to pass amendments like the annual abortion funding ban and proposals that in the 1970s cut off funding for the Vietnam War.

The next assault on a member's right to move legislation outside of the majority's tightly controlled schedule was the 1987 rule change forcing a day's notice for any attempt by a member to call up a rule reported more than seven days before. This procedure had been used successfully several times in the past to bring up such issues as aid to the Contras when the majority objected. Eliminating the element of surprise restricted the usefulness of this technique.

Some of these rule changes were in direct response to efforts by the minority to move legislation that had been long pending or to force votes on issues the Democrats wanted to avoid. Other changes were to strengthen the power of younger Democrats to enact their personal agendas.

Throughout this period the Democrat majority increased the use of closed rules to conduct business on key issues. A closed rule restricts or prohibits amendments to a committee bill. The Rules Committee, appointed by the Speaker with the consent of the Caucus, was given a permanent majority of more than two to one to ensure there would be no slip-ups. Creative rule-making also became more common. The purpose here was to limit the right of the minority to offer amendments or to have their amendments considered on a straight up or down vote.

Finally—the height of arrogance. The majority party refused to seat a member-elect with a legitimate election certification from his state.

The Democrat response to charges of ethics violation on the part of Speaker of the House Jim Wright amply demonstrates the arrogance of perennial majority status. As long as the attacks came only from isolated Republican members, they were simply ignored. However, once Common Cause, a liberal lobbying group, issued a call for an investigation by the House Ethics Committee, the threat was taken more seriously, and answered in kind.

First, a key aide to the Democratic leadership stated flatly that Common Cause was through on Capitol Hill. "It kills them on the House side," the *Washington Post* quoted the aide as saying, "suggesting strongly that Democratic leaders would be loath to work with the organization" on issues of importance to Common Cause. There is evidence that this threat was taken seriously. A few weeks later, Vic Fazio (D-CA), a member of the Ethics Committee supposedly investigating Wright, hosted the Speaker at a fundraiser in California. The money raised went to an organization chaired by Mr. Fazio. In fact, Speaker Wright had appointed Mr. Fazio to this chairmanship. Despite the impropriety of an investigator benefiting from the activities of his subject, as of this writing Common Cause has made no comment on the matter.

Second, the Democrat leadership targeted Wright's most prominent critic, Congressman Newt Gingrich (R-GA), for political extinction. The Democratic Congressional Campaign Committee agreed to devote maximum resources to defeat him. These resources included hiring a private investigator to investigate Mr. Gingrich's background and personal life and producing a series of negative ads to be aired in his district.

The Wright Way

It is instructive to review some recent case studies to understand how the liberalization of the Democratic majority, the arrogance of power, and the diffusion of power work to affect the actions of the Democrats, and how the lack of leadership and the failure of the minority to serve as the loyal opposition results in Republican impotence.

The elected Democrats in the Congress are themselves more liberal than the Democrat Party at large. Furthermore the caucus of elected Democrats is controlled by an even more liberal majority. The Caucus elects all of the leadership and the committee and subcommittee chairmen. By and large, to gain these positions, the candidates vie to see who can make the strongest appeal to the liberals who control the Caucus. This extends even to the Speaker's position.

Thus several years ago the young, liberal Democrats lectured then Majority Leader Jim Wright "schoolmarm" style on the House floor, in public. His errant vote in favor of the MX missile program had caused this reaction. It doesn't take long for an ambitious man to understand what he needs to do to rise to the top with a crowd like that. A reading of the vote ratings for Congressman Wright shows a strong trend over time to a more liberal voting record. This trend was capped off by his support of the liberal Lloyd Doggett in the run-off election for the Democrat Senate nomination in Texas in 1984, even though his opponent was conservative Kent Hance, one of Wright's House colleagues.

Speaker Wright's leadership of the House has been characterized by increased partisanship and a more marked liberal trend. On issues from trade policy to Central America he has used the power of his office and his influence to secure liberal victories.

The Greening of Les Aspin

A second example of how the trend toward liberalism in the Democrat Caucus focuses more on liberal policy choices is the case of Les Aspin's (D-WI) service as Chairman of the Armed Services committee.

Known as one of the liberal technocrats in the party, Aspin challenged Congressman Melvin Price (D-IL) for the chairmanship of the committee in 1985. He was elected over Price by securing the votes of the liberal antidefense wing of the Democrat Caucus. In his first term as chairman he committed the unforgivable sin of voting against this bloc of liberals on the funding for the MX missile compromise. They also blamed him for giving up too much on the Defense Department authorization conference report. Aspin was challenged in 1987 for the chairmanship of the committee by two members who both pledged to be more pure in their support of the liberal agenda.

Although Aspin was reelected chairman, there was a policy price tag. In 1987 Aspin moved aggressively to support the liberal agenda. He successfully added a number of arms control restrictions to the Defense authorization bill. It has been charged that these restrictions amount to a subversion of the power of the Senate to advise and consent to treaties negotiated by the executive branch. There is no doubt that his action limited the authority of the president and the Department of State as well as the Defense Department.

Taming The Boll Weevils

The third, and perhaps clearest example of how the liberalization of the Democratic caucus works to crush individual philosophical beliefs is the evolution of the Boll Weevil Democrats.

From the early 1970s there was a group of conservative southern Democrats who worked to help pass more moderate legislative proposals, or worked in coalition with Republicans to stop some of the extremely liberal committee proposals.

When Ronald Reagan won the presidency in 1980 and brought in a new Senate Republican majority, he also increased the number of Republicans in the House. At that point, the conservative Democrats (the Boll Weevils) were the balance of power in the House. They sympathized with President Reagan's commitment to reducing the size and scope of the government, cutting spending, and, to a lesser degree, cutting tax rates.

In 1981 and 1982 the Boll Weevils played a critical role in helping to develop and pass some of the Reagan proposals. They were willing to take the political risk in the Democrat Caucus to achieve the Reagan policy goals they supported.

The Republican loss of 33 House seats in the 1982 elections meant that the Boll Weevils no longer held the balance of power. This gave the Democrat Caucus a chance to enforce some discipline on their errant brothers. They chose as their target Phil Gramm of Texas, one of the most effective and the most abrasive of the Boll Weevils. They stripped him of his Budget Committee position. And just as the keelhauling of the mutinous sailor serves both as a punishment to the sailor and as a warning to the rest of the crew, these actions against Gramm scared the rest of the Boll Weevils. Gramm was the only one unfazed. He resigned his seat, switched parties, was reelected, and now serves as a Republican in the Senate. The other members of the Boll Weevil fraternity were suitably chastised and went underground for two years.

The Boll Weevils reemerged after the 1984 presidential elections. Once again Reagan's landslide had helped to increase the Republican House contingent, this time to 182 seats. The Boll Weevils, while not holding a clear balance of power, could make any vote a dead heat if they joined the Republicans. It was at this moment that Charlie Stenholm of Texas announced that he would challenge Tip O'Neill for the position of Speaker. Under heavy pressure, Mr. Stenholm eventually withdrew from the race.

If you are going to strike at the king, you had better vanquish him. If you fail, the best advice is to become his most obsequious servant. The Boll Weevils (and their leader, Congressman Stenholm) struck at their king (the Speaker of the House) and failed to complete the dispatch. They appear now to be engaged in an effort to save their political lives. Since 1985, while there have been occasions in which the Republicans and the conservative Democrats have won votes, there is neither an effective strategy nor an ongoing relationship, as there was in 1981. Putting together a majority for a Republican administration position becomes very difficult, and a regular working relationship is out of the question. Many of these conservative Democrats want to preserve their subcommittee chairmanships more than they want to enact a legislative program.

ESCAPING ACCOUNTABILITY

The changes in the rules and the arrogance of the majority serve not only to limit the rights of the minority, but they serve equally to protect the liberal majority from an electorate which is measurably more conservative. These factors contribute to the strength of incumbency, and combine with Republican timidity to hide the truth from the voters.

The Power of Incumbency

The numbers tell the story: In 1986, more than 98 percent of the members of Congress who ran for reelection were returned to office. In 1792, 60 percent of members were reelected, and the number has increased since then in an unbroken upward line. In other words, over the years, the members have been studying the science of reelection, and they are now approaching perfection.

Some of their techniques include:

• *Gerrymandering* of legislative districts, as discussed in Chapter 5. Gerrymandering has benefited the majority, but minority seats remain nearly as safe as majority seats.

• *Staff increases.* Since the middle 1960s, spending to support the legislative branch has multiplied almost ten times. The bulk of this expense is for personal and committee staff. Congress now employs almost 12,000 people, not counting many support agencies such as the Library of Congress. These staff members work on legislation and constituent cases, of course, but a great deal of what they do provides political benefits to the member.

• *The franking privilege.* The free mailing privileges available to incumbents are worth millions of dollars. The average member of Congress sends thousands of letters for each one received. In 1986, Congress as a whole received 62,756 letters and mailed out 758,700,000 pieces of mail. That is a ratio of more than 12,000 responses to every piece of citizen input.

• *Political campaign contributions.* There is nothing wrong with political action committees, but evidence is overwhelming that PACs give their money to incumbents by large margins. For example, in 1986, the average Democrat incumbent received more than 26 percent of his campaign money from PACs. By contrast, the average Republican challenger received only a little more than 10 percent of his money from PACs.

• *Public relations help.* Members of Congress have their own press secretaries and speechwriters, of course, but they can also get professional coaching, as well as the use of congressional studios to make tapes and videotapes for use on local radio and television stations and in campaign commercials. There are professional photographers employed by the House and Senate as well to take the member's picture with constituents.

The Minority's Failure

As indicated, this program of incumbency protection serves some Republicans just as well as it does the Democrat majority.

Republicans who serve as ranking members on committees tend to be more liberal than the party as a whole. They have often served the role of the loyal opposition, with the emphasis on the "loyal" and often forgetting completely the "opposition." They have become a minority in mindset as well as in numbers.

The pattern for the Old Bull Elephants is all too familiar. Get a good committee assignment, build your seniority, develop a close working relationship with the Democrat chairman, and don't rock the boat. Don't rock the boat on issues, on committee staffing, on internal committee rules. Finally, help the Democrat chairman get a few things done and wait to be fed the best table scraps.

On those rare occasions when the Republicans fought the Democrats over legislation, what was at stake was usually at most a minor modification of the Democrat proposal. The losses suffered in the elections of 1974 made the Republican leaders even more docile.

Republicans have little leadership, no vision, no strategy, and no unified sense of purpose. Therefore, Republicans have failed to take advantage of the opportunities to exploit Democrat weaknesses and arrogance.

One of the worst failures is permitting liberal members to disguise their true colors. For example, the 7th District of Pennsylvania voted for Ronald Reagan by a margin of 62-38 percent. Yet that district is represented in Congress by a man to whom the respected *National Journal* gives the highest liberal ranking on economic and social policy, and who ranks as more liberal than 92 percent of the other House members on foreign policy. Unfortunately, this is not an atypical example.

Conservative members are not encouraged by their leadership to make explicit these disparities. One of the reasons is that some members of the minority party might also be embarrassed. Another is simply a failure of nerve.

Nothing else can explain the refusal of Republican leaders in the House to object to the election of George Crockett (D-MI), whose loyal adherence to the Communist Party line is legendary, to the chairmanship of the Subcommittee on Western Hemisphere Affairs.

Even worse was the treatment by Senate Republicans of a report on Senator Howard Metzenbaum's (D-OH) youthful flirtations with communist organizations. These flirtations are not a matter of dispute. Yet when the report was accidentally made public, instead of defending its accuracy, Republicans cowered, publically denouncing a researcher for the Senatorial Campaign Committee who had since left after five years of service.

THE CONSERVATIVE RESPONSE

The happy symbiosis between a liberal majority and a placid minority has not been universally accepted in the House. Beginning about the time of the Vietnam War, which was a catalyst to so much else, a reaction began in the Congress.

Republicans took a page out of the Democrats' book. They began to work together in fits and starts, sometimes at the leadership level, and with more certainty among conservatives. This was the period when the Republican Study Committee and the Senate Steering Committee were formed. These *ad hoc* groups of conservatives provided a way for congressmen to use scarce resources to develop conservative policies. To a great extent these groups were a copy of the Democratic Study Group and a reaction to the moderate Republican control of the committees and the liberal domestic agenda put forward by the Nixon Administration, such as the Family Assistance plan.

New welfare and food stamp proposals were developed, the jobs creation act took shape, and, very importantly, Congressman Henry Hyde (R-IL) and Senator Jim Buckley (R-NY) fought the leadership on both sides of the aisle to stop federal funding for abortions.

The next major victory for these activists was the defeat on the House floor in March 1977 of common site picketing. Although the Democrats had gained the presidency and large majorities in both houses of Congress, a key part of the labor agenda was stopped in the first 100 days of this new era. This turned out to be a prelude to things to come. The Carter Administration was incompetent, and the Republicans were beginning to build the ideas of a new movement. Even more than that, the Republicans were showing surprising unity in the House and the Senate. Ronald Reagan's victory in 1980 cemented the young Turks who had forced new ideas on the Republican party into a leading role, especially in the House of Representatives. A completely new leadership team took over in the House, and even more profound was the capture of majority control in the Senate.

The first half of 1981 saw the implementation of two major pieces of the Reagan economic agenda: tax rate cuts and a change in the focus of government spending. While spending was not reduced, its momentum was slowed. Unfortunately, the second half of 1981 showed that these changes were not going to be accepted without a fight by the Democrats and some of the senior establishment Republicans on the Hill.

The best example was the political battle in the fall of 1981 on the Continuing Resolution. President Reagan took the step of closing down the government when he vetoed the Continuing Resolution just before Thanksgiving. He wanted $12 billion more in cuts. After shutting down the government, Ronald Reagan had the upper hand. But his own party leadership on the Appropriations Committees compromised at only a $4 billion cut and pulled the rug out from under the president.

The battle cry, "that's all we could get," and the philosophy that every vote must be won, no matter what compromise it took, was to be a costly siren song for the administration and its hopes for change.

The Rise of the Conservative Opportunity Society

In the House many of the more aggressive conservative members continued to fight these battles full force. A small group of members calling themselves the Conservative Opportunity Society (COS) came together to try to set an agenda for the House. Unhappy with the administration-supported tax increases in 1982 and 1983, they focused their attention on the House Democrats and often ignored the administration. They fought the nuclear freeze bill, using a series of individual amendments which kept the debate alive for weeks and uncovered many weaknesses in the bill.

A greater success was their fight to bring a comprehensive drug control act to the floor of the House in 1984. After it had passed the Senate overwhelmingly, the Democrats in the House stonewalled the bill. Not until six weeks before the election were the Republicans able to get a vote on this package, and even then only through a rare and usually unsuccessful legislative action. The greatest shock was saved for last, because the bill actually passed, with Democrats jumping ship and changing votes at the last minute to be on the side of tougher police powers against drug trafficking.

The fight was successful because it was taken out of the normal committee and leadership atmosphere, and because the issue was clearly defined and polarized. There was no confusion as to which side of the issue a member supported or what his vote meant. It was handled by a group of junior members, most of whom were not on the committee of jurisdiction. But they were very disciplined in their actions. They had a plan and a goal. They were superb at doing basic things well, from one-minute speeches, to special orders, to setting up their own hearings. They built a case for their proposals and then when the opportunity presented itself, they were able to succeed.

Conservatives have been markedly less successful in the past four years. Some of those, like the Conservative Opportunity Society, seem to have given up on the basic, but focused, step-by-step strategy they employed so well in 1983 and 1984. The administration has had little in the way of a program and the Republican leadership has not been willing to engage the Democrats directly. In the House this is due to the style of leadership which emphasizes the building of "consensus."

When there is a plan and a specific target, consensus leadership can help to bring about the support needed to achieve the goal. But when there is no well-defined goal, consensus leadership brings about indecision, a loss of purpose, and disunity in the ranks. This is the state of the Republican Party in the House today. Worst of all, the Republicans face a very aggressive and highly determined group of Democrats.

THE NEED FOR LEADERSHIP

As the 101st Congress approaches, Congress seems incapable of addressing the problems that face our country. No doubt the institution could use some changes, but its inability to act largely is due to a lack of leadership and to a failure of will. The Democrats control the House and the Senate, but their liberal ideas are not acceptable to most of the country now. Yet the Republicans did not offer any vision for America in the elections, of 1984 or 1986, nor in the Congressional elections of 1988.

As a result the leadership has concocted a series of black box solutions: continuing resolutions which fund virtually the whole government, budget compromise negotiations that deal with symptoms not problems, and formulas like Gramm-Rudman. Solutions are supposed to spring full-blown from those black boxes as Venus from the Cyprian Sea. Instead, these magical devices provide a convenient way to hide from the tough decisions that must be made. The massive size of the continuing resolution makes it virtually impossible to take anyone to task for the specifics in the bill. The bipartisan cloak over the nonsolutions to the budget problem masks accountability. The reliance on formulas removes the responsibility for solving the problem.

Recommendations for Change

To encourage openness and accountability in the House, there must be a return to more open debate and open rules. The right of the minority to offer amendments for straight up or down votes, without parliamentary tricks or limits must be restored. The right of all members to offer amendments during consideration of bills on the floor should be revived. In committee, where the real work is done, proxy voting must be eliminated and the number necessary for a quorum to do business should be increased to 50 percent. Equitable committee ratios and a reduction in the number of subcommittees and staff would result in more order and better laws.

Restrictions on debate and amendments in the House come not from a desire to limit disruptions and move legislation forward but from a desire to avoid discussing certain issues. The basic rules of the House are adequate to move debate forward.

The matter could easily become part of the national agenda if it were to be taken up by the major political candidates. Presidential candidates who in the past have run against Congress

(Harry Truman, Ronald Reagan) have done very well. Certainly the Congress of today is more ripe for presidential picking than any in recent memory.

Any procedural changes, no matter how necessary, ultimately lead back to the people in the institution. No procedural changes will compensate for a lack of will. Only leadership and a willingness to allow an honest discussion of differences—and the guaranteed right to offer alternatives and vote on them—will solve the problem. When the goal is to limit discussion and confuse the voters, it is very difficult to find solutions. It is not necessary to inject more partisanship, but it is necessary to open up the discussion of issues and to define the differences clearly.

When that is done, the people are able to decide whose vision and whose program they prefer.

9. Legislative Lords: Gag Rules and Permanent Staff

MICHAEL E. HAMMOND AND

PETER M. WEYRICH

As the House has become less and less representative, and less obser-vant of minority rights, the Senate has been following at a slower pace. In this chapter, two experts on Senate rules discuss that body's move-ment towards lessening its protection of ideological minorities. They also discuss how professional staff influence the ideological orientation of the Senate. There are serious implications of this ideological and policy narrowing. When open debate is shut off, it becomes much more difficult to decide policy questions in accordance with the wishes of the ultimate political power: the people. It also makes easier the encroach-ment of congressional power on the realm of the executive branch. The rules changes thus are a part of the erosion of the separation of powers.

Because procedure is the channel through which substance flows, its parameters determine whether the legislative process ultimately produces fertility or inundation. This chapter will deal with the ways in which arcane points of parliamentary pro-cedure in the U.S. Senate and House of Representatives have been major determinants of policies which have done signifi-cant damage to the country and to the democratic process itself.

Although the question of legislative staffing may initially

seem remote from issues of legislative procedure, we will also seek to establish that the staffing policies of various legislative offices have much to do with the comparative abilities of liberal and conservative offices to use and preserve those rules which are to their advantage—and to use the legislative process itself. To understand the importance of procedure, it is instructive to examine the difference between the Senate and the House.

Because the Senate grants relatively free access by the minority to the policy-making process, the Jesse Helmses and the Ted Kennedys are able to air and, in some cases, enact their concerns, even when they are in the political or philosophical minority. Their names are known to most Americans, even though neither has occupied the top echelons of Senate leadership for over a decade.

The House, on the other hand, is more of a totalitarian regime. In connection with the House Rules Committee's recent consideration of a pornography issue, for example, the acting chairman of the committee told antipornography members that, while he sided with them on the issue, "he had his orders" from the House leadership. Those orders directed the deletion of the antipornography amendment. Thus, the acting chairman recessed the committee rather than allow a vote that would bring displeasure from the House Democratic leadership. Such ironclad control means that many able and talented members of the House remain relatively anonymous because, to paraphrase the words of Delaware Senator Joseph Biden (D-DE), they "lack a platform on which to stand."

HOW NON-REPRESENTATIVE IS THE HOUSE?

The U.S. House of Representatives is rapidly replacing the Soviet Union as the paradigm of an institution which has the shell, but none of the substance, of democracy.

Here is a body which is selected under carefully rigged rules, mostly established by one political party to insure that that party remains in power. Once elected, the body proceeds to shower its members with the taxpayer-funded perquisites needed to fight off virtually any political challenge.

Within the House, the system is jury-rigged so that the minority party, with 41 percent of the seats, has only 22 percent of the committee staff and only 30 percent of the seats on the Rules Committee, which determines the terms under which legislation is considered. On the Appropriations Committee, which has rapidly supplanted the other standing committees as the engine of legislation, the minority party is allowed only 38 percent of the seats.

The oligarchic leadership structure in the House uses its predominance on the Rules Committee to bypass the other committees entirely, to completely waive the House rules with respect to the consideration of legislation, and to limit or eliminate the possibility of amendment on the floor. In the second session of the 100th Congress, for example, 62 percent of the measures considered on the floor were never considered by the appropriate committee. Either they were brought directly to the floor by suspending the rules, or the Rules Committee issued a rule to permit their consideration without deliberation by a standing committee.

All of this—and the extent to which it has gotten considerably worse under the regime of House Speaker Jim Wright—has begun to stir up even some of the more bovine members of the House minority. On Tuesday, May 24, 1988, a wide range of Republican House members, including leadership and nonleadership, activists and pacifists, conservatives and moderates, took to the House floor to denounce such treatment. Their complaints, which have been echoed by many outside observers, include the following:

• *The composition of the House—and the extent of the Democratic majority—is the result of an incredible exercise in banana republic-style electoral politics.* The number of seats which are controlled by one party or another solely as a result of fanciful drawing of legislative districts can, of course, never be definitively determined. But according to GOPAC—admittedly a Republican political action committee formed for the express purpose of achieving Republican control of the House—as many as 23 House seats are Democratic rather than Republican, strictly as a result of gerrymandering by Democrat state legislatures. These include five seats in California as a result of a redistricting plan pushed through by California Democrats, which the United States Supreme Court has recently refused to review.

In addition, these districts include three seats each in Illinois and Michigan, two in Florida and Oklahoma, and one each in Georgia, Massachusetts, Missouri, North Carolina, Tennessee, Texas, West Virginia, and Wisconsin. Understandably, GO-PAC fails to mention such states as Indiana, where gerrymandering has favored Republicans, but it is undoubtedly true that the practice has disproportionately helped Democrats, and that the seats lost to Republicans due to gerrymandering, when coupled with the seventeen seats which are expected to shift from the Northeast and Midwest to the South and West as a result of the 1990 census, would clearly put the Republicans within striking distance of control of the House.

• *The perquisites that House members grant themselves to facilitate reelection are spiraling to record levels, even in the era of Gramm-Rudman.* These have been discussed in some detail in Chapter 8.

• *The bulk of legislation increasingly consists of commemorative, private relief, and other insubstantial matters, while important legislation is lumped into huge, immutable bills.* Example: While more than 90 percent of the legislation passed in the 95th Congress was substantive legislation, only 53 percent of the legislation passed by the second summer of the 100th Congress had been substantive. Instead, Congress enacts such vital legislation as bills declaring National Pickle Week and National Stuttering Awareness Week.

In 1986, moreover, all thirteen of the regular appropriations bills were rolled into one huge continuing resolution—a continuing resolution that also addressed virtually all of the contentious defense-related questions, including satellite testing, chemical weapons testing, and nuclear testing. That shameful result was repeated in the first session of the 100th Congress, when not a single regular appropriations bill passed, and the president was once again presented with approving or vetoing an omnibus Continuing Resolution funding the entire government.

Coupled with the Rules Committee's limitations on amendments and points of order during consideration of such mammoth legislation, about the only alternative open to the minority is to vote against final passage of the entire federal budget. It is significant that even in 1955, when the budget of the federal government was less than $69 billion a year, Congress passed two and a half times as much legislation as it did in 1986.

It is also significant that, notwithstanding the sizable number of commemorative and largely private bills considered by the 100th Congress, legislation passed was, on the average, six times the length of the measures passed in 1955.

The continuing resolutions of fiscal years 1987 and 1988, which resolved virtually every legislative issue in their respective sessions—and which were not available for review until, in one case, a week after passage—have to be regarded at the top of the list of recent legislative travesties. But in close contention was the Omnibus Trade bill, which was finally written in a conference including over 200 members from 9 Senate committees and 14 House committees. The conference was so large, in fact, that the daily calendar finally stopped printing all the names.

• *The number of bills and resolutions considered under the "suspension calendar"—where all of the House rules are suspended and no amendments allowed—also has continued to climb.* As a result of "suspensions" and other procedural tools, an increasing amount of legislation is bypassing the House committee system entirely. In fact, the number of House committee reports has generally declined during the last decade—shrinking from a high of 731 during the first session of the 96th Congress to 499 during the first session of the 100th Congress.

Examples of such legislation that passed the House without report, hearings, or committee consideration of any type include: S. 557, the Grove City bill, which was perhaps the most significant civil rights legislation in a decade; H.J. Res. 523, the Central America Aid package; and H. Con. Res. 293, an attempt to change the Omnibus Trade bill *after it had already passed*, in order to gain the votes to override an expected presidential veto.

In addition to the growing number of bills considered under suspension of normal rules, the number of rules that prohibit all or some germane amendments and motions has risen precipitously. This is a relatively new phenomenon, since as recently as the 97th Congress, 80 percent of all rules were open rules which freely allowed the offering of all germane amendments. In the 98th Congress, however, that percentage fell to 72 percent. It was 64 percent in the 99th Congress, and up to July 1988 of the 100th Congress, only 56 percent of the 94 rules reported were open rules. Of the open rules reported during the 100th Congress, very few have pertained to the most controversial pieces of legislation.

Furthermore, rules have recently been enacted that prohibit a traditional minority prerogative—the right to offer instructions to motions to recommit legislation. Before the 99th Congress, this sort of prohibition was virtually unheard of. In the 95th, 96th, 97th, and 98th Congresses combined, there was only one rule in eight years that stripped the minority of the right to offer instructions on a motion to recommit. By contrast, there were twelve such rules during the 99th Congress and thirteen so far in the 100th Congress.

Another particularly troubling development is the "self-executing rule," a rule which purports to enact legislation without the House having to vote separately on the legislation itself. One such "self-executing rule" provides that the enactment of a First Concurrent Budget Resolution increasing the federal debt beyond the statutorily permissible level automatically sends a House-passed increase in the debt limit to the Senate, even though the House did not vote for such an increase.

During the 95th, 96th, and 97th Congresses, there were only three self-executing rules considered by the House, out of a total of 667 rules granted. That number climbed to 5 in the 98th Congress, 20 in the 99th Congress, and 18 by the second summer of the 100th Congress.

STIFLING DISSENT IN THE SENATE:
EMULATING THE HOUSE

Given that the Senate is not without its considerable egos, one would have thought there would be more resistance to a tendency to divide the Senate into first-class senators and second-class senators. Nonetheless, the elevation of a few senators at the expense of the others has moved forward equally during periods of Republican and Democratic control of that chamber, with neither party apparently giving much thought to the fact that the beatification of the majority party's leadership may produce undesired results should the Senate once again fall into opposition hands.

The Senate after Mansfield

The departure of Majority Leader Mike Mansfield (D-MT) in 1977 spelled the end of an "era of good feeling"—a period during which the easy-going Mansfield bemusedly tolerated the Senate's cumbersome and sometimes unwieldy ways.

With the arrival of the more result-oriented Robert Byrd (D-WV), things changed. The first thing that changed was the bipartisan reverence for the Senate's existence as a "continuing body," which, until shortly before, had been something of a sacred cow. By threatening to treat the Senate of the 95th Congress as a completely new institution with no rules, Byrd succeeded in forcing concessions consolidating the power of the Democratic leadership, the most notable of which was a crackdown on the traditional rules of unlimited debate.

Largely at the instigation of Byrd—first as whip, then as leader—the Senate, between 1975 and 1978, adopted restrictive rules changes:

• reducing the number of votes required to shut off Senate debate from two-thirds of the senators present and voting (or 67, if all senators are present) to three-fifths of those chosen and sworn (or 60, if no seats are vacant);

• reducing the total time for debate under cloture to 100 hours, no matter what amendments were pending at the expiration of that time;

• granting the Senate majority and minority leaders an additional four hours each to dispense after the invocation of cloture;

• severely limiting the types of amendments which could be offered after cloture, requiring them to be not only germane (under a new, tougher standard) and nondilatory, but also filed by 1:00 P.M. the day after cloture was filed (one hour before the invocation of cloture in the case of second-degree amendments).

Those not expert in the ways of the Senate may think many of these changes reasonable, but the increasing willingness of both political parties to tamper with the fundamental underlying rules of the democracy itself, when it suits their political ends, suggests that a highly threatened and agitated minority should have some recourse. Given that deciding what is "dilatory" and "germane" is both arbitrary and the under the control of the majority leader, these changes go a long way towards silencing dissenting voices.

The Senate Under Republican Control

When the Republicans took control of the Senate in 1981, they proved less inclined toward explicit rules changes, but their tendencies to consolidate power in the leadership proved no less pronounced.

The Republicans' first move under Majority Leader Howard Baker (R-TN) was to further tighten the definition of germaneness. And, while this would not ordinarily matter because the Senate has no standing rule requiring germaneness, it did effectively eliminate most amendments in those restrictive contexts in which germaneness *is* required, such as after the invocation of cloture, or when the Senate has agreed by unanimous consent to consider only germane amendments, or when the Senate is considering appropriations bills.

The Republicans also pushed another procedural technique to unprecedented lengths. The Republican leader took advantage of the custom of first recognizing the majority leader or manager of a bill to offer so many amendments that any further amendments were precluded, except by unanimous consent. Thus, the committee chairman could simply sit on the Senate floor and automatically exclude any amendment unacceptable to him. This tactic was perfected in connection with legislation to impose a five cent per gallon gasoline tax in December 1982.

Finally, in 1986, having staved off Democratic challenges to their Senate hegemony for two election cycles—and perhaps feeling a sense of invulnerability—the Republicans, under Robert Dole (R-KS) attached a series of rules changes to the resolution authorizing the televising of Senate debates. Ostensibly, the rationale for the changes was to make the Senate look less silly on TV by eliminating or reducing those situations in which it could be tied in procedural knots for long periods of time.

The three most radical alterations to come out of this exercise were: (1) reduction of post-cloture debate from 100 hours to thirty hours, (2) severe revamping of rules for treaty consideration, and (3) easing of circumstances under which the Senate leadership can move directly to a bill without debate. The magnitude of the treaty changes only began to become apparent to consenting senators in the spring of 1988 when they began to plan their opposition to the Intermediate-Range Nuclear Forces Treaty.

The Democrats' Return to Power

The Democrats returned to power in the Senate following the 1986 elections. The experience of being out of power, complete with the recurrent whining about the inability to offer amendments in connection with critical legislation during the Dole regime, seems to have left the Democratic leadership unslaked in its thirst to consolidate its power through more Senate rules changes.

The centerpiece of the new Democrat effort to silence dissent is a proposal to allow the Senate to quickly declare most amendments out of order by imposing a germaneness requirement on a piece of legislation. This proposal, Senate Resolution 41, was introduced on January 6, 1987. There have been negotiations between Republicans and Democrats on it, and an effort to mark up the resolution in the Senate Rules Committee, but as of this writing, the committee had still not been able to report the resolution.

If passed, this resolution would disenfranchise the Senate minority in somewhat the same way that the resentful minority in the House has already been disenfranchised. Even most "sense of the Senate" resolutions would be out of order. About the only difference between the Senate and the House—a difference which would be easily correctable by future resolutions—is that in the Senate the action to stifle dissent would have to be taken by a three-fifths majority vote.

Equally troubling is the fact that, under S. Res. 41, the majority will still be able to protect *its* right to offer amendments. That is so because the resolution would exempt "committee amendments" from its provisions. We can get some idea of how this exemption would work by looking at current exemptions granted "committee amendments" to appropriations bills.

From time to time, subcommittee chairmen and floor managers have considered offering floor amendments and fraudulently labeling them "committee amendments." The Senate parliamentarian has indicated that he will accept the statement of the floor manager of a bill that an amendment is a "committee amendment," even if this is patently not the case.

In practice, then, the adoption of Senate Resolution 41 would allow the majority to block virtually all substantive amendments opposed by the leadership, while permitting consideration of those supported by the majority party's leadership. Once again, we see the trend towards a two-tiered system of rights in the Senate.

There are a number of other proposed rules changes pending before the Senate. All of them, to one extent or another, share the same defects as S. Res. 41.

Efficiency at What Cost?

All legislative bodies are messy, and there is no denying that the Senate of the United States is messier than most. Over the years, its rules have carefully evolved to provide the most complete protections to minority views of any parliamentary body in the world. It is true that the use of these rules has often thwarted the will of the majority, producing situations so complicated that the whole legislative situation has imploded, grinding to a halt with much wailing and gnashing of teeth.

Both ends of the ideological spectrum, however, have used such rules to their advantage. Conservatives have often done it over civil rights issues; liberals did it over Vietnam; liberals again over the death penalty. And, at the end of each session, one of the most liberal members of the Senate, Howard Metzenbaum (D-OH), stands on the floor and uses the rules to keep what he views as special-interest legislation from sailing through in the rush to adjournment.

There is no doubt that much good legislation has been slowed up, often for years. But it is also undeniable that when it finally has passed, it has been much improved by its passage through the legislative screen of Senate procedure.

These beneficial effects are now very much in danger. The desire to appear "efficient" before the television cameras, the frustration over intractable budget deficits, the declining consensus over foreign policy—all these and other factors combine to produce an irresistible pressure to streamline, to concentrate power in the hands of leaders whose job it is to "move legislation." It is not at all clear that the nation's interests, and in particular its minority viewpoints, are well served by this "efficiency."

THE CONGRESSIONAL STAFF DYNAMIC

We have seen how the rules are being used in the House to restrict access to power, and how the Senate is moving in the same direction. But why have the Democrats been so much more successful in using the rules to their advantage? There is probably no single answer, but many have suggested that their success in building up a smart, experienced staff cadre is an important factor.

Why does one member develop a good, experienced staff, and another not? Based on their own observations, many "Hillwatchers" have pointed out that the relative longevity and power of each congressional staff member has depended on a variety of factors: the longevity of the member himself, the activism and seniority of the member, the tightness with which the member supervises the minutiae of his office's operation, the irascibility of the member, the quality of the staff, and the relative interest the staff places on personal wealth versus power.

Many Hill veterans have further supposed that the synergism of these factors has combined to create an institutionalized, experienced, savvy liberal staff oligarchy, which is pitted against a more business-oriented, shorter-term conservative staff. If this hypothesis is true, it would go a long way toward explaining the relative success of Democrats and liberal lawmakers in attaining their legislative objectives, even during periods when the White House and the Senate are both in the titular control of the Republican Party.

To test this hypothesis, we have tried to clarify the relationship between longevity and ideology on Capitol Hill. To do this, we first identified the policy-making staff in the United States Senate during the 100th Congress. We have defined "policy-making staff" to include all administrative assistants, all legislative assistants and legislative directors, and all committee professional staff members.

We then proceeded to determine which of the policy-making staff during the 100th Congress had been employed by the Senate at the beginning of the 97th Congress (1981) and which had been employed by the Senate during the 94th Congress (1975-1976).

The Senate was selected because it is a smaller and more manageable body, and because we felt that any findings applicable to the Senate would apply, *a fortiori*, to the House. Although the senior members of both houses are disproportionately Democrat, the disproportionality is greater in the House than in the Senate. It is true that eight of the ten most senior senators are Democrats, but thereafter the seniority of Democrats falls off rapidly. In the House, by contrast, not only are 70 percent of the 79 most senior members Democrats, but Democrats constitute a whopping 68.7 percent of roughly the most senior one-third (131 members) of the House.

Because the Senate has changed hands twice in the last thirteen years, and because at least half of Senate Democratic committee staff were theoretically purged by the Republicans in 1981, we have operated under the assumption that, if the senior staff in the Senate proves to be disproportionately Democrat and liberal, the same tendency will almost certainly apply with even greater force to the consistently Democratic House.

This exercise is something less than a science, as evidenced by the fact that we have not tried to account for name changes due to marriage, for temporary departures from the Senate by persons accepting jobs in private industry and in the bureaucracy, and for inadequacies in the internal Senate phone directory (there are some). It is also true that a few senators—presumably in an exercise in egalitarianism—refuse to label some or all of their policy-making staff.

In addition, although we make observations about administrative assistants, legislative directors, legislative assistants, professional committee staff members, and other policy-making staff, these terms mean different things in different committees and personal offices. In some offices, the titles of "legislative assistant" and "legislative aide" are given out rather freely; in others, rather sparingly. In some offices, there is a difference between the two, with "legislative aides" ranking barely above the clerical personnel. In other offices, there is no difference. The role of the administrative assistant also varies widely, with some wielding almost more power than their respective senators, and others serving as barely more than repositories of supplies and other nonlegislative services.

Any effort to particularize our observations to too great an extent will necessarily run up against the limitations of our study. Nevertheless, our efforts come closer than anything we have seen in attempting to quantify recent characteristics in the decision-making staff in the Senate and, within a very broad context, trying to make some tentative observations about their careers.

Length of Service Among Senate Policy Staff

In the 100th Congress, we identified 90 administrative assistants, 68 legislative directors, 504 legislative assistants, 281 committee staff members, 38 miscellaneous staff within the senators' personal offices and five other policy-making staff in the Senate. Of these, 45 of the administrative assistants were employed by Democrats, as were 36 of the legislative directors, 275 of the legislative assistants, 101 of the 140 committee professional staff members who could be identified by party (some committees maintain a fiction of "nonpartisan, professional staff"), and 21 of the other personal office policy-making staff. This means that 45 of the administrative assistants were employed by Republicans, together with 33 of the legislative directors, 229 of the legislative assistants, 39 of the identifiable professional staff members, and 17 of the other policy-making staff.

High Turnover

Our first finding was that turnover among Senate staff was occurring at an almost astronomical rate. Of those 986 policymaking staff whom we identified in the 100th Congress, only 209 (or 21.2 percent) were employed by the Senate in 1981. Only 86 members of the Senate policy-making staff (or 8.7 percent) were around at the beginning of the 94th Congress in 1975.

Thus, there was only an 8.7 percent longevity rate between 1975 and 1988—a period of thirteen years. This period of time is hardly more than one-quarter of a person's working career, and it is only 60 percent of the career span for even those jobs requiring relative youth and physical stamina, such as police, fire, and military personnel. This rate of turnover might be expected of an undesirable dead-end job involving tedious manual labor, but hardly of a job for which there are between several hundred and several thousand applicants at virtually all times.

Retaining Committee Staff

By far, the single largest career bureaucracy in the Senate is the Appropriations Committee. Of a total of 48 policy-makers identified on the Appropriations Committee in the 100th Congress, 18 of these (or 37.5 percent) had been employed by the Senate in 1981, and 9 (or 18.75 percent) were Senate employees at the beginning of the 94th Congress.

It is hardly a novel idea to suggest that the Senate Appropriations Committee has replaced most of the Senate standing committees as both the body that determines the size of each program and as the body which sets the policy for each program. Our findings suggest that this long-term career bureaucracy in the Appropriations Committee, which constitutes over one-quarter of the long-term Senate staff employed by standing committees of the Senate—and roughly one out of every nine long-term Senate staffers—may partially explain why the Senate Appropriations Committee has been so successful in appropriating power from the other committees.

Our second finding is that it is the issue specialists who tend to become entrenched in the Senate bureaucracy. In 1987-88, the 281 decision-making staff working for standing, select, and special committees constituted only 28.5 percent of all Senate policy-making staff. However, this committee staff constituted 75 out of 209 policy-making staff who have been employed by the Senate since 1981 (35.9 percent). Furthermore, committee staff represented 38 of 86 policy-making staff who have been with the Senate since 1975 (44.2 percent).

A Dearth of Experienced Conservatives

Our third observation has to do with the relative longevity of Senate staff located in the personal offices of the senators. We took those staffers with eight years' longevity and those with thirteen years and separated them on the basis of ideology and party. Of the 132 personal staff who had been with the Senate since 1981, 35 of these staffers worked for the most liberal third of the Senate, 35 worked for the most conservative third, and 62 worked for the moderates, as defined by the 1987 ranking of senators by the American Conservative Union. The underrepresentation of more experienced staff among Senate liberals is the result of the fact that 16 of those 34 liberals are first-term senators; only eight of the conservatives are in their first term.

The figures are even more pronounced when liberals, conservatives, and moderates are examined for staff who have been with the Senate since 1975. Only seven conservative staff fall into that category, compared to thirteen liberal staff and twenty-five moderates. In other words, Senate moderates employ three and a half times the number of long-term staff as Senate conservatives. Viewed another way, the average moderate Senate office has at least one policy-making staff member—normally the administrative assistant—who has been with the Senate for at least two Senate terms. Only about one in five conservative offices has such a person.

Conclusions on Staffing

The results of our brief study should certainly not be taken as the definitive examination on Senate staffing, ideology, and longevity. However, we were frankly surprised by the extent to which our original hypotheses were true:

• First, even at the level of legislative assistant, it appears that most service by Senate staffers is regarded as little more than a clerkship used to launch recent college graduates into more lucrative careers in the bureaucracy or the private sector.

• Second, despite the fact that a vast majority of Senate policy-making staff resides in the personal offices of the senators, a disproportionate share of the senior staff is employed by the committees—and particularly the Senate Appropriations Committee—which seems to have used its seniority and special relationship with the bureaucracy to supplant the roles of other committees.

• A moderate or liberal office of a senator who is not a freshman is three times as likely as a conservative office to have a staff member who has been with the Senate more than two full Senate terms.

A CONSTITUTIONAL PERSPECTIVE

The tendency of power to enhance itself by destroying centers of opposition has been the rule, rather than the exception, in human history. The Founding Fathers blessed the United States with a government in which competing centers of power have precluded any one branch or person from normally exercising a dictatorial level of authority.

Yet, contrary to the expectations of the Founding Fathers, the House of Representatives has become a self-perpetuating oligarchy in which the political choices of a majority of Americans have been offset by an elaborate system of electoral jury-rigging, and in which the interests of a few districts predominate in the decision-making process. The Senate is moving in the direction of the House, but more slowly.

Perhaps it is the increasing dissatisfaction of the American people with their government that has convinced some in the

Senate that, through a consolidation of power, the continuing ideological impasses which seem to beset the institution can be broken and effective government can be restored. If this is their notion, it is based on what is clearly becoming the central political fallacy of our generation: that in legislation lies salvation. In fact, salvation—or, at least, political salvation—lies in wresting power away from the few narrow autocrats who have done so much damage already, and placing it in a broader and, hopefully, wiser set of hands.

10. The Criminalization of Politics

GORDON CROVITZ

This chapter explores a new congressional technique for achieving power over the executive branch. This technique grew out of the "reforms" adopted in the wake of Watergate. Mr. Crovitz describes the "independent counsel" as a dangerous, irresponsible institution. He argues that this weapon has been used by Congress to criminalize its policy differences with the executive branch. The dangers in creating a powerful institution theoretically uncontrolled by either the executive or legislative branch are well described here. This chapter should be read in connection with Chapter 11, since the independent counsel is really just a particular kind of independent agency.

The criminalization of policy differences by a liberal-dominated Congress against a conservative Reagan Administration took the separation of powers battle into a new and politically dangerous dimension. In the eight years of the Reagan Administration, Congress developed and perfected the art of transforming political differences into potentially indictable offenses. What better way to intimidate executive branch officials than to threaten them with jail? Even as President Reagan made good on his pledge to strengthen the nation's economy and defenses, it is indeed ironic that he will leave the office itself even weaker than he found it.

This "prosecutorial"politics[1] could constrain the presidency in ways that would soon make the government increasingly ineffective. The risk is paralysis in the branch that the Founders intended would have the "energy" to ensure effective government. Excessive legal controls, extending to possible criminal indictment, will naturally tend to divert attention from substantive policy issues to the formalities of legal compliance. The results already include less of the discretion that is necessary to carry out executive branch functions, a long list of officials made victims of irresponsible criminal investigations, and a continued weakening of a branch of government in decline.

PROSECUTORIAL POLITICS: THE INDEPENDENT COUNSEL

The modern era of criminalizing of policy differences dates from the 1978 Ethics in Government Act. Passed as post-Watergate legislating of "good government," the law has actually led to a demeaning of politics by transforming what are often entirely innocent events and activities into "ethical" concerns, some of which also become legal matters. The law mandated new financial disclosures that were so complex and cumbersome that innocent mistakes became almost inevitable. These completed forms served as time bombs, primed to go off when an official's political opponents decide the timing is right.

Double Standards

The law is entirely hypocritical. Only executive branch officials are subject to the law's most threatening innovation, the institution of the independent counsel, originally given the more accurate title of special prosecutor. In cases ranging from the Iran-Contra affair to an infamous dispute over executive privilege during congressional testimony, these specially appointed lawyers have investigated and prosecuted Reagan Administration officials with a vengeance. Congress made the most of these prosecutors by frequently lobbying for their appointment and, perhaps even more importantly, drafting new laws so that future executive branch officers would inevitably run the risk of accusations that they "violate the law" simply in the natural course of doing their jobs.

These counsel are unique prosecutors in many ways. They do not investigate *ethics* in *government*, but only alleged breaches of law that may or may not have anything to do with common conceptions of ethics, and that were committed only by executive branch officials. The most notable characteristic of these prosecutors is that they are the only ones in the federal system who are not under the control and supervision of the Department of Justice. Also unlike other prosecutors, they are given the names of officials they must investigate, not merely events that might be crimes, committed by suspects unknown. They have unlimited resources; indeed, one independent counsel employed a staff of 50, spending at the rate of $5 million in taxpayer funds a year. There are thus no other cases against which to balance otherwise limited prosecutorial resources. This is a recipe for extremely aggressive prosecutions, and even the most widely respected private lawyers have been guilty of prosecutorial indiscretions once anointed as independent counsel.

Aggressive prosecutors were indeed the apparent goal of Congress, which chose to take a lesson from the Watergate affair that would justify expanding the legislative reach over executive functions. Citing the Archibald Cox incident, Congress wanted to avoid future firings of special prosecutors inside the executive branch by taking these special prosecutors out of the control of the presidency. The firing of Mr. Cox, of course, was in fact followed by the appointment of another special prosecutor inside the Department of Justice, who continued to gather evidence until the resignation of President Nixon.

Guilty Until Proven Innocent

Congress wrote the Ethics in Government Act to force the appointment of an independent counsel with a very low threshold of evidence of a crime. Under the law,[2] "whenever the attorney general receives information sufficient to constitute grounds to investigate," he has 90 days to consider whether a crime might have been committed. The law expressly gives a majority of either the minority or majority members on the Judiciary Committee of either House of Congress the power to request the appointment of an independent counsel. In this case, the attorney general then has 30 days to explain in writing the results of his investigation.

The only way for the attorney general to avoid naming an independent counsel is if "upon completion of the preliminary investigation, [he] finds that there are no reasonable grounds to believe that further investigation or prosecution is warranted." This is well below the standard for asking for an indictment, which is the standard of probable cause. In addition, unlike the usual procedure in alleged federal crimes, the attorney general is expressly prohibited from using the most important investigative tools. The law says that during this preliminary investigation to determine whether an independent counsel must be appointed, the attorney general "shall have no authority to convene grand juries, plea bargain, grant immunity, or issue subpoenas."

The courts also have a unique role in appointing and overseeing these prosecutors. Once the attorney general concludes under these circumstances of extremely cursory investigation that there may conceivably be reasonable grounds to think a crime may have occurred, he must notify a specially created division of federal judges. These judges then define the independent counsel's prosecutorial jurisdiction. These independent counsel are required to "comply with the written or other established policies of the Department of Justice," the law says, "except where not possible." Breach of this vague prohibition could in theory lead to a removal of an independent counsel by the attorney general "for good cause," but this has never happened. Even such a removal could be overruled by the special court.

As a practical matter, independent counsel understand that their true supervisors are not the executive branch or even the special division of the court, but members of Congress. During his investigation, the independent counsel sends to Congress reports on his investigation. These reports "shall set forth fully and completely a description of the work of the independent counsel, including the disposition of all cases brought, and the reasons for not prosecuting any matter." Clearly, the incentive is to prosecute. This is the unsubtle message of the clause in the law that says "the appropriate committees of the Congress shall have oversight jurisdiction with respect to the official conduct of any independent counsel...and such independent counsel shall have the duty to cooperate with the exercise of such oversight jurisdiction." The clear message is that an independent counsel works for Congress, and had better be prepared for "oversight" if he chooses not to prosecute an executive branch official.

The Constitutional Issue

Every president and attorney general has opposed independent counsel on constitutional and practical grounds. One reason is the clear sole authority under the Constitution of the executive branch to execute the laws, including prosecuting offenders. The problem is illustrated by incidents in which these "independent" counsel have created serious threats to the civil rights of their targeted executive branch officials. This was the theme of the *amicus* brief former Attorneys General Edward H. Levi, Griffin B. Bell, and William French Smith filed in the Supreme Court in the *Morrison v. Olson* case on the constitutionality of independent counsel. Their argument was simple, yet compelling. They noted that criminal prosecutors have great power over their targets, and their decisions can affect other government interests, such as foreign policy considerations. The principal checks on prosecutors are supposed to come from the executive branch, but independent counsel are intentionally freed of such constraints. The former attorneys general concluded by showing the link between their constitutional and pragmatic concerns about independent counsel:

> These internal checks and balances are the direct result of the Framers' decision to establish a unitary executive branch. They function precisely as the Framers intended the system of checks and balances to function: they prevent a prosecutor from being overtaken by an excess of zeal or ambition, or by the loss of perspective caused by too narrow a focus on one case.[3]

This argument against an overly aggressive prosecutor should appeal to civil libertarians. It is hard to imagine any one governmental power over individual rights greater than the power to prosecute.

Indeed, concerns about overly aggressive prosecutors prompted by political considerations predated the establishment of independent counsel. Back in 1940, Supreme Court Justice Robert H. Jackson, then attorney general, warned the federal prosecutors under his supervision that, "The prosecutor has more control over life, liberty, and reputation than any other person in America. His discretion is tremendous."⁴ The modern independent counsel is the creation of the single-minded, single-tasked prosecutor, which Justice Jackson considered the greatest domestic threat to civil rights.

Prosecuting People, Not Crimes

The former attorneys general appended a copy of Justice Jackson's speech in their brief to the Supreme Court. It is worth excerpting to show how the concerns that always exist for normal federal prosecutors must be greatly exacerbated in the case of independent counsel. Justice Jackson warned:

> Law enforcement is not automatic. It isn't blind. One of the greatest difficulties of the position of prosecutor is that he must pick his cases, because no prosecutor can even investigate all of the cases in which he receives complaints. If the Department of Justice were to make even a pretense of reaching every probable violation of federal law, ten times its present staff will be inadequate. We know that no local police force can strictly enforce the traffic laws, or it would arrest half the driving population on any given morning. What every prosecutor is practically required to do is to select the cases for prosecution and to select those in which the offense is the most flagrant, the public harm the greatest, and the proof the most certain.
>
> If the prosecutor is obliged to choose his case, it follows that he can choose his defendants. Therein is the most dangerous power of the prosecutor: that he will pick people that he thinks he should get, rather than cases that need to be prosecuted. With the law books filled with a great assortment of crimes, a

prosecutor stands a fair chance of finding at least a technical violation of some act on the part of almost anyone. In such a case, it is not a question of discovering the commission of a crime and then looking for the man who has committed it, it is a question of picking the man and then searching the law books, or putting investigators to work, to pin some offense on him. It is in this realm—in which the prosecutor picks some person whom he dislikes or desires to embarrass, or selects some group of unpopular persons and then looks for an offense—that the greatest danger of abuse of prosecuting power lies. It is here that law enforcement becomes personal, and the real crime becomes that of being unpopular with the predominant or governing group, being attached to the wrong political views, or being personally obnoxious to or in the way of the prosecutor himself.[5]

The problem becomes entirely political in the case of independent counsel because congressmen often choose the targets of investigation. Justice Jackson's fear as applied to independent counsel might be as follows: It is here that law enforcement becomes political, and the real crime becomes that of being unpopular with the predominant group in Congress, being attached to wrong political views, or being personally obnoxious to or in the way of the legislative branch itself.

Although the Supreme Court upheld the constitutionality of independent counsel in *Morrison* v. *Olson*, this did not end the controversy about whether such institutionalized independent prosecutors are good policy. Judge Laurence Silberman interpreted independent counsel as political creations serving Congress's political purposes. In his opinion for the Court of Appeals for the District of Columbia Circuit, which invalidated the independent counsel law as a violation of separation of powers and a threat to civil rights, Judge Silberman found a vivid metaphor for the use by Congress of its institution of independent counsel. "If the president's authority is diminished," Judge Silberman wrote, "Congress's political power must necessarily increase vis-a-vis the president. In practical terms, repeated calls for the appointment of a statutory independent counsel may, like a flicking left jab, confound the executive branch in dealing with Congress."[6]

INDEPENDENT COUNSEL INVESTIGATIONS

The history of independent counsel shows that they rarely disappoint their congressional taskmasters. The ten independent counsel investigations under the Ethics in Government Act to date have all seriously embarrassed their targets, and several have led to indictments, plea bargains, and convictions. Below is a short review of the status of each investigation and a detailed analysis of the two most widely followed investigations: the investigation of former Justice Department official Theodore Olson arising from his 1983 congressional testimony, which led to the case that reached the Supreme Court, and the Iran-Contra investigation and prosecution.

Drugs in the Carter Administration

In 1979, Arthur H. Cristy was appointed as the first independent counsel under the Ethics in Government Act. His job was to investigate Hamilton Jordan, President Carter's chief of staff, on drug charges. The appointment was to investigate allegations that Mr. Jordan had used cocaine at the New York night club Studio 54, and "any other related or relevant allegation." In May, 1980, a grand jury found insufficient evidence to prosecute Jordan, who in the meanwhile had run up a legal bill of some $67,000. This was certainly the first time the entire resources of the federal law-enforcement community were devoted to investigate one person's alleged drug use. The second such massive investigation of drug use was by an independent counsel focused on Timothy Kraft, who in 1980 had been President Carter's reelection campaign manager. Independent Counsel Gerald Gallinghouse announced in March, 1981, that there were no grounds to proceed.

Ray Donovan

The first independent counsel investigation of the Reagan Administration led to a series of events that included the leave of absence by a cabinet official, his being cleared by the independent counsel, then indicted by a state prosecutor citing the press speculation surrounding the two-year investigation by the independent counsel, his resignation from the cabinet and, finally—seven years after his nomination as Secretary of Labor—the finding that Raymond Donovan was not guilty on all charges. Mr. Donovan then asked to which office he should go to get back his reputation. His is a cautionary tale for anyone considering an executive-branch appointment in this new era.

Almost immediately upon President Reagan's asking him to serve as his Secretary of Labor following the 1980 election, Donovan became the subject of much press speculation raising questions about his ethics. The allegations concerned his role at Schiavone Construction Company, a New Jersey firm that he and his partners built into one of the largest heavy construction firms in the Northeast. There were rumors of ties to organized crime and questions about contracts with a firm that had, allegedly, fraudulently obtained minority set-aside government contracts.

Many congressmen continued to raise questions about Donovan after the Senate confirmed him in 1981. Meanwhile, as Labor Secretary, Mr. Donovan was not making himself popular with many Democrats or organized labor. He cut the department's budget by one-third, and in the process reformed programs beloved by many liberals, such as the inefficient CETA job program. The constant barrage of rumors about Schiavone clearly interfered with his proper administration of the department and his relations with Congress.

By 1981, Attorney General William French Smith had no choice but to appoint an independent counsel. Leon Silverman was instructed to investigate all the charges. He convened a grand jury and spent nine months looking into some 50 allegations of wrongdoing. Silverman issued a more than 1,000-page report to Congress dismissing all the charges. He wrote that "no prosecution of the Secretary on any of the allegations investigated is warranted or could successfully be maintained." Donovan was cleared in the eyes of the law, but nevertheless his reputation was clearly tarnished.

Then came what could have served as the inspiration for Tom Wolfe's best-seller about abusive prosecution, *The Bonfire of the Vanities.* In October, 1984, Bronx District Attorney Mario

Merola had Donovan indicted in New York state court on 137 counts arising from one of Schiavone's minority set-aside contracts. One month before the 1984 presidential election, Donovan thus became the first sitting cabinet member ever indicted. He went on unpaid leave. Merola, a Democrat, told the press that Mr. Donovan had committed "a fraud upon minorities." This led to calls from congressmen for another federal investigation, and Mr. Silverman was called back into service. By 1987, he could again report that all charges, including kickback charges, were meritless.

With the prospect of a long trial, Donovan in March, 1985, resigned from government. The Bronx trial lasted nine months. The defense attorneys were so confident there was no case against the defendants that they adopted the unusual strategy of refusing to call any witnesses. On the first ballot, the jury found all defendants not guilty on all counts. Indeed, the jurors stood up and applauded the defendants after announcing the verdict.

Mr. Donovan and his partners were left with a legal bill of $13 million and nagging questions. Would any of this have happened if Donovan had not been President Reagan's Labor Secretary? Would Merola have had the courage to bring such a weak case if it weren't for the earlier allegations and Silverman's lengthy investigation, despite the independent counsel's conclusion that there was no case? Finally, the day he was acquitted, Donovan asked the question that must be on the lips of all the ultimately cleared targets of independent counsel. "Which office do I go to," he asked, "to get my reputation back?"

Ed Meese

The next independent counsel investigation centered on Edwin Meese III, who was to become the most frequently investigated executive branch official in history. By the time President Reagan nominated Mr. Meese to become his second attorney general, he was already a well-known figure in Washington. He had served Governor Reagan in California, was chief of staff for the 1980 Reagan campaign and served as counselor to President Reagan. He was widely considered to be President Reagan's closest confidant and as attorney general promised he would change the composition of the federal judiciary.

Before he was confirmed, however, his political enemies in Congress unleashed the big gun of criminal accusations and issued a demand for an independent counsel to investigate. The Senate Judiciary Committee began confirmation hearings for Meese in March, 1984. Democrat Senators Howard M. Metzenbaum (OH) and Joseph R. Biden Jr. (DE) led the questioning about Meese's activities, including accusations that he helped arrange federal jobs for people who had helped him financially, that he used official influence to get a promotion in the Army Reserve, and that he had failed to report a $15,000 interest-free loan to his wife, Ursula.

Jacob A. Stein was appointed independent counsel in March, 1984, and spent five months investigating these and other charges, including ones as trivial as his "retention of cufflinks given to him by the Government of South Korea." He and his staff interviewed more than 200 witnesses, 45 of whom, including Mr. and Mrs. Meese, testified before a grand jury. In September 1984, Stein issued a 385-page report clearing Meese on all charges. Meese did err in completing the required financial reporting documents, but these errors were minor and Stein concluded that they were inadvertent. Certainly, there was no evidence that he intended to mislead or withhold information.

Mr. Meese's political opponents were not defeated by this report clearing their nemesis. Several Democrat senators had demanded that Meese's lawyers ask Stein to comment on the ethics of Meese if he found there were no violations of federal law. Stein refused to take this bait, citing his limited brief. In response to this demand, Stein included this section in his official report:

> The statute authorizing the appointment of independent counsel confines the inquiry to the question of whether a Federal law has been violated by the respondent. The court's order directs independent counsel to investigate violations of Federal criminal law. Nowhere in the statute or the order is there a directive to investigate and report on the propriety or the ethics of the respondent's conduct. Neither the statute nor the order af-

fords a basis for me to submit an evaluation of fitness for public office or to express opinions of the type requested by Mr. Meese's counsel.

The result was that the Stein investigation and report hardly disarmed Meese's opponents. Senator Metzenbaum, for example, said, "If the report does anything it strengthens my view that Mr. Meese should ask the president to withdraw his name." He added, "The Judiciary Committee will once again have to conduct lengthy and detailed hearings."[7] Meese was eventually confirmed by the Republican-controlled Senate, but not before his wife and daughter were reduced to tears as they watched his savaging by liberal senators.

This was not the last time Mr. Meese was investigated by an independent counsel. His actions also were later scrutinized by Lawrence Walsh in his investigation of the Iran-Contra affair. One side-issue in that investigation arose from the fact that Meese, with a small team of Department of Justice officials, were the ones who uncovered the fact that some of the profits from the arms sale to Iran were diverted to aid the democratic resistance in Nicaragua. There were allegations by members of the joint congressional committee on Iran-Contra that Meese allowed targets including Lt. Col. Oliver North to destroy relevant material. Walsh found no evidence of any such coverup efforts by Meese. Mr. Meese also became a subject of investigation by independent counsel James McKay, who was instructed to investigate the lobbying activities of Lyn C. Nofziger, a former White House official. Yet again, no grounds to prosecute Meese were found.

White House Aides

Former White House aides Michael Deaver and Lyn Nofziger were investigated by independent counsel for alleged violations of the Ethics in Government Act's prohibition against executive branch officials lobbying immediately after they leave office. Mr. Deaver was convicted not of illegal lobbying, but of perjury. In the process, independent counsel Whitney North Seymour showed the dangers of allowing prosecutors to operate outside the Department of Justice. Seymour involved the country in a skirmish with a foreign government when he twice tried to subpoena Allan Gotlieb, the Canadian ambassador to the United States, to testify about discussions with Deaver on the subject of acid rain. After the Department of State intervened on Ambassador Gotlieb's behalf, the court ruled that these subpoenas were a clear violation of diplomatic immunity. Mr. Nofziger was convicted by independent counsel McKay of illegal lobbying on behalf of Wedtech Co., a defense contractor in the Bronx, New York, that had minority set-aside contracts. In addition to these better-known cases, Department of Justice aide W. Lawrence Wallace was investigated for alleged tax irregularities by Carl Rauh and James Harper, who found no evidence of wrongdoing.

THE PERSECUTION OF THEODORE OLSON

Perhaps the best example of how Congress has criminalized its policy differences with the executive branch is the extraordinary persecution of Theodore Olson, a former Department of Justice official. The relatively low profile of this case highlights the personal risks that all executive branch officials now face when they dare to do their jobs, perhaps especially when this requires defending the presidency against legislative usurpations.

Mr. Olson's crime was trying to protect the executive privileges of President Reagan against an overreaching Congress. His reward has been several years under the threat of indictment first by Congress and later by independent counsel Alexia Morrison. His case has special resonance. As Assistant Attorney General for the Office of Legal Counsel, Olson was the chief adviser on issues of separation of powers for the presidency. Previous occupants of the position include Chief Justice William Rehnquist and Associate Justice Antonin Scalia. And his case, *Morrison* v. *Olson*, was the challenge to the constitutionality of independent counsel in the Supreme Court.

The Olson controversy began when two subcommittees in the House of Representatives issued broadly worded subpoenas in 1982 for volumes of documents from the Environmental Protection Agency and the Land and Natural Resources Division of the Department of Justice. These documents concerned Superfund, the big-budget hazardous-waste removal program. Most of the documents were produced, but President Reagan sent a memorandum to the Administrator of the EPA, Anne Burford, instructing that many of the subpoenaed files were covered by executive privilege. These were the documents "generated by attorneys and other enforcement personnel within the EPA in the development of potential civil or criminal enforcement actions against private parties," which are traditionally kept confidential between investigators and possible violators. The Reagan memorandum concluded that "dissemination of such documents would impair my solemn responsibility to enforce the law."[8]

This assertion of executive rights sparked fireworks in the House of Representatives. There was already a history of budget battles, with the Reagan Administration urging limits to increased budgets for the EPA in general and the Superfund program in particular, which had made Ms. Burford a frequent target of Democrat complaints. The documents themselves came to seem less important than the battle over them. In mid-December 1982, the House passed a resolution finding Burford in contempt for invoking executive privilege and refusing to turn over the documents. The executive branch tried to sue the House over the matter, but the case was dismissed as non-justiciable.[9] A deal was struck that gave Congress restricted, nonpublic access to the controversial documents. The House purged its contempt resolution. The embattled Ms. Burford resigned on March 9, 1983.

This set the scene for Mr. Olson's testimony to Congress on March 10, 1983, the day after the Burford resignation. Olson was called to testify in a previously scheduled hearing on the Department of Justice authorization—a budget hearing. Olson testified without being sworn, voluntarily, not in response to any subpoena, and without any forewarning that the authorization hearing would largely become a hearing on the Superfund matter. The tone of the hearing was extremely hostile, with most of the accusations concerning Olson's role in defending the executive privilege claim.

During the hearing, Olson was asked about the extent of the release of the subpoenaed documents. He said that his office had delivered all such "finalized" documents that "were relevant to the questions that you have asked and to the formal advice that we have given." He emphasized that not all the documents had been made public, which reflected the compromise struck between the two branches of government. Several congressmen urged that more documents be turned over. His testimony, despite its contentiousness, was not considered important enough even to be printed by the subcommittee.

The next time Mr. Olson heard about the Superfund matter from Congress was December 11, 1985, when the House Judiciary Committee released a highly critical 3,000-page report on the Department of Justice's role in the executive privilege claim. This was the result of a more than two-year investigation by committee staff members who held informal interviews and reviewed the documentary records. The report criticized several Justice officials, including Olson, Deputy Attorney General Edward Schmults, and Assistant Attorney General for Land and Natural Resources Carol Dinkins. It rejected the advice they gave to President Reagan on the executive privilege claim and accused them of failing to cooperate with the committee staff.

This report would have been dismissed as simply another case of the legislative branch taking umbrage at executive branch officials who dare to question the appropriateness of congressional subpoenas except for the charge that the Justice officials had committed crimes in the process. The report charged that Olson's March 10, 1983, testimony at the authorization hearing was false and misleading, that Schmults had wrongfully withheld Department of Justice handwritten notes from the Judiciary Committee, and that Dinkins had wrongfully withheld a chronology.

The report itself was controversial from the start, with 13 dissenting congressmen dismissing it as sensationalized. Indeed, the dissenters noted that there was no committee or subcommittee meeting to discuss the objective of the investigation and no vote to authorize what looked from the start like a political hatchet job. The Republican dissenters said that the report was "solely the work of three majority staff counsels."[10] No case could be clearer than this: Democrat staffers crafted a report to criminalize the political differences between the liberal majority on the House committee and representatives of a conservative administration.

The next step came the following day, December 12, 1985, when the chairman of the House Judiciary Committee sent a copy of the report to Attorney General Meese with a demand under the Ethics in Government Act that he appoint an independent counsel to investigate the three Department of Justice officials. In other words, based on a dubious staff report, congressmen criminalized the matter by making the request, under the ethics law, for appointment of a prosecutor. Even without being able to conduct any investigation because of the prohibitions against subpoenas or a grand jury, Attorney General Meese was able to dismiss as frivolous the accusations against Schmults and Dinkins. But because Olson did testify and there was a question, no matter how far-fetched, about that testimony, Attorney General Meese felt obliged to ask the special court panel to appoint an independent counsel to investigate Olson for his 1983 testimony.

James McKay was appointed to investigate in April 1986, but he was replaced by his deputy in May 1986, when he developed a conflict. Alexia Morrison then investigated Mr. Olson for about six months. In November, 1986, she requested that Meese expand her range of investigation to include Schmults and Dinkins to see if they had unlawfully withheld documents from Congress. Meese refused on the ground that it was clear that they had not.

What was most interesting about Morrison's application for an expanded investigation is that it included an acknowledgement that Olson had done nothing wrong. In her request, she stated that "standing in isolation...Mr. Olson's testimony of March 10, 1983 probably does not constitute a prosecutable violation of any federal criminal law." Despite this affirmation of Olson's innocence, she continued her investigation; in the process spending about $1 million of taxpayer funds. She also has caused Olson to run up legal bills for his defense of about $1 million.

In this context, an incident that amounts to the blackmailing of Mr. Olson is especially illustrative of the abuses these prosecutors, ultimately accountable only to Congress, can perpetrate against their executive branch targets. The statute of limitations for the crime of giving false and misleading testimony to Congress is five years, and thus would have expired on March 10, 1988. By this date, Morrison's case was on appeal to the Supreme Court after the Federal Court of Appeals had invalidated independent counsel as unconstitutional. Ms. Morrison was worried that her own status would not be resolved until after the Supreme Court ruled, so she set out to intimidate Olson into waiving his right to claim that the statute of limitations had run out.

First, she threatened in court papers that she would seek what she termed a "sealed protective indictment" against Olson if he didn't waive the statute of limitations. By this concept she presumably meant that she would ask a grand jury to indict Olson despite her having insufficient evidence under the federal guidelines for prosecutors to seek an indictment. The protection would be for her own case, to give her time to resolve the constitutional problems with the office of independent counsel, and then to develop a case against Olson several years after acknowledging that there was no case against him.

Mr. Olson had a hard decision to make. He has claimed all along that he broke no law, and the statute of limitations was passed to prohibit just such stalling by prosecutors. But even to be indicted "protectively," even by a prosecutor of dubious constitutionality, would be a serious embarassment. Olson, the managing partner of the Washington office of the Los Angeles law firm Gibson, Dunn & Crutcher, might have a hard time continuing his legal practice. There was also the financial calculation. One of the peculiarities of the Ethics in Government Act is that a target can get his legal expenses reimbursed by the government only if he is never indicted. Once indicted, even if never convicted, a target must pay his own legal fees. Therefore, Mr. Olson would have no prospect of getting reimbursed if he were indicted.

On March 10, 1988, Olson signed a secret agreement with Morrison, agreeing to waive the statute of limitations claim until 60 days after the Supreme Court ruled on the constitutionality of independent counsel[11] in exchange for her agreement not to seek an indictment in the meantime. This coercion was especially outrageous because the courts have hesitated to uphold such waivers of statute of limitations even when it is the target of a criminal investigation who seeks more time in order to try to persuade a prosecutor not to file charges.

In one leading case, the federal appeals court in Washington, D.C. upheld such a waiver but only because it originated with the target. Oil executive Claude Wild was accused of violating a campaign-finance law, but thought that he could offer new evidence that would show he was innocent. He agreed to waive the statute of limitations to get more time to bring evidence to the prosecutor's attention. The court upheld the waiver, but wrote that "We consider it of prime importance to our decision here that Wild was the one who sought to waive this defense. . . . It was not the government attorneys who sought the extra time in which to make their case." The opposite is true in the case of Morrison, who needed the extra time to pursue Mr. Olson.

THE REAL IRAN-CONTRA SCANDAL

Certainly the most notorious case of prosecutorial politics is what has come to be known as the Iran-Contra affair. The arms sales to Iran and diversion of profits to the democratic resistance in Nicaragua led to the almost immediate appointment of an independent counsel, followed by a massive congressional investigation, and eventually to the indictment of now-retired Lt. Col. Oliver North, former National Security Adviser John Poindexter, Richard Secord, and Albert Hakim. The episode represented the low point of the Reagan Administration, and not just because of the disparity of President Reagan's rhetoric and practice in dealing with the terrorists holding American hostages and the sales to Iran. In the long run, perhaps the greater sin will have been the complete failure of the executive branch to protect its privileges or its officials against a Congress driven by blood-lust headed by an extraordinarily aggressive prosecutor.

North described the congressional enterprise with precision

in the opening statement to his testimony in July, 1987. "This is a strange process you are putting me and the others through. Apparently the president has not asserted his prerogatives and you have been permitted to make the rules," he began. "You call before you the officials of the executive branch. You put them under oath for what must be collectively thousands of hours of testimony. You dissect their testimony to find inconsistencies." North perfectly captured the one-two punch of congressional investigation plus independent counsel: "It is mind-boggling to me that one of those investigations is criminal and that you have attempted to criminalize policy differences between co-equal branches of government and the executive's conduct of foreign policy."

The Boland Amendment

Unraveling the Iran-Contra affair requires first understanding the roots of the problem. What led North in a June 1986, computer message to his boss, Adm. Poindexter, to complain pathetically that, "What we most need is to get the CIA re-engaged in this effort so that it can be better managed than it now is by one slightly confused lieutenant colonel"? In a fundamental sense, the entire episode can be traced back to 1982, when Congress first tried to condition U.S. foreign policy toward Nicaragua by limiting which executive branch officials could be involved in helping the Contras. From the early days of the Reagan Administration, its policy was to encourage the Democratic resistance against the Marxist-Leninist Sandinista government. This policy was resisted by several leading liberal congressmen who opposed any aid for the Contras. Congress as a body, however, straddled the fence. There was never a long- or even medium-term consensus for aid, yet at the same time Congress did not want to be blamed for losing Nicaragua to the Soviet bloc. The result was a compromise, embodied in what came to be known as the five Boland Amendments: the president would do whatever he could, using the powers of his office to keep the Contras alive and in the field without constant congressional appropriations, and Congress would not be accountable for any identifiable policy of its own.

The Iran-Contra affair can thus be dated from the dubious

compromise that was Boland One, which was attached as a rider to the fiscal 1982-83 Defense Appropriations Act. Then-Representative Tom Harkin (D-IA) failed to gather support for his unambiguous proposal, which would have prohibited any U.S. aid for "carrying out military activities in or against Nicaragua."[12] Similarly, Sen. Christopher Dodd (D-CT) wanted a provision that "no funds should be obligated or expended, directly or indirectly . . . in support of irregular military forces or paramilitary groups operating in Central America." Senator John Chafee (R-RI) rejected the Dodd proposal on the ground that any such blanket prohibition would be too extreme. "Is this body going to insert a complete prohibition of activities against this nation?" he asked. "Are we going to tie the hands of the president? After all, it is the president who is at the top of the heap in this . . . . I do not believe we have ever proposed a draconian restriction such as proposed by the Senator from Connecticut in the past with 'no activities, direct or indirect.'"

The compromise crafted by Representative Edward Boland (D-MA) instead was a vague prohibition against military aid "for the purpose of overthrowing the government of Nicaragua." Presumably anything short of an actual overthrow was allowed. The Reagan Administration pledged that some of the funds would be used to interdict the flow of arms from Nicaragua to Marxist guerrillas in El Salvador. Indeed, this compromise was such a meaningless prohibition that it passed the House of Representatives by a unanimous 411-0 vote.

Interpreting the Law

In a forewarning of misunderstandings to come, however, Rep. Lee Hamilton (D-IN), the future co-chairman of the Iran-Contra congressional committee, soon claimed that provisions such as the Harkin-Dodd proposals had become law. "Covert action against Nicaragua is against the law. The first law in question is the Boland Amendment, passed last year," he said in 1983. Rep. Michael Barnes (D-MD) declared that aid to the Contras "is illegal under domestic law as we all know." These interpretations came as a shock to Rep. Kenneth Robinson, then the ranking Republican on the Intelligence Committee, who criticized the liberals for revisionism. "I took some of those 411 votes with me," he said. "I argued some of my colleagues into going along at that time because I thought I understood it, and I still think I understand it, and I do not believe the Boland amendment has been violated." The second Boland Amendment arose from the desire in the House to ban all aid and the Senate preference for overt and covert aid, with the result that Congress authorized $24 million in military aid in the 1983-84 Defense Appropriations and Intelligence Authorization Acts.

Then came the infamous Boland Three in effect during 1984-85, which was arguably the most restrictive of the Bolands and became notorious during the congressional investigation into the Iran-Contra affair. This banned the Central Intelligence Agency, Department of Defense, or "any other agency or entity of the United States involved in intelligence activities" from using appropriated funds to aid the Nicaraguan resistance. Once the activities of North became known, the question arose whether this applied to him as a staff member of the National Security Council. The best answer is that it did not, and indeed that the reason the Marine working out of the Old Executive Office Building became a one-man Contra-aid workaholic is that the agencies that were better prepared to help the Contras were precisely the ones Congress intended to prohibit from the job.

Evidence for this interpretation that the Boland Amendments did not apply to the NSC comes from the fact that Boland Three was not a catchall prohibition of the kind that are often worded with language beginning, "Notwithstanding any other provision of law, no funds may be appropriated under this or any other act for the purpose of" [aiding the Contras]. Instead, the prohibition was a rider attached to the Defense Appropriations and Intelligence Authorization Acts, acts which by their terms only covered ten specified intelligence agencies. The National Security Council was not among these. Instead, the provision was part of a funding package that applied to the CIA, Pentagon, Defense Intelligence Agency, National Security Agency, Army, Navy and Air Force, State Department, Treasury Department, Energy Department, Federal Bureau of Investigations, and the Drug Enforcement Administration. The NSC was similarly excluded from the list of intelligence agencies covered by a 1981 Executive Order.

Rewriting the Constitution

Even if a Harkin-Dodd type of complete bar to aiding the Contras had ever been passed, whatever the statutory construction, any provision that purported to restrict the foreign-policy authority of the NSC would run up against severe constitutional problems. As the staff of the president, with his broad Commander-in-Chief powers, the NSC cannot be banned from activities that are part of the enumerated or unenumerated prerogatives of the president. Congress cannot create a new separation of powers different from the one the Founders created merely by passing a statute, and certainly not by vaguely worded provisions like the Boland Amendments that become part of veto-proof continuing resolutions.

The Constitution, Supreme Court precedents, and two centuries of practice make clear that the president, and through him his staff, has wide and indeed plenary powers in the foreign affairs field.[13] Chief Justice John Marshall, then a member of Congress, told his colleagues in the House in 1800 that the Constitution makes the president the "sole organ of the nation in its external relations, and its sole representative with foreign nations." This language was approved in the 1936 Supreme Court case, *U.S.* v. *Curtiss-Wright Export Co.* The 1946 Supreme Court case of *U.S.* v. *Lovett* underscored in particular the limits of the exceedingly blunt congressional power of the purse to condition executive branch power. Congress tried to insert a condition into an omnibus appropriations act that would deny payment of the salaries of three executive branch officials suspected of subversive activities. The Supreme Court held that this usurped the president's power to hire and fire his own staff. The lesson of *Lovett* is that Congress cannot effectively usurp core executive branch functions via its power of the purse. Otherwise, Congress could prohibit expenditures for a pen for the presidents to sign a veto that invalidates legislation.

Framing the Issue

With this political and legal background, the news conference Attorney General Meese held on November 25, 1986, to announce his discovery the previous weekend of the diversion to the Contras was a disaster for the executive branch. In his understandable concern to avoid charges of a cover-up, Meese fell into the trap laid by congressmen who hoped to make executive branch aid for the Contras illegal. He announced that Lt. Col. North had been fired and Admiral Poindexter reassigned. One of the first questions the press asked was posed by ABC's Sam Donaldson. "Did what Col. North do, is that a crime? Will he be prosecuted?" Meese responded that, "We are presently looking into the legal aspects of it." The appointment of independent counsel Walsh and the televised congressional hearings were soon to follow.

It's worth considering in retrospect how different the last two Reagan years might have been if instead Meese had explained the diversion as overexuberance by patriotic Reagan officials trying to pursue the policy of keeping the Contras alive despite congressional fudging on the issue. What if Meese had responded in language that North himself used in the congressional hearing when the role of prosecutorial politics became clear. Imagine if Meese had said,

> It is mind-boggling to me that Congress has attempted to criminalize policy differences between co-equal branches of government and the executive's conduct of foreign affairs. I suggest to you that it is the Congress which must accept the blame in the Nicaraguan freedom fighter matter. Plain and simple, Congress is to blame because of the fickle, vacillating, unpredictable, on-again, off-again policy toward the Nicaraguan democratic resistance.

Instead, one slightly confused lieutenant colonel was left to try to perform the tasks that Congress had prohibited the CIA and other capable agencies from performing.

This criminalizing of policy differences eventually led to the indictments. The Boland Amendments were not criminal statutes, and they envisioned no criminal punishments. Yet Walsh argued that aiding the Contras was against government policy, and that a conspiracy to aid the Contras therefore amounted to a crime.

PROTECTING EXECUTIVE POWERS

The system of checks and balances obligates each branch of government to use its constitutional authority to properly limit the powers the other branches exercise. This control on government officials is the leading protection for limited government and, ultimately, for our political freedom. Thus, the prime responsibility of each branch must be to protect its own powers and privileges so that it is not powerless to stop the abuses of the other branches. The greatest failure of the Reagan Administration may be this failure to guard the powers of the executive branch. Ironically, although President Reagan won two landslide elections promising to reinvigorate the office, he will have left the office of the presidency even weaker than he found it. A very large part of this weakening of the executive office stems from the Reagan Administration's failure to protect innocent officials who became caught up in the web of independent counsel investigation.

In addition to the cases discussed above, many other officials escaped the potential criminalizing of their activities only by ultimately agreeing to be sacrificial lambs. Richard Allen left his job as national security adviser after $1,000, apparently meant for first lady Nancy Reagan from Japanese journalists was found in his safe. Allen explained that he had simply intercepted the funds, and had done nothing wrong.

Leslie Lenkowsky withdrew his name from nomination to deputy director of the U.S. Information Agency when there were allegations of a "blacklist" of liberals whom USIA would not send abroad to speak for the government. This list made much sense—why send John Kenneth Galbraith to speak for supply-side Reaganomics?—but in the mud-slinging environment of Washington, D.C., this was enough to blacken Lenkowsky's reputation. Faith Ryan Whittlesey, a fervent conservative, had to take time from her post as ambassador to Switzerland to defend herself from similarly baseless attacks. Yet the accusation that she had wrongly used private funds for the purpose of entertaining official guests made headlines for several weeks.

James Beggs was forced to step down as administrator of NASA when he was investigated and eventually tried for alleged fraud related to his previous job at General Dynamics. Only after Beggs was forced to run up a ruinous $25 million legal bill were the charges dropped as groundless. It transpired that the accusations were based on a misreading of the contract by a special procurement fraud division of the Justice Department that had been created in answer to ubiquitous congressional accusations of $400 hammers and $600 toilet seats. This prosecutorial abuse in the name of responding to Congress may have had a tragic cost to the nation as well as to the Beggs family. Beggs was forced to resign shortly before the Challenger shuttle disaster. He had been watching the preparations for the lift-off on television and when he saw there was ice on the pad told his wife that the launch should have been scrubbed. "I would have scrubbed," he said afterward. "It's as simple as that."

Presidential Leadership

There will almost certainly be more victims of prosecutorial politics in later administrations. President Reagan contributed to this risk when he failed to veto the renewal of the Ethics in Government Act, despite the recommendations of the Department of Justice. He signed the bill adding that he thought independent counsel were unconstitutional, yet expressing the hope that the courts would eventually invalidate them. This hope was proved vain when the Supreme Court upheld these prosecutors in *Morrison* v. *Olson*. The Reagan Administration saw other new legislation that could well guarantee a later scandal similar to the Iran-Contra affair. A proposed bill requiring congressional notification by the president of any covert activity within 48 hours is all but sure to be ignored when lives and national security are at stake. Senator Malcolm Wallop (R-WY) argued on the Senate floor that "clearly in the age of special prosecutors [the bill] may be grounds for prosecution."[14]

There were also many provisions in the massive budget continuing resolutions during the Reagan years putatively based on the congressional power of the purse that could easily lead to prosecutions. There was a provision in the 1988 budget bill, for example preventing the Federal Communications Commission from using any appropriated funds to grant waivers of the cross-ownership prohibition against owning both a newspaper and broadcast outlet in the same market. This provision was not discovered until after President Reagan signed the budget bill. It transpired that Senator Edward Kennedy (D-MA) had it inserted to punish Rupert Murdoch, who had temporary waivers for Boston and New York City. An appeals court eventually invalidated this as unconstitutionally aimed at one individual. But staff members of the FCC would have risked going to jail if they had tried to grant a waiver before the provision was invalidated. The Anti-Deficiency Act prohibits any unappropriated activities by government employees, and the Kennedy provision against Murdoch was a flat prohibition against using appropriated funds for the purpose of granting waivers.

Where We Are Headed

The abuses of prosecutorial politics led to some of the most vicious attacks against the Reagan Administration. By the end of the second term, the nature of this new, low level of politics became clear to many political observers. For some, the question was not simply Democrat versus Republican, liberal versus conservative. It was whether the best qualified individuals would risk serious dangers to their reputations simply by coming to Washington to serve in the government. It also became an issue of what the demeaned tenor of our political debate would do to the substance of that debate. Only an ultra-safe and risk-averse individual could be completely confident of avoiding prosecutorial politics. How many more Anne Burfords or Ray Donovans would come to Washington to implement policy changes once people saw how great the personal price had become?

One of the most eloquent criticisms of this phenomenon came from what may seem an unlikely source: one of the most liberal members of the Congress that passed the original Ethics in Government Act, Father Robert Drinan, who spoke at a bipartisan conference of lawyers and ethicists on ethics in government sponsored in March 1988, by the Administrative Conference of the United States. He said:

I'm going to suggest that maybe the day has come for a little bit of deregulation . . . . I would like to have something come out of this conference that suggests a cautious note that maybe we've gone too far in some things. Regardless of who is elected, I can foresee some government bureaucrats saying, 'We don't want any scandals in this new administration,' and they are going to put on the form, 'Have you ever smoked pot, yes or no?' Question two: 'Have you ever been unfaithful to your wife? If so, how many times?' Three: 'Do you have any homosexual tendencies?' I think we've come to a point where a group like this should say quietly that enough is enough.[15]

Despite these sentiments, however, Congress has considered a new Ethics in Government Act that would stiffen prohibitions further. Some proposals do have the benefit of ending some of the hypocrisy by also subjecting Congress to the possible appointment of independent counsel. Still, having even more public officials subject to prosecutors who are not bound by the usual federal guidelines of prosecutorial discretion does not seem the best solution.

Reviving the Constitution

There is a pressing political issue here that goes to the core of our democracy. The Constitution makes the president both politically accountable for the conduct of high-ranking administration officials and legally responsible for investigating and if necessary prosecuting these officials. The constitutional devices for ensuring that the president enforces the laws include a free press to report alleged violations of law and shortcomings in law enforcement, a Congress with investigative powers, and the ability of the voters to punish any offending president and his political party. It is not part of this scheme that Congress should presume to enforce the law on its own through politically unaccountable independent counsel.

The Constitution is not silent on the issues that led to the criminalizing of policy differences. The Founders put a great onus on the presidency to punish conflicts of interest or other alleged offenses by high-ranking executive branch officials. The responsibility to enforce the laws clearly lies with the president, and Congress and the voters have the power to hold him accountable to meet this responsibility. The system worked well prior to the Ethics in Government Act. At that time, presidents were forced to appoint their own special prosecutors. These prosecutors, firmly within the executive branch, successfully prosecuted officials for wrongdoing in the administrations of Presidents Jefferson, Grant, Hayes, Theodore Roosevelt, Harding, Coolidge, Truman, and Nixon.[16]

The Next President

There are two pledges the next president should take. First, he must promise to veto any "minefield" legislation. For example, in retrospect, the Boland Amendments were a crisis waiting to happen. Congressional micromanaging of foreign policy intentionally cut the most effective agencies out of the Contra aid program, leaving it to a small band of presidential national security staff members and their private agents.

Second, the next president should make the modest-sounding but in fact radical pledge to veto any legislation that he believes is unconstitutional. President Reagan opposed independent counsel on constitutional grounds, for example, yet he allowed the Ethics in Government Act to be reauthorized. The courts are much more likely to help protect the powers of a branch of government that is willing to help protect itself.

The next president, regardless of his political party, must carefully nurture the powers of the presidency. This must include protecting his sole authority to enforce the law, even if opposing any independent counsel apparatus creates short-term political costs to the president. Similarly, the next president must protect falsely accused executive branch officials, no matter how great the political pressure to sacrifice the innocent. The next president must take responsibility for the institution of the presidency. One excellent way to gather the political courage and resolution that will be required to defend the presidency from a usurping Congress is for a candidate to campaign on a platform that includes a pledge to fight the new prosecutorial politics.

Notes

1. For an excellent discussion of prosecutorial politics, see Garment, "The Guns of Watergate," *Commentary,* April 1987.

2. 28 United States Code Section 591.

3. Brief for the United States as Amicus Curiae supporting appellees in the Supreme Court, October term 1987, *Morrison* v. *Olson,* pp. 2-3.

4. *The Federal Prosecutor,* Address delivered at the Second Annual Conference of United States Attorneys, April 1, 1940, p. 1.

5. Ibid., pp. 4-5.

6. In Re Sealed Case, looseleaf, p. 66.

7. *New York Times,* September 21, 1984, p. 1.

8. Memorandum from President Ronald Reagan to Administrator, Environmental Protection Agency, Nov. 30, 1982.

9. *U.S.* v. *The House of Representatives,* 556 F. Supp. 150 (D.D.C. 1983).

10. Report of the Committee on the Judiciary of the House of Representatives, Investigation of the Role of the Department of Justice in the Withholding of Environmental Protection Agency Documents From Congress in 1982-83, H.R. Rep. No.99-435 (Dec. 11, 1985).

11. For more details, see Crovitz, "The Blackmailing of Ted Olson," *The Wall Street Journal,* March 23, 1988, editorial page.

12. Parts of this section are based on Crovitz, "Crime, the Constitution, and the Iran-Contra Affair," *Commentary,* October, 1987. See also a compilation of the congressional debates on the various Boland Amendments in Congressional Record, June 15, 1987, Vol. 133, No. 97.

13. See, Rotunda, Nowak & Young, "Treatise on Constitutional Law: Substance and Procedure," Section 6.9-10 (West Publishing 1988).

14. Congressional Record, March 15, 1988, p. S2234.

15. Working Conference on Ethics in Government, Administrative Conference of the United States, March 1, 1988, transcript, pp. 52-53.

16. Brief for the United States as Amicus Curiae Supporting Appellees in the Supreme Court, October Term 1987, *Morrison* v. *Olson,* p. 48.

11. The Headless Fourth Branch

NOLAN E. CLARK

Chapter 10 discussed a special kind of independent regulatory agency, the independent counsel. Here, Nolan Clark broadens the argument to the point of eliminating the rationale for all the independent agencies. As he demonstrates, the functions that they exercise properly belong to the executive branch. Their "independence" simply serves to remove their accountability to those most intimately affected: the voting public.

For more than a century, Congress has been in the business of creating independent regulatory agencies. The grandfather of them all was the Interstate Commerce Commission, established in 1887. It was followed by the Federal Trade Commission in 1915. Since then, the numbers have proliferated, providing us the acronyms with which we are vaguely familiar: FCC, FERC, CAB, NRC, ITC, OSHA, HLBB, FRB, FEC, CRC, FDIC, SEC, CFTC, etc. What are independent regulatory agencies? What do they do? How well have they performed? Why were they created? For whom are they agents? From whom are they independent? How do they fit into a constitutional scheme providing for three branches of a federal government? Do they belong to the judicial branch? To the legislative branch? To the executive branch? Or don't they fit under our Constitution at all?

WHAT IS AN INDEPENDENT REGULATORY AGENCY?

Independent agencies bear a variety of designations, but are usually called commissions or boards. All appear to share five features: 1) they are financed by taxpayers; 2) they regulate some aspect of the economy; 3) they are multiheaded; 4) their heads have a vast range of discretion; and 5) the heads cannot be removed at the pleasure of the president. As we shall discover, these common features are not accidental.

WHAT DO INDEPENDENT REGULATORY AGENCIES DO?

To detail the workings of all of the independent agencies would require a textbook. But a brief glimpse of a few independent agencies at least hints at the vast powers and incredible discretion vested in them.

• *The Federal Communications Commission* regulates interstate and foreign communications by radio, television, wire, and cable. The Federal Communications Commission Act, among other things, authorizes the FCC to "assign bands of frequency, prescribe the nature of service, . . . determine the location of . . . stations, and . . . regulate the kind of apparatus used as . . . public convenience, interest, or necessity requires."

• *The Commodity Futures Trading Commission* regulates trading on all U.S. futures exchanges. It approves the rules of all exchanges and must approve the terms of any futures contract offered.

• *The Consumer Product Safety Commission* regulates the safety of consumer products. Under the Consumer Product Safety Commission Act, it is empowered to set rules that "prescribe reasonable testing programs for consumer products." If the CPSC determines that a product "presents a substantial product hazard," it can order recall, replacement, or refund if it determines that such action "is in the public interest."

• *The Federal Reserve Board* regulates banks that are members of the Federal Reserve System. For example, it is authorized to require "such statements and reports [from member banks] as it may deem necessary." The Federal Deposit Insurance Corporation provides insurance coverage for bank deposits and regulates banks that are not members of the Federal Reserve System. The Federal Home Loan Bank Board regulates savings institutions. It is given broad discretion to "prescribe rules governing the payment and advertisement of interest or dividends on deposits, shares, or withdrawal accounts" and to set liquidity requirement in such amounts "as, in the opinion of the Board, is appropriate."

• *The Interstate Commerce Commission* regulates interstate surface transportation, including trains, trucks, buses, water carriers, freight forwarders, transportation brokers, and a coal slurry pipeline. Under the Interstate Commerce Commission Act, it certifies carriers and regulates rates to ensure that they are "fair and reasonable." Under similarly broad authority, the Federal Maritime Commission regulates waterborne foreign and domestic offshore commerce.

• *The Federal Trade Commission* enforces laws that prohibit "unfair or deceptive acts or practices" and "unfair methods of competition." The Federal Trade Commission Act gives the FTC power to enact rules defining unfair acts and practices. Under this authority, the FTC has even asserted the power to invalidate state statutes.

• *The National Labor Relations Board* regulates collective bargaining, election of labor representatives, and all unfair labor practices.

• *The Federal Energy Regulatory Commission* has broad authority to regulate natural gas production and transportation, and the transportation of electrical power. Under the Natural Gas Act, FERC controls rates and charges for the transportation or sale of natural gas subject to the requirement that the rates "shall be just and reasonable." FERC may order a natural gas company to extend or improve facilities, or sell gas to specified parties if it "finds such action necessary or desirable in the public interest" and "that no undue burden" will be placed on the company.

• *The Federal Election Commission* regulates the campaign financing industry. It oversees disclosure of information and enforces limitations of contributions and expenditures.

- *The Nuclear Regulatory Commission* regulates the use of nuclear energy for private consumption.
- *The Securities and Exchange Commission* regulates securities markets and the disclosure of information to investors.
- *The United States International Trade Commission* regulates the prices of imports, unfair methods of competition, and unfair acts committed in the importation of goods.

HOW WELL HAVE THEY FUNCTIONED?

It may seem unfair to pass judgment upon the performance of a multitude of agencies in a few paragraphs. It may also seem that any answer will inevitably be partisan. There is, however, a fair and nonpartisan judgment. Virtually every analyst, of every political leaning, has been dissatisfied with the performance of the independent regulatory agencies. Almost without exception, independent regulatory agencies have failed to develop coherent, principled bodies of substantive law. Deciding litigation case by case, common law courts have developed coherent bodies of tort, contract, and property law. But there is no coherent body of international trade law, transportation law, occupational safety law, or energy regulation law.

Almost without exception, independent regulatory agencies have failed to promote the public interest. Numerous analysts, for example, have concluded that the economic regulatory agencies have historically protected incumbent businesses, thwarted entry, and led to prices above those that unregulated competition would produce. The failure of agencies regulating specific industries has often been attributed to "capture" by the regulated industries. However, even those agencies that do not regulate a specific agency also have been severely criticized. For example, the Federal Trade Commission has been examined almost every 20 years, and each time has been found wanting. In 1968 an American Bar Association Commission studying the Federal Trade Commission concluded that its study should be the last; if the Commission did not improve its performance, it should be eliminated. Twenty years later, in 1988, the ABA Antitrust Section is making another study of the FTC.

Analysts of the regulatory process have regularly bemoaned

the quality of the personnel named to head independent regulatory agencies. Study after study has criticized the competence of commissioners. The ritual call repeatedly has gone forth for improved appointments. Occasionally the quality of appointments seems to improve, but history continues to repeat itself: within a few years, yet another report calls for improved appointments to the independent regulatory agencies.

Commissions that engage in case-by-case adjudication are also regularly faulted for their lack of fairness when they act as both prosecutor and judge. Although independent regulatory agencies both try and decide cases, they artificially adjust their procedures to provide a semblance of fairness. Commissioners authorize an investigation, review the staff's results, and decide whether they have reason to believe that a proposed respondent has violated the law. If so, they authorize the filing of a complaint. If the proposed respondent has the temerity to litigate rather than capitulate, the case is tried before a commission employee, an administrative law judge. During this trial, the commission erects a "Chinese wall." Members of the staff who try the case are prohibited from discussing the litigation in the presence of the commissioners. This elaborate and inefficient barrier is created to preserve the appearance of fairness and lack of prejudgment, even though the commission has already judged that there is reason to believe that there is a violation. After trial, the case comes on appeal to the commission, which then decides whether it was right when it issued the complaint. One of the best critiques of this process was provided by Philip Elman, a former Commissioner of the Federal Trade Commission:

> On the basis of my own experience and observations, the strongest argument I would make against agency adjudication of alleged violations of law is that the blending of prosecutorial and adjudicative powers in a single tribunal imposes intolerable strains on fairness. The problem of avoiding prejudgment, in appearance or in fact, constantly hovers over all agency activity, and is troublesome to agency members in almost every kind of action it takes. It can arise in the most subtle as well as obvious forms.
>
> Consider, for example, the so-called test case where the agen-

cy issues a complaint in order to establish a new legal principle or remedy—precisely the "rule in Shelley's Case" type of adjudication which agencies have been urged to undertake as an essential and proper method for developing new regulatory policies. Agency members frequently take an active part in the pre-complaint investigative and prosecutorial phases of these cases; and the complaint is usually issued with the knowledge that, because of the novelty and importance of the issue, it will be fully litigated and be back for adjudication on the record. When such a test case does come up on appeal to the agency members, while there is no bias or prejudgment of guilt in the classic sense, there is an inescapable predisposition in favor of the agency position, as set forth in the complaint. After all, the whole point of starting a test case is to let the case go forward into the reviewing courts, where the issues may be finally settled. To put it bluntly, once such a complaint is issued, one should ask for long odds before betting against issuance of a final order. While a test case may be and usually is vigorously contested, the result—at least in the agency phase—is likely to be a foregone conclusion.

Indeed, in such a case an agency member may vote for an order not because he is personally convinced that there is a violation of law, but because he feels, perhaps in an excess of humility, that since it is a test case involving a doubtful or unsettled question of law, his duty is to find against the respondent so that the case may go on to the court for definitive solution. This Catch-22 process may reach full fruition when conscientious judges on the reviewing court affirm the agency ruling, whatever their own doubts about its merits, because they feel obliged to defer to the agency's expert judgment and discretion.

WHY WERE INDEPENDENT REGULATORY AGENCIES ESTABLISHED?

Historians, political scientists, and economists still debate why independent regulatory agencies were established. The principal arguments tend to be oriented toward one of two polar views: the "public interest" explanation and the "public choice" explanation. The public interest explanation is, of course, that the agencies were created to serve the public interest. The public choice explanation is that elected officials made choices that served their own interests.

The Public Interest Explanation

According to the public interest explanation uncontrolled capitalism ran roughshod over many segments of the population: consumers, workers, investors, and television viewers. In light of the intricacies of a complex and dynamic economy, Congress was unable to prescribe specific and detailed rules governing private rights and responsibilities. Recognizing its own inability to regulate the details of a vast and growing economy, Congress created administrative agencies to act as its "arms." The agencies were not given specific rules to enforce. Rather, the authorizing statutes merely set forth basic principles that were to guide the commissioners as they evolved a set of rules and regulations.

The independent regulatory agencies were to be surrogates or extensions of Congress, exercising quasi-legislative power delegated by Congress. Expertise was needed for the wise development of a body of administrative law. That expertise was to have two sources. First, wise commissioners were to be selected for the important task of developing whole new bodies of law. As stated in the legislative history of the Federal Trade Commission Act: "The work of this commission will be of a most exacting and difficult character, demanding persons who have experience in the problems to be met—that is a proper knowledge of both the public requirements and the practical affairs of industry." Second, the agencies were to have continuity so the wise commissioners could continue to develop their expertise. Once again, in the words of the legislative history of the FTC Act: "It is manifestly desirable that the terms of the commissioners shall be long enough to give them an opportunity to acquire the expertness in dealing with these special questions concerning industry that comes from experience." With continuity and growing expertise, the commissioners would progressively acquire the information and the wisdom needed to develop an integrated body of administrative law to regulate an entire sector of the economy.

Since quasi-legislative powers were extended to the independent regulatory agencies, it was necessary to structure the agencies as mini-legislatures. Their multimember structure allowed for deliberative and collegial interchange, distilling the wisdom of a group of experts. Members of these mini-legislatures were not to be elected by the public, but this was a virtue not a vice. The experts in the independent regulatory agencies were to be removed from partisan politics. They needed to be appointed by someone, so that task was assigned to the president. But the president's powers were deliberately limited. Only a bare majority of the commissioners could be members of one party. The commissioners were appointed for fixed terms. And, most importantly, the commissioners could not be fired at will by the president. Some removal power was needed lest the commissioners proved to be a total embarrassment. Typically, a commissioner can be removed by the president only "for inefficiency, neglect of duty, or malfeasance in office."

Congress was aware that deliberation, study, and analysis might not suffice to develop a full-blown body of substantive law. In addition, Congress was concerned that the necessary flexibility for the agencies would not be achieved if the agencies were required to bring all of their enforcement proceedings in federal courts. Thus, the agencies were given quasi-judicial powers and authorized to engage in individualized adjudication in addition to the legislative function of promulgating rules and regulations. In their case-by-case adjudication, the agencies would not be hampered by the rules of evidence nor encumbered by the necessity to base decisions upon established legal rules. As the expert commissioners decided individual cases, they would develop new legal rules that adequately protected the public interest.

Since it was commonly agreed that courts were not appropriate bodies for policy-making, Congress also sought to limit the ability of the courts to control the workings of the independent regulatory agencies. Administrative action was subject to judicial review, but great deference was to be granted to decisions by independent regulatory agencies. The Administrative Procedures Act provides that an agency determination cannot, as a general rule, be set aside by a reviewing court unless it is "arbitrary, capricious, an abuse of discretion, or otherwise not in accordance with law," or, in cases involving an adjudicative hearing, if "unsupported by substantial evidence. . . ."

The Public Choice Explanation

The public choice perspective is quite different from the public interest perspective. From the public choice perspective, the first question is: what do congressmen gain by setting up independent regulatory agencies? The beginning premise for public choice analysis is that the first job of a congressman is to get reelected. As it turns out, independent regulatory agencies are extremely valuable in the perennial quest for reelection. To gain reelection, one must, of course, please enough voting constituents. From the perspective of constituents, the justification of congressmen is that they solve problems. But some problems, particularly economic problems, appear very hard to solve. Railroads charge farmers too much. Securities become valueless. Toys injure children. Broadcasters' frequencies conflict. Banks fail. Investors lose money in futures markets. Campaign contributions unduly influence elections. Labor unions face difficulty in being accepted as exclusive bargaining agents. These perceived problems are brought to Congress for solutions. After all, under our Constitution the power to enact laws is vested in Congress.

The historical and authorized method for Congress to deal with a problem was to pass a law. Some limitations, however, are imposed upon this legislative power. Laws must be forward-looking and general. Congress is prohibited from passing *ex post facto* laws (laws that impose sanctions for past conduct) and bills of attainder (laws that penalize particular individuals).

These constitutional restrictions might in theory provide an effective constraint upon Congress. If Congress in unable to enact a general and forward-looking statute, congressmen might just leave a problem alone, allowing private parties to rely upon existing legal principles and enforce their rights in courts of law. But if congressmen stay within the bounds established by the Constitution, they face a severe quandary. If they fail to take action to "solve" a perceived problem, some constituents will perceive themselves to be losers. The losers are likely to be alienated and vote for an opponent. But if Congress passes a general and forward-looking statute, other constituents will become losers, and will be similarly alienated. Alas, it is extremely difficult to draft laws of general applicability that will solve complex economic problems in a manner that will not antagonize a major constituency. Congressmen appear to be in a "lose-lose" position.

From the public choice perspective, the congressional solution to this quandary is truly ingenious. Instead of creating new rules, Congress creates a new agency. The problem that Congress has been asked to solve is delegated to a new agency under a broad general mandate that will not offend any constituency. Action has been taken. Congress has been decisive. In the process, speeches are given, hearings are held, and press releases are issued. Congressmen gain positive exposure, credit for dealing with a major problem of public concern, and, with good luck, no major constituencies are offended. Sometimes, the risk of offense cannot be totally eliminated, as was the case with the creation of the National Labor Relations Board, and the size of the constituency that is "helped" is always larger that the one injured.

From a public choice perspective, it does not matter that the newly minted commission does not eventually solve the problem that provided its *raison d' être*. That prospect need be of no great concern to Congress. When an agency is perceived to have failed, Congress is not blamed for having failed by having created the agency. The failure is laid at the feet of the commissioners. And, like good soldiers, they are supposed to take the heat.

Indeed, perceived failures by independent regulatory agencies can, from the public choice perspective, be a boon to the oversight committees. If failures did not exist, they might have to be invented. When a regulatory failure has been spotted, the members of the oversight committees can write letters, give speeches, hold oversight hearings, and pass appropriation riders.

When necessary, a new law can be passed, dumping a slightly altered problem into the lap of the agency. All of this guarantees additional exposure for members of the oversight committees and continuing campaign contributions from the industries that are regulated. From the public choice perspective, one is not surprised that congressional committees seldom want to give up their oversight authority over an independent regulatory agency.

Indeed, from a public choice standpoint, independent regulatory agencies are akin to the goose than laid the golden egg; benefits continue to flow so long as the goose is not killed off. (Congressmen are, you will note, wiser than the king who owned the goose; agencies are never killed off unless the agency lays only rotten eggs rather than golden eggs, and the rotten eggs fall into the lap of Congress. The demise of the Civil Aeronautics Board is the exception that proves the rule.)

One benefit is that the independent regulatory agencies provide a forwarding address for complaints from constituents. A congressman can send a reply to the constituent assuring that the complaint has been forwarded to the appropriate agency. And as the importance of the constituent increases, the congressman can increase his involvement, by writing a follow-up letter, making a speech calling for agency action, or, if appropriate, even holding hearings. This last benefit, however, is reserved for controlling members of the oversight committees, thereby increasing the value of certain positions, such as Chairman of the House Commerce Committee.

Key congressmen can be perceived to derive a second important and continuing benefit from the independent regulatory agencies. Key members of oversight committees, particularly the Senate oversight committees, are in a position to influence, sometimes even control, appointments to those agencies. Since the advice and consent of the Senate is required, key members of the Senate oversight committees are often in a position to block appointments that are not acceptable. In addition, presidents seldom place much value on appointments to independent boards and commissions. Since the president cannot control an independent regulatory agency, he obtains little credit if the agency does well and little blame if the agency does poorly.

By contrast, the appointments are often of great value to senators, particularly when the agency affects major interests within senator's state. For example, appointment to the Federal Energy Regulatory Commission may be of great importance to senators from energy-producing states. Since the appointments are frequently more valuable to key congressmen than to the president, both the congressman and the president can potentially gain from a political trade. The president can get, for example, a vote on a key bill while the senator can get an appointment. The public may be unaware of any such political trade, but key interest groups are surely aware. A public choice analyst might even expect that the interest groups would be ready, willing, and able to demonstrate their appreciation. The hypothesis that interest groups benefit from regulatory action and make campaign contributions that reflect their interests can, of course, be tested by examining the sources and destination of political action committee money. While congressmen, the president, and the special interest may all gain from the trade, the quality of personnel heading independent regulatory agencies may suffer. From the public choice perspective, one would not be surprised to find that political hacks amenable to the views of particular constituent groups frequently receive appointment as commissioners of independent regulatory agencies.

Public choice analysts are likely to argue that one of the greatest benefits to key congressmen on oversight committees is that the independent regulatory agencies are akin to money machines. Millions of dollars are at stake in some decisions made by regulatory agencies. Certain senators are able to influence those decisions, by letters, telephone calls, speeches, legislative proposals, hearings, and perhaps most importantly by controlling appointments. For example, in a decade when foreign imports are an important issue, public choice analysts would predict that appointments to the International Trade Commission will be influenced by members of the Senate Finance Committee. Access to the ears of such senators may be sufficiently valuable that lobbyists are willing to pay $10,000, for occasional breakfasts with them.

FROM WHOM ARE THEY INDEPENDENT?

Independent regulatory agencies may be good for Congress, but for whom do these agencies act? To whom are they responsible and from whom are they independent? The concept of agency is that one is an agent for someone else (except for a free agent who can act for himself). An agent acts for his principal and is legally authorized to bind his principal. Who is the principal for whom regulatory commissioners act? To whom they are accountable? In the executive branch, every employee's authority ultimates derives from the president. Each person has a superior and the line of authority goes all the way to the top. Any employee can be fired for failing to do his or her job. But persons in policy-making positions, those who have the most discretion, serve at the pleasure of the president or a top level figure who reports directly to the president. Every policy-maker in the executive branch can be fired—or, as is more common, asked to resign—for good reason, for bad reason, or for no reason.

By design, agency commissioners are not responsible to the president. The president has very limited control over what they do and hence is not responsible for what they do. The Supreme Court's decision in *Humphrey's Executor* v. *United States* confirmed that the president cannot remove a commissioner at will. In December 1931, William E. Humphrey was nominated by President Hoover to fill a second term as a Commissioner of the Federal Trade Commission. He was duly confirmed by the U.S. Senate, took the oath of office, and entered upon his duties. On July 25, 1933, President Roosevelt requested Humphrey's resignation on the ground "that the aims and purposes of the Administration with respect to the work of the Commission can be carried out most effectively with personnel of my own selection." Additional correspondence ensued. Among other things FDR stated:

> You will, I know, realize that I do not feel that your mind and my mind go along together on either the policies or the administering of the Federal Trade Commission, and, frankly, I think it is best for the people of this country that I should have a full confidence.

After consideration, Humphrey declined to resign. Accordingly, the president on October 7, 1933 wrote him: "Effective as of this date you are hereby removed from the office of Commissioner of the Federal Trade Commission." The Treasury stopped Mr. Humphrey's biweekly paycheck, but Humphrey did not acquiesce. Instead, he sued for his back salary. Although Humphrey did not live to receive the check, his executor won the lawsuit on appeal to the Supreme Court. The check went into the estate, the decision went into the law books, and independent agencies' independence from the president seemed assured. The Supreme Court had given a ringing endorsement to the concept of independence from the president. According to the Court, "The Federal Trade Commission is an administrative body created by Congress to carry into effect legislative policies embodied in the statute in accordance with the legislative standard therein prescribed, and to perform other specified duties as a legislative or as a judicial aid." The agency was not "an arm or an eye of the executive." Indeed, it was "wholly disconnected from the executive department" and was designed to act "in part quasi-legislatively and in part quasi-judicially."

The Supreme Court viewed the independent regulatory agencies to be arms of Congress. But are commissioners agents of Congress? Congress has high degree of control over the independent agencies, and often seems to think that the commissioners work for Congress. But commissioners are not agents of Congress in the sense that they can bind Congress. They cannot. In addition, although members of oversight committees can make life unpleasant for commissioners who fall from their graces, commissioners cannot be fired by either the Speaker of the House or any other member of Congress.

According to the Supreme Court's reading of the legislative history of the Federal Trade Commission Act, "the commission was not to be 'subject to anybody in the government but ... only to the people of the United States.'" Every commissioner undoubtedly likes to think that he or she is an agent of the public. Commissioners can certainly bind the public. But it is equally clear that *the public cannot fire a commissioner.* If there is a principal-agent relationship between the public and independent agencies, the relationship runs the other way. The agency is the principal and the public the agents; the agency gives the orders and the public must obey.

Of whom then are the independent regulatory agencies independent? In a formal, legal sense, they are in large part independent from the president, the Congress, and the courts. They can be removed only by impeachment or "for inefficiency, neglect of duty, or malfeasance in office," seemingly ensuring their virtual independence during their term of office. In addition, the scope of judicial review is narrowly circumscribed.

In a practical sense, however, while independent regulatory agencies are independent of the president and the courts, they are generally minions of Congress. Congressional committees can and do haul commissioners up for hearings and figuratively beat them on the head. They can and will ask for any document that they want. If the documents are not turned over upon request, they will be subpoenaed. From the standpoint of Congress, no document is considered privileged. The president does not protect the agencies. The commissioners, not surprisingly, are not willing to risk jail sentence to avoid turning over privileged documents. With rare exceptions, Congress can exercise as much control over the agencies as they desire. Indeed, Congress has the best of both worlds. Congressmen can yank commissioners' chains without having to accept the responsibility for the actions of those commissioners.

HOW DO THE AGENCIES FIT WITHIN THE CONSTITUTION?

The independent regulatory agencies have often been called the fourth branch of the government. With all due respect to *Humphrey's Executor* v. *United States*, whence the term originated, the appellation makes no sense from a constitutional perspective. The constitution provides for a legislative branch, an executive branch, and a judicial branch. There is no fourth administrative or regulatory branch.

Nevertheless, one can understand why the independent regulatory agencies are referred to as a fourth branch of the government. First, they are not formally within the control of either the legislative or judicial branch and Congress has tried to weaken the control by executive branch officials, thereby creating the appearance that they must belong somewhere else. Second, the mix of powers exercised by the independent regulatory agencies suggests that they do not lie clearly within any one branch of government. They engage in individualized investigations and begin enforcement proceedings against individual parties—powers that appear to lie within the executive branch. They prepare reports for Congress, such as might be done by employees in the legislative branch. They promulgate rules and regulations, exercising what have been called "quasi-legislative" powers. They decide whether individual parties have violated rules, regulations, or statutes and enter orders that impose sanctions, exercising what have been called "quasi-judicial" powers.

Rather than ask whether the independent regulatory agencies are in the legislative branch, the judicial branch, the executive branch, or no branch of the government, it is more informative to examine the various functions served by the independent regulatory agencies and ask in which branch, if any, those functions belong.

The Investigatory and Reporting Functions

Independent regulatory agencies conduct investigations and make reports to Congress. These functions obviously can come within the legislative branch. Since Congress can make all laws necessary and proper for carrying out any of the powers mentioned in the Constitution, Congress certainly can create agencies to gather information, conduct information, and provide reports to Congress. For example, it is perfectly legitimate for Congress to create a Library of Congress or a General Accounting Office.

However, just because "arms of Congress" can be created to gather information, conduct investigations, and provide reports and recommendations to Congress, it does not follow that these functions are necessarily legislative functions. The Constitution specifically provides that the president "shall from time to time give to the Congress information of the state of the Union, and recommend to their consideration such measures as he shall judge necessary and expedient. . . ." In addition, it seems self-evident that Congress can, by virtue of the "necessary and proper" clause, enact laws providing for departments and agencies of the executive branch to gather information, prepare reports, and provide information for Congress. Gathering information and preparing reports for Congress can be either a legislative or executive function.

The Quasi-Legislative Function

Another major function of the independent regulatory agencies is to promulgate rules and regulations. This function has often been called quasi-legislative. The prefix "quasi-," however, merely short-circuits analysis. The proper question is: does an agency exercise legislative powers when it issues rules and regulations? Under our Constitution, one thing is clear. An independent regulatory agency cannot be enacting a law when it issues a rule or regulation. While Congress can create "arms" for itself to gather information, conduct information, or make investigations about how the money appropriated by Congress is spent, Congress cannot create an "arm" to enact laws for it. The Constitution specifically provides that a law must be passed by the House of Representatives and the Senate and presented to the President of the United States.

It is said that Congress can delegate its power, implying perhaps that it can delegate the power to enact laws. To speak of delegation of powers, however, is actually a misnomer. Congress cannot delegate its power to enact laws. What it can do is enact laws that are relatively vague and leave wide discretion for the agency that enforces those laws to interpret the mandate of Congress. The appropriate constitutional question in such cases is whether the legislation is unconstitutionally vague. The Supreme Court has allowed Congress extremely wide leeway. Legislation can be very vague and the courts still will not strike it down as unconstitutionally vague.

Since laws can only be enacted through the passage of a bill by Congress that is presented to the president, the promulgation of rules and regulations cannot be the enactment of law. Therefore, the so-called "quasi-legislative" function is not legislative at all. Instead, it must be seen as a part of the executive power to enforce the laws that have been enacted by Congress. Executive branch departments and agencies regularly promulgate rules and regulations, interpreting and making more specific the laws they enforce.

When viewed from the perspective of allocation of powers among the branches of the federal government, one cannot fault the Supreme Court for its unwillingness to police vague statutes. Wide discretion given to the executive branch is not irrevocable. Congress can at any time enact a more specific statute. Vagueness and lack of specificity may raise constitutional questions, but the major concern has nothing to do with the allocation of power. Instead, the concern is that private parties may not be adequately apprised of the laws that govern them. An allocation of power issue only arises if the president does not have the power to control the operation of an agency that is enforcing a vague statute.

The Quasi-Judicial Function

The last major function exercised by independent regulatory agencies is that of adjudicating individual cases. Independent regulatory agencies conduct investigations regarding possible violations of laws, rules, or regulations; make determinations whether there has been a violation, and enter administrative orders. The function of deciding whether third parties have committed violations is frequently referred to as a "quasi- judicial" function. Once again, the prefix "quasi" begs the question. The initial question is whether agencies are exercising a judicial power when they review a factual record and determine whether a violation has occurred.

Under the Constitution, clearly the answer is no. The Constitution provides that "[t]he judicial power of the United States, shall be vested in one Supreme Court, and in such inferior courts as the Congress may from time to time ordain and establish." So far, so good. In theory, the Congress could create inferior courts and call them the Interstate Commerce Commission, the Federal Trade Commission, etc. But the Constitution goes farther and provides: "The judges, both of the Supreme Court and the inferior courts, shall hold their offices during good behavior. . . ." Article III judges have life tenure and can only be removed by impeachment. Since Congress provides set terms for commissioners, those commissioners cannot be Article III judges. And since they are not Article III judges, they cannot exercise the judicial power of the United States.

One can then ask: are the independent regulatory agencies exercising a legislative function when they engage in case-by-case adjudication? On this question the Constitution is equally clear. Congress's power to try cases is limited to impeachment. The House of Representatives has "the sole power of impeachment." The Senate has "the sole power to try all impeachments." The penalties for impeachment are clearly limited: "Judgment in cases of impeachment shall not extend further than to removal from office, and disqualification to hold and enjoy any office of honor, trust or profit under the United States. . . ." Aside from this power of impeachment, Congress has no power to punish an individual. The Constitution specifically provides that: "No bill of attainder or ex post facto law shall be passed." Congressional specification of penalties must be generalized and forward-looking. Congress itself cannot impose an individualized penalty except through the exercise of its power of impeachment.

What then is the constitutional status of case-by-case adjudication by independent regulatory agencies? Since commissioners are not Article III judges, their case-by-case adjudication cannot be an exercise of judicial power under the Constitution. Nor can case-by-case adjudication by independent regulatory agencies be an exercise of legislative power under the Constitution. Thus the question becomes: is case-by-case adjudication an exercise of the executive function? Or is it an unconstitutional merging of the powers of the executive and judiciary?

The Due Process Requirement

The executive power of the federal government is vested in the president, and the scope of the executive powers is not fully defined by the Constitution. But Article II clearly specifies that the president "shall take care that the laws be faithfully executed. . . ." Law enforcement is clearly an executive function.

The scope of judicial power is delineated more extensively than the scope of executive power. Among other things, Article III provides that judicial power extends "to all cases, in law and equity, arising under. . .the laws of the United States. . . ." In criminal cases, the boundary between the executive function and the judicial functions is rather clearly drawn. The Constitution itself provides: "The trial of all crimes, except in cases of impeachment, shall be by jury. . . ." In the case of civil offenses, the boundary between the executive function and the judicial function is less clear. The fifth amendment provides: "No person shall be. . .deprived of life, liberty, or property, without due process of law." Due process is somewhat vague. Nevertheless, from its context, the clear inference is that due process is judicial process. Thus, one must conclude that the executive branch is constitutionally prohibited from imposing a final order, unreviewable by a court, that would impose a penalty that deprives any person of liberty or property.

Since independent regulatory agencies are not Article III courts, constitutional problems would arise if an independent regulatory agency were empowered to impose a final order, unreviewable by a court, that would impose a penalty that deprives a person of liberty or property. Congress, however, has not conferred such power. Some form of judicial review is always provided in administrative orders. In some cases, the scope of judicial review is very limited. Indeed, one can question whether the Administrative Procedures Act's limitations upon judicial review accord with the constitutional requirement for due process. The issue whether judicial review of agency action meets the due process test has been camouflaged. In place of judicial due process we are given administrative due process, the convoluted process whereby an agency acts as prosecutor and judge while trying to separate the two functions. Administrative due process, however, is no substitute for judicial process, the kind of due process guaranteed by the Constitution. If the scope of judicial review meets the due process requirement, the internal procedures of an administrative agency are of no constitutional concern. An agency, whether executive branch or independent, can, without any constitutional need to worry about due process, enter a preliminary order that would, absent judicial review, impose sanctions so long as the available judicial review meets the due process test.

There may be good reasons for a regulatory agency, whether independent or not, to bifurcate (or not to bifurcate) its internal decision-making procedures. It may (or may not) be more efficient or more accurate for an agency to make decisions when the internal prosecutorial and decision-making functions are separated. The issue whether to separate the prosecutorial and decision-making functions, however, relates to fairness and efficiency, not to constitutional due process.

As we have seen, administrative adjudication cannot possibly be an exercise of judicial power or legislative power. By contrast, individualized initial decisions of violations are routinely made by executive branch officials. Executive law enforcement officials constantly face the question whether there has been a violation of the laws, rules, and regulations they enforce. Often they make initial determinations that, subject to judicial approval, would deprive persons of their life or liberty. The Immigration and Naturalization Service determines whether aliens can legally remain within the country. The Internal Revenue Service determines that taxes are due. Absent any further action by the private parties involved, these determinations by executive branch officials become binding and enforceable orders. These determinations are subject to judicial review; it is this opportunity for judicial review that satisfies the requirement of due process. Despite the camouflage, administrative agencies do not exercise Article III judicial power. Their issuance of decisions does not turn them into Article III judges. Whatever administrative procedures they use, when commissioners engage in case-by-case adjudication they are simply enforcing the law, thereby exercising an executive branch function.

RESTORING THE CONSTITUTIONAL DESIGN

Having examined the individual functions of the independent regulatory agencies, the totality becomes quite clear. In this case, the whole is no greater than the sum of the parts. Every single function that independent regulatory agencies exercise can legitimately be exercised by the executive branch of the government. The principal function that they exercise, the enforcement of laws, is clearly an Article II executive function, not Article I law-making nor Article III judging. Whether they promulgate rules and regulations or engage in case-by-case adjudication, regulatory agencies are exercising executive functions that properly belong within the executive branch.

The understanding that the so-called independent regulatory agencies exercise executive branch functions clarifies the significance of the terms "independent" and "fourth branch of government." The independent regulatory agencies are independent only insofar as Congress is able to create agencies that exercise executive branch functions and make those agencies free from control by the president and by the courts. The independent regulatory agencies are a fourth branch of government only insofar as Congress is able to divide the executive branch in two.

Thus, the key policy and constitutional questions presented by independent regulatory agencies are: what limits should and can Congress constitutionally impose upon the power of the president and the courts to control regulatory arms of the executive branch? Congress has limited the president's power to fire at will the key policy-makers in regulatory agencies. Congress has limited the scope of judicial review of the decisions of regulatory agencies. Are these limitations good policy? Are these limitations constitutional? No, these limitations are neither good policy nor good constitutional law.

The historical judgment has been that the independent regulatory agencies have not functioned well. The lesson that we should learn from history is that this near-universal failure is attributable to the to the departure from the scheme of governance provided by the Constitution. The president ignores the regulatory agencies because he is not accountable for what the agencies do. Congress can safely convert the regulatory agencies into their own mini-fiefdoms because Congress is not accountable for what the agencies do. This lack of accountability is not within the constitutional design. The corroding lack of accountability, and the accompanying irresponsibility, arise because the mandates of the Constitution have been ignored.

The creators of the independent regulatory agencies have ignored the mandates of the Constitution in three respects. The president of the United States, who has the responsibility to "take care that the laws be faithfully executed . . . ," has been denied the power to remove the policy-makers of certain agencies that enforce the laws of the United States. The courts, whose due process is required before persons can be deprived of their life, liberty, or property, have been limited in their power to review the decisions of administrative agencies. Congress, which has the power and responsibility to enact legislation, has passed legislation that is incredibly vague and which "delegates" broad power of interpretation to agency officials that are not responsible to Congress, to the courts, to the president, or to the public.

Using Presidential Power

A president who takes seriously the oath to "preserve, protect and defend the Constitution of the United States" can and should take steps to reassert his constitutional authority to oversee the enforcement of law. The president can and should assert his direct authority over the independent agencies and discharge those commissioners who will not follow his direction.

One may think that executive direction and removal are foreclosed by *Humphrey's Executor* v. *United States*. This was once the case, but unbeknownst to most observers, the Supreme Court in *Morrison* v. *Olson*, the independent counsel case (discussed in Chapter 10), swept the logic of *Humphrey's Executor* into the dust bin of history. According to the Supreme Court:

> We undoubtedly did rely on the terms "quasi-legislative" and "quasi-judicial" to distinguish the official in *Humphrey's Executor* and *Wiener* from those in *Myers,* but our present considered view is that the determination whether the Constitution allows Congress to impose a "good cause" type restriction on the president's power to remove an official cannot be made to turn on whether or not that official is classified as "purely executive." The analysis contained in our removal case is designed not to define rigid categories of those officials who may or may not be removed by the president, but to ensure that Congress does not interfere with the president's exercise of the "executive power" and his constitutionally appointed duty to "take care that the laws be faithfully executed" under Article II.

The constitutional question regarding the president's removal power has now been reframed. It is whether it is "essential to the president's proper execution of his Article II powers that these agencies be headed up by individuals who [are] removable at will." The Court held that this was not the case with regard to independent prosecutors. As the Court noted, "the independent counsel is an inferior officer under the Appointment Clause, with limited jurisdiction and tenure and lacking policy-making or significant administrative authority." But the same cannot be said of the heads of regulatory agencies. Who can doubt that they are policymaking positions with significant administrative authority? Since commissioners and the like are policymakers in the fullest sense of the term, they must be amenable to removal by the president at will.

The Next President

A newly elected president with sufficient nerve could, in accordance with the Supreme Court's test in *Morrison* v. *Olson*, simply assert his power over the heads of independent agencies and discharge every single one when he takes office, giving basically the same reason that FDR gave in requesting the resignation of William Humphrey: his lack of confidence that they will enforce the law consistent with the will of the president. To avoid chaos, the president could name each incumbent to serve in an acting capacity while the president decides which he will reappoint and which he will not. A sweeping discharge, accomplished during the honeymoon period and not aimed at any particular agency, might avoid challenge. If challenged, the president has an excellent opportunity to obtain an overruling of the exact holding of *Humphrey's Executor*, the holding that the president cannot remove a commissioner of an independent regulatory agency at will.

Lacking the stomach for a wholesale dismissal, the president should direct the Office of Management and Budget to identify existing independent agency rules and regulations that are contrary to the public interest. Once an appropriate rule or regulation has been identified, the president should direct the applicable agency to change its rule or regulation. If the agency heads fail to do so, the president should promptly fire the commissioners who fail to follow the direction of the president.

For political reasons, OMB should try to identify rules or regulations that are generally discredited. But even if there is lack of consensus, the president should not fail to assert the authority of his office. If Congress is dissatisfied with the rule or regulation imposed by the direction of the president, Congress has the power to act. The power to enact laws has not been stripped from Congress. Indeed, only by exercising authority over the regulatory agencies can the president force both the agencies and Congress to act responsibly. Only if the president takes steps to see that the independent regulatory agencies cease to be independent can the Constitutional system of regulation be restored.

PART

III

Reclaiming
American Politics

Introduction by

GORDON S. JONES

*I*n Part I we looked at the historical development of the separation of powers doctrine and its theoretical usefulness. In Part II we examined the actual workings of the two more active branches of the American government, and found the separation of powers in disrepair. Now we will propose what can be done to restore the areas of responsibility to their proper boundaries.

In the following chapters, three different authors will give their prescriptions for the future. All three agree that it will require creativity and energy, and that it is unlikely that either of these will come from Congress without prodding. Consequently, all three of the authors suggest remedies that originate primarily in the executive branch.

There is considerable uncertainty as to the exact boundaries between the three branches (and, as Nolan Clark suggests in Chapter 11, between the constitutional branches and the independent agencies). This uncertainty invites conflict, and the history of government in the United States is certainly marked by conflict, with first one, then another, of the branches asserting supremacy. On balance, this situation of uncertainty and conflict is a healthy one for the freedoms of an independent people. The problem comes when one of the branches declines to defend its own rights.

In our present circumstances, no one can blame the legislative branch for doing what it has done; but one can blame the executive branch for its failure to protect its own constitutional turf. Our authors do criticize the executive, and then suggest ways to turn the situation around. Our book concludes with a chapter of recommendations based on the analyses provided by the authors of this volume.

12. Overthrowing Oligarchy

GORDON S. JONES

Several of the authors have suggested that there is a breakdown in the governing consensus in the United States, and that that breakdown lies at the heart of the executive-legislative battle. In this chapter Gordon Jones identifies five defining issues which need to be settled in the political realm. He argues that there was once consensus on these issues, and that this consensus is what permitted self-government in the United States. Unless that consensus can be regained, self-government will become increasingly problematic. This chapter makes a strong plea for open, vigorous, political debate over these issues.

CONSERVATIVES AND CONGRESS

It will not have escaped the attention of the careful reader of the preceeding essays in this book that, while critical of Congress, the authors are also very critical of the executive branch. The succeeding chapters are even more explicit in their prescription for solving the crisis of the separation of powers: strengthen the executive. It may seem strange that conservatives, writing in a book published by policy groups with conservative leanings, should bemoan the weakness of the executive. After all, it was not many years ago that books were being written by conservatives decrying the Imperial Presidency. It has been an article of faith for conservatives that the constitution really does give an edge to Congress in the battle with the executive for supremacy. It is, after all, the branch closest to the people, and a more diffused power center than a robust executive.

At the heart of conservatives' concern is their distrust for concentrations of power. Beginning in the 1940s and continuing through the 1950s and 1960s, conservatives saw power flowing to the executive, and they instinctively sought a check on that power, first in the courts, and when that avenue failed, in Congress. However, their preference for Congress was less a general preference than a situational one. That is, it was a preference for the branch that was striving to counter the dominant branch.

There is another reason, rooted in history, why conservatives prefer a strong, if not a dominant executive. Americans tend to take too seriously the bill of particulars against George III contained in the Declaration of Independence. In fact, George did none of the things he was charged with in the Declaration, and Thomas Jefferson knew it perfectly well. The true culprit in the mid-18th century was a Parliament in which all power had become concentrated. The monarch's power to act arbitrarily had been stripped away over centuries, and Parliament was acting virtually without check. In his need to stir up the American colonists, Jefferson knew enough to focus on a single target; it was much easier, and more productive, to attack a single tyrant than to make the much more complex case against an unrepresentative Parliament.

As a result, a major aim of the Founders in crafting the new national government was to create an executive with enough power to check a legislature otherwise unbridled. That much is very clear from the debates of the constitutional convention in 1787 and from the ratification debates, including the *Federalist Papers*. (These are discussed in detail in Chapters 1 and 2.)

The Founders did not place much faith in the power of the judiciary to check either Congress or the executive, seeing it as the "least dangerous branch." In that judgment they were wrong, but it is not clear that they would have rejected the result: a tripartite national government with all three of the branches scrambling for influence, if not supremacy.

And that is what most conservatives want: a divided power and limits on the scope of government. The problem is always a concentration of power in one branch to the extent that the liberties of Americans are threatened. A generation ago, the threat came from the executive. Today, it comes from Congress. Perhaps another day will come when it will be the executive again. (The power of the courts is always a concern, unchecked—and apparently uncheckable— as they are, but that is a subject for another book.)

Americans voters today are unlikely to assert control over Congress, for the reasons outlined in Chapter 8. Their only hope, if power is again to be diffused, is to wield the weapon of a reinvigorated executive. Only a single executive who understands the stakes can focus attention on the derelictions of an oligarchic Congress to the degree that the electorate can exercise its prerogatives, and throw the rascals out.

Is there a danger that the reinvigorated executive sought by these conservative theorists and practitioners will threaten the freedoms of all Americans? There is indeed, but that can not be an excuse for acquiescence to legislative tyranny. Eternal vigilance is the burden we bear to be free.

We should note that there is a strain of conservatism which prefers a strong executive for its own sake, in a kind of atavistic monarchism. That strain was present at the time of the Founding, and while it is undoubtedly weaker today, it remains. Thus it is not only liberals who prefer a powerful central government, but they are certainly its primary source of support. Centralizing conservatives (outside of the area of national defense, as explained in Chapter 3) are numerically few.

In the 1940s, 1950s, and 1960s, it was the liberals who championed a powerful chief executive, freed from the restraints of a Congress ruled by entrenched barons. Elaborate schemes were devised to channel more power to the president, and if these schemes were not succesful, it was not from want of trying.

This faith in the executive persisted right up to the election of Ronald Reagan, though the seeds of congressional power were sown in the soil of the 1960s cultural revolution (and even earlier, as a number of our authors show, in the Progressive era) and irrigated by Watergate. When Reagan was elected in 1980, he shattered the myth that the president was, should, and would be the repository of institutionalized liberalism in the United States. Immediately the search was on for a new charger on which liberalism could ride. Congress was ripe and ready, with an ascendant liberal leadership unafraid to use whatever power was at hand to battle the reactionary invaders.

THE PASSIVE EXECUTIVE

It was, in a word, war. War was declared before Ronald Reagan ever arrived in Washington, by an establishment that could not abide the thought that a third-rate actor could epitomize the policy aspirations of a majority of Americans. For eight years, this establishment has attempted to peddle the idea that Reagan was popular *despite* his views, rather than *because* of them. The components of this establishment include the opinion leaders of America, editorial boards, pollsters, academics, and political pundits. They also include congressional leaders—of both parties—who were unwilling to implement the policy program represented by the Reagan mandate.

As a war, however, it has been curiously one-sided. The president himself seems to have only gut instincts, an inbred sense of the rightness of things. He does not have the intellectual firepower, or the temperament, to mount a philosophically consistent defense of his ideological position. Unfortunately, for eight years most of his advisers have not shared his policy positions, and so they have not contributed to the defense. His congressional allies largely have been silent.

One reason for this last phenomenon is that Reagan policy positions involve some tough choices, and it is easier for members of Congress to dodge those issues than to vote on them. Voting for the Reagan program on national defense, on social issues, on economic issues, involves making somebody mad, usually a well-organized minority. Insufficient thought has been given to the need to provide a counter to these special interests by mobilizing a significant sector of the general public. The result is that voting on a sensitive issue—abortion, for example, or union violence—will anger an organized group no matter which way one votes. No one has generated the political cover a nervous politician needs to cast such votes of conscience.

In the absence of a firm policy position from the executive branch, Congress has managed to expand its role in a number of areas, as has been amply demonstrated in earlier chapters. This congressional activism has vitiated the Reagan policy mandate, which remains popular despite the efforts of public opinion pollsters to obscure the fact. After all, Lloyd Bentsen (D-TX) was not chosen Democrat vice-presidential nominee in 1988 because he is the photographic negative of the sitting president. Quite the contrary. He was chosen to provide camouflage to Michael Dukakis on the very issues of critical interest to most voters. The Dukakis acceptance speech at the Democratic Convention definitively illustrates the political danger Democrats perceive in attacking Reagan's (conservative) policies.

As has been suggested by others in this volume, the fact that the policy views of the center-right majority of Americans have not been translated into policy itself reflects a failure of conception and execution by the president. In other words, the executive branch has almost totally failed to defend itself against legislative branch depredations. It is clear that Ronald Reagan leaves the presidency weaker than he found it. The presidency is weaker in foreign policy, where Congress has usurped the treaty power, and arrogated to itself the conduct of foreign and defense policy in area after area; it is weaker in economic policy, because it has acquiesced in the destruction of budget-making, conceding preeminence to congressional leadership and budget committees; and it is weaker in social policy as its failure to counter liberal initiatives has permitted consolidation of the liberal status quo in the areas of affirmative action, education, judicial philosophy, and abortion, and it has given in to the judiciary on church-state relations. There simply are very few areas where the conservative position—the position conservatives argue is the constitutional position—has been aggressively defended.

RECONSTRUCTING THE POLITICAL CONSENSUS

Government is always a messy business. The reality of governing does not always, or even often, lend itself to neat organizational charts and job descriptions. Quite often arrangements just develop by happenstance, or through inertia. The Department of the Interior, for instance, operates a theater in the Virginia countryside, called Wolf Trap Farm Park for the Performing Arts. Why is this facility operated by the U.S. Park Service? It could just as easily be a commercial facility, or, if it has to be run by the federal government, it could be run by the Smithsonian Institution. The answer is not a rational one. The answer is that that's just the way it developed, and we have a general consensus that it is a good, or at least an acceptable, idea.

Presidential Power and Political Consensus

President Thomas Jefferson bought the Louisiana Territories; during the Civil War, President Abraham Lincoln suspended the writ of *habeas corpus* and freed the slaves; President Franklin Roosevelt sold ships to Great Britain before Congress declared war. Their power to do any of these things was suspect, but their actions were supported by substantial majorities of the citizens, and the actions stood.

More problematic was the internment of some Japanese-Americans and the relocation of others after Pearl Harbor. At the time, it was a popular move, taken by what we would today call a liberal president on the recommendation of a liberal governor who later became Chief Justice of the United States and the epitome of activist liberalism on the Supreme Court. The consensus of support has since eroded (along with the distinction between internment and relocation), and the action is now almost universally regarded as a mistake, although one that can be explained.

Still more problematic was the war in Vietnam. Although it is hard to remember, the Gulf of Tonkin Resolution was passed with only one dissenting vote in the Senate, giving President Lyndon Johnson an effective declaration of war. Within a few years, the consensus unraveled, and Johnson was the object of obloquy at home and the subject of an "International War Crimes Tribunal" conducted mainly by U.S. citizens.

Consider the Oliver North case. There was never any consensus in support of the Nicaraguan Contras; neither was there a consensus against aid. The result was, as Gordon Crovitz shows in Chapter 10, the development of a *modus operandi* by which

Congress would legislate against military aid to the Contras while leaving the president with enough options that he could keep them alive.

Because there was no consensus, however, a slight shift in the relative power of the executive and legislative branches of government offered an opportunity to the political opponents of the declining president to launch a legal attack on a policy without firm support in the populace. The criminalization of this policy difference was the result. It is revealing that the battle is being fought in courtrooms, and not in political campaigns.

In theory, there is no reason why a special prosecutor could not be appointed to look at the Louisiana Purchase, Lincoln's wartime actions, Roosevelt's disposition of our naval hardware, or any of the thousands of other actions not neatly authorized by the Constitution or basic law but taken by former presidents anyway. There isn't much point to it, because the people involved are all dead, but it could be done.

But there are still people alive who were involved in the Japanese-American relocation, in the Vietnam War, and, of course, in the Iran-Contra affair, where this criminalizing process is still going on. And as the political consensus crumbles, the attraction of this kind of criminalization grows.

One result of the failure of political consensus is a turn toward excessive legalism, as Congress, no longer willing to trust the executive, strives to circumscribe the range of his discretionary action. Congressional unwillingness to trust the executive has forced more and more detailed content into general laws, resulting in the micromanagement complained of in many of the chapters of this book.

Avoiding Political Consensus: Democracy by Commission

A second result is the search for a *deus ex machina* to save us from chaos and to reestablish legitimacy. Too many of our leaders seem to have lost confidence in the major instrumentalities of governance and no longer take seriously the democratic framework established by the Constitution. The legitimacy of the entire constitutional order has been undermined. The crisis of legitimacy, the search for consensus, has produced a number of suggestions of extraconstitutional mechanisms (even quite silly ones) as a way of distracting attention from the fact that our constitutional framework no longer operates.

Some of these mechanisms are merely extensions and perversions of processes and procedures previously used, such as the "bipartisan, blue ribbon commissions" convened to deal with any subject that the political world finds difficult. There have been commissions in the past, of course, such as the Hoover Commission during the Truman Administration, which examined the structure of the executive branch and suggested reforms. Still, there has been a tendency in recent years, to resort to these commissions in all sorts of cases where one of the constitutional branches of government ought to be able to act.

It is one thing for one of the branches to appoint an outside group of advisers to make suggestions about how to improve performance. It is quite another to appoint commissions jointly with other branches to make the kinds of judgments and proposals that the constitutional branches themselves are supposed to make. It now seems to be the case that commissions are named when a hot political issue arises that politicians would like to avoid. They are no longer sources of expertise, but ways of passing the political buck.

Thus we have seen commissions in recent years dealing with social security, with race relations, with pornography, with drugs, with the economy, and a host of other subjects. These commissions are all advertised as "independent, bipartisan, blue ribbon," and so on. Whether they are or not is open to question. There is considerable evidence that they are quickly captured by the interest groups most closely involved in the issue. The President's Commission on the Outdoors and the Commission on Acquired Immune Deficiency Syndrome are cases in point.

More important is the fact that these are extraconstitutional mechanisms. The commissioners are not elected; they are irresponsible in the sense that the objects of their policy, the people, cannot fire them, and can have only the most tenuous effect on their selection. They constitute an important shield for politicians, who can point to these commissions as a way of deflecting criticism from dissatisfied constituents when government imposes unpopular policies. True, commission recommendations are not usually self-executing, but occasionally, as in the case of the commissions on congressional salaries, they come very close to it. In one recent case, all that was necessary was to delay a vote in Congress until after the pay raise took effect. That way representatives could enjoy the pay raise and tell their constituents that they voted against it.

Recognizing the Political Crisis

The crisis in the budget process, so amply chronicled by Margaret Davis in Chapter 6, has produced its own set of proposals for black box fixes. Dr. Davis discusses line item vetoes, balanced budget amendments, and similar mechanical solutions. The fact is that these *are* mechanical solutions, but the crisis is political. There is no reason to think that any of these important rule changes would solve the basic problems of political disintegration. They address means, rather than ends.

Other extraconstitutional mechanisms are nothing more than gimmicks, but they are more and more common. Their increasing currency is troubling. There was, for example, the idea of a Ford-Reagan co-presidency, a proposal which surfaced during the Republican convention of 1980. It was fostered by the news media who couldn't accept the idea that Ronald Reagan could seriously be considered presidential material. The Democrats took their turn during the 1988 nominating process in suggesting a Vice President-Secretary of Defense joint appointment, in order to persuade Senator Sam Nunn of Georgia to join the ticket. The Republicans came back with the idea of putting Elizabeth Dole on the ticket as Vice President while her husband was still the Senate Minority Leader.

The periodic proposals to replace our formal governmental structure with a parliamentary system, most recently being advanced by prominent members of both political parties are intellectually more serious, but they are no more satisfactory as an answer to the problem, which is again, *political*, not *mechanical*.

These various ideas and trends all reflect a fundamental mistrust of the constitutional system devised by the Founding Fathers, and of that stroke of genius, the separation of powers. Note that to one extent or another all of these proposed remedies blur the lines between the branches. They all seek to avoid the need to seek popular legitimacy for policy choices. Under such proposals, politicians would never again need to engage the people on the policy level, to make their case for general and specific policies, and to seek electoral approval for those policies. Above all, conflicting views of the *ends* of government would never have to be laid before the people. *Ends* would be obscured by a focus on *means.*

Reviving the American Majority

Even when Jefferson bought Louisiana, or Roosevelt sold Liberty ships, the nation as a whole was agreed on the general ends of government, on what things were "American" and on how we should deal with one another and with foreign nations. Lincoln did not enjoy that degree of unanimity, but he was spared the necessity of developing a consensus through the secession of the dissenting citizens.

Today the consensus has broken down across a broad front, at least with respect to elite opinion. It is no longer true that "all Americans" respect the country, and believe it to be fundamentally good; it is no longer true that all Americans support free enterprise, and are agreed that private property is the foundation for civil and personal liberty. All Americans no longer accept the words of the Pledge of Allegiance, that this is "one nation under God." The common roots of our polity are increasingly challenged both in word and in deed, as our ethnic groups assert separate identities, seek separate legal structures, and as religious expression is systematically extirpated from our public life.

From world population policy to the Berlin Wall, from sex education to housing, from civil rights to tax policy, the centrifugal forces at play in our society threaten to tear it apart.

This war is, in reality, being waged by elites on ordinary people. The vast majority of the American people, what we used to call "all Americans," remain agreed on what our society ought to look like, but their beliefs are under continual siege by the elites, and there is a real danger that even this "silent majority" will be deceived.

In 1980, the delegates to the Democratic convention were criticized as not reflecting the average member of the Democrat Party, let alone the average American. The Democrat delegates in 1988, while closer to the Party, were still very far removed from it on almost all issues, and they were even farther from the average American.

There is ample documentation of similar disjunction between mass organizations such as churches and labor unions and their elite leadership. For instance, the rank and file of the National Education Association voted for Ronald Reagan in 1980 and again in 1984. However, the NEA leadership was overwhelmingly opposed to his candidacy, and in fact, the union endorsed his opponent in both years. What is true of the NEA is also true of other unions.

Challenging the Establishment

Ronald Reagan's popularity derived from his willingness to speak to the people on specific policy options. He seemed on the verge of reconstituting a national consensus. It is hard to imagine how his mandate could have been stronger or more explicit. His failure to capitalize on it reflects a failure to make the attempt. With the exception of the first two years, he really failed to challenge the major institutions of establishment Washington.

Consider the case of one of his supposed successes, the judiciary. While it is true that Reagan's appointees to the federal bench were more conservative than his predecessor's, it is not true that they were uniformly conservative, or even uniformly good appointees, in terms of intellectual power and scholarship. More importantly, Reagan did nothing whatever to break the American Bar Association's stranglehold over the process of judicial appointment.

For many years, potential judicial nominees have been submitted to a committee of the ABA for review as to professional competence. More recently, as the bar association has experienced the same disjunction between general membership and activist leadership as the rest of our major institutions, this committee has begun to examine nominees for ideological acceptibility. This new criterion was most evident in the nomination of Robert Bork to the Supreme Court, but it came into play in numerous other cases, not all of which were made public.

In fact, this review committee was often able to kill nominations out of the light of day simply by threatening to issue a negative report. In those cases, the Reagan Justice Department would offer the nominees a choice between withdrawal of the nomination and a long and bloody fight with the bar association and its Capitol Hill allies.

This last point is important, because the review committee works very closely with the staff of the Senate Judiciary Committee, which considers judicial nominations. In effect, the ABA review committee became a part of the liberal arsenal against conservative Reaganite nominations. In fact, so entrenched in the process has the ABA become that a suit was brought to require its deliberations to be public, as the deliberations of public bodies must be under the Sunshine Act.

It seems undeniable that the power of the president to make judicial nominations, conferred by the Constitution, has been severely weakened, ceded in some measure to a nongovernmental institution.

An even more fundamental attack on the prevailing legal establishment could have been mounted by a change in the way law schools are accredited. It is a little-known fact that the Secretary of Education establishes the accrediting bodies. At the present time, and for some years, he has designated the American Bar Association as the accrediting institution, but there is nothing that requires him to do so. He could just as well designate regional or state bar associations, which tend to be much more conservative than the ABA, or even some other neutral body. By continuing the present system, Ronald Reagan missed a tremendous opportunity to break the choke-hold liberal lawyers and law professors have on the legal establishment.

As the course of the Reagan presidency ran, the Senate Judiciary Committee exercised more and more power over the process of judicial nomination. The Democrat chairman of the Committee, Delaware Senator Joe Biden, at the time a candidate for president himself, established a four-man, all-Democrat screening committee to decide which nominees would even qualify for consideration by the committee. Not only is this maneuver completely unprecedented, and not provided for in either Senate or Committee rules, it was a declaration of war on the Republican members of the Committee, and on the right of the President of the United States to make nominations to the federal bench. By failing to fight this move, Reagan acquiesced in another massive intrusion by Congress into the prerogatives of the executive branch.

PRESIDENTIAL LEADERSHIP

Five political dichotomies divide the center-right majority and the liberal minority in America:

1) The individual (usually in his family setting) is important, competent, and powerful; or *the individual is weak, powerless, and in need of help from government.* On the policy level, this dichotomy is clear in conservative proposals that view the individual as citizen, versus liberal proposals that view the individual as client.

2) National weakness threatens freedom; or *national strength threatens peace.*

3) The traditional family is essential to the health of the society; or *"family" is an illusive and malleable concept, and no particular configuration is better for society than any other.*

4) The United States is morally superior to the Soviet Union; or *the U.S. and the U.S.S.R. are morally equivalent.*

5) Private property is essential to political liberty and the private sector is superior to the public sector; or *the private sector is a necessary evil, to be controlled by the government, and private property is only tolerated.*

The function of the issueless politics of the last 20 years has been to obscure these great dichotomies. Politics has camouflaged the fact that specific policies being put into place

through congressional and judicial usurpation of the prerogatives of the executive are in fact moving our society from one
pole of the dichotomies to the other. Decisions between these
pairings are being made on the basis of mechanics and dry legal-
isms such as those discussed in Chapter 10. During the debate
over the two interpretations of the ABM Treaty, for example,
one potential Democratic candidate for president was quoted as
saying that if the ABM Treaty prohibited U.S. testing and deployment of SDI, he assumed we would abide by it. The implication was that we would so abide *even if SDI were our only hope
for a defense of the nation.*

Only in America would the nation's survival be made a matter of *legal* analysis. This is fundamentally a *political* matter, one
that should be in the hands of the people to decide. If they are to
make decisions of this kind, we will have to find leaders willing
to talk to them in political, that is, policy terms.

Reaching Ordinary Americans

To recast the political consensus, a popular president will have
to reach beyond the existing elites, to ordinary Americans,
grass-roots members of America's social and religious organizations, and communicate directly with them. Chapter 14 offers a
number of specific suggestions as to how this communication
can take place. The process consists of nothing more than relating specific policies to the great dichotomies outlined above.
No doubt there are others, with serious philosophical and religious implications. But these will do for a start, and a start is
badly needed.

There is some evidence that the 1988 presidential campaign
will be fought on the issue of "leadership," and indeed, leadership is required if the body politic is to be restored to health.
But true leadership goes beyond assertion. It involves the courage to tell the truth about what divides us and where the divisions will take us.

13. Restoring the Separation of Powers

THOMAS G. WEST*

The idea that Congress might usurp the power of the executive branch occurred to the Framers of the Constitution. They saw the remedy in a check on the legislative branch exercised by the people through regular elections. But when reelection is a virtual certainty, as is now the case, that check is removed. In this chapter, Thomas West argues that the president can reinvigorate that check by appealing directly to the people about "the mess in Congress." This technique has come to be known as "running against Congress," and it has been used effectively by presidential candidates from Harry Truman to Ronald Reagan.

CONGRESS TODAY

The heart of today's federal government is Congress. Power in Congress is exercised primarily by an aggregation of individual committee and subcommittee chairmen. Each chairman is responsible for a particular subject area, such as agriculture subsidies, welfare, air pollution, or defense procurement. Congress as a body deliberates infrequently over policy. Instead, it prefers to establish sweeping but vague mandates for a multitude

* Thanks to John Marini for explaining how Congress works and to Charles Heatherly for substantial contributions.

of agencies. For example, the law establishing the Consumer Product Safety Commission (CPSC) makes no attempt to define consumer product safety, although the Commission is therein directed to provide for it. Then each of Congress's many little leaders makes policy for his limited area of concern. (CPSC regulations are determined by phone calls and behind-the-scene meetings between businessmen, congressmen, and bureaucrats.)

The various devices by which Congress sustains this system of control, including the abuse of the criminal law to punish executive branch officials who resist the will of members of Congress, have been described at length throughout this book.

Deal-Making, Corruption and Automatic Reelection

The Constitution requires Congress to make the laws. Laws in the constitutional sense are general rules which apply to large classes of people. They are supposed to embody broad policy decisions promoting the common good of the nation. These rules are to be deliberated on and voted on publicly, and congressmen are to be accountable to the people for their votes.

Today, however, Congress typically refuses to make these controversial decisions as a body. Instead, individual members determine them piecemeal in private through their control of administration, or they allow them to be decided by the courts. In effect, Congress has turned over much of its lawmaking power—which it is supposed to share with the president, who has the constitutional power to recommend legislation and to veto—to the Court in exchange for control by particular members over administrative details. Congress has exchanged its constitutional task—securing liberty and justice for all by passing laws in broad daylight—for private maneuvering over such matters as sewer-plant construction, personnel decisions, and federal grants for local businesses. In the words of Rep. Gillis Long (D-LA), Congress has turned

> ... from an institution that was supposed to be a broad policy-making institution with respect to the problems of the country and its relationship to the world, into merely a city council that overlooks the running of the store every day.[1]

The worst aspect of this system is the corruption it fosters and thrives upon. Congressmen become brokers between private lobbies and bureaucracy, giving and receiving favors as a matter of routine. The 1987 revelation that Senator Lloyd Bentsen (D-TX) was mailing invitations to special interests inviting them to pay $10,000 apiece to have breakfast with him, raised few eyebrows in Washington. An executive branch official caught in this position would have been immediately subjected to intense scrutiny from Congress, the media, probably an independent counsel, and very likely driven from office. But everyone in Washington knew that this sort of thing happens every day in Congress.

This system of governance was consolidated in the early 1970s. It is now hard for Washington to remember or even imagine it any other way. And the system has amazing staying power. In the 1986 election, 98 percent of House incumbents who ran for reelection won. It did not matter whether they were ardent constitutionalists or apologists for communist expansion. The results were the same. Until this pattern of automatic reelection changes, senators and congressmen have no incentive to change.

Constitutional Remedies

There is nothing inevitable about the current state of affairs. On the contrary, as long as we live under the Constitution, the remedy for its abuse is always within reach. The Constitution's authors anticipated its abuse, and they anticipated the quarter from which encroachment would most likely come: Congress. A "dependence on the people" was expected to be "the primary control on the government."[2] Properly aroused, the people will defeat corrupt or lawless government officials running for reelection. But how can the people be aroused? The problem is that

> The representatives of the people, in a popular assembly, seem sometimes to fancy that they are the people themselves, and betray strong signs of impatience and disgust at the least sign of opposition from any other quarter; as if the exercise of its rights, by either the executive or judiciary, were a breach of their privilege and an outrage to their dignity.

Above all, since these representatives

> commonly have the people on their side, they always act with such momentum as to make it very difficult for the other members of the government to maintain the balance of the Constitution.[3]

The answer, the Founders thought, was to provide the president with the necessary "constitutional means" to defend his office against Congress, which his "personal motives" of ambition and private interest would encourage him to apply. If the president takes the lead, the people's eyes can be opened to congressional abuses of authority. They will then be in a position to vote out of office those of their representatives who fail to govern in accord with the people's fundamental law, the Constitution.

That is why the Constitution established separation of powers, and that is how the separation of powers is supposed to work. Today that separation has broken down. The consequence is a government which meddles in the details of everyday life, but which cannot act strongly when it needs executive energy. Dominated by Congress, government is eager to regulate matters more appropriate to local or private control—such as speed limits, home appliances, and the wages of city employees—but is incapable of dealing with such prominent national issues as Soviet expansion in Central America.

THE POWER OF POLITICS

A hint of what could be done about all this came in the election of 1980. A half-dozen congressional leaders were defeated, such as Senators McGovern (D-ND), Magnuson (D-WA), Bayh (D-IN), and Church (D-ID), and even a few prominent House members such as Ways and Means Chairman Ullman (D-OR). These leaders had been publicly tied to congressional policies of centralized administration and foreign-policy weakness, dominant themes of the Reagan campaign.

Republicans, for example, ran a campaign commercial in 1980 picturing a Tip O'Neill look-alike riding in a big limo, looking out of his window contemptuously at the common people, with the voice-over asking the people to "vote Republican, for a change." This enormously successful commercial is sometimes dismissed as a clever public relations ploy. The real reason it worked so well was that it symbolized perfectly the worst tendency of today's government: fat congressmen lording it over the people, using the people's taxes to pay for their own elite privileges.

The congressional losses in the 1980 campaign made possible the unusual legislative year of 1981, when Congress was willing to follow the president's lead for the only time in his eight-year tenure. Pundits like to attribute this to vague notions like "the honeymoon period" or "the mandate," but the dramatic defeats of prominent liberal legislators are a much more obvious and likely explanation. Congressional Republicans voted in 1981 with a much higher degree of party unity than they have for many years before or since, while many Democrats deserted their party's leadership in crucial 1981 votes.

Never again in Reagan's presidency did the Republicans run against Congress. And never again did Congress cooperate with him. Congressional Republicans and Democrats alike routinely sneered that the president's budget was "dead on arrival"—an unmistakable sign of their contempt for him. The 1982 tax increase, put through at Congress's insistence with Reagan's reluctant support, undercut in advance any effort the president might have made to continue the 1980 assault on congressional excess.

When the Democrats recaptured their Senate majority in 1986, Reagan was weakened still further. Prominent congressmen used the first opportunity that came their way—the Iran-Contra affair—to attempt to destroy the administration's foreign policy and if possible the administration itself. Some in Congress were even beginning to speak of impeachment right up to the moment that Oliver North's testimony dissolved the lynch-mob atmosphere. Even so, Congress came out ahead. After Iran-Contra, many of Reagan's top-level executive appointments were made in deference to Congress's will. Among the friends of Congress appointed during that period were Howard Baker, the chief of staff of the White House; the directors of the National Security Council and the CIA; and Frank Carlucci, the Secretary of Defense.

As the Reagan Administration came to its end, Congress was

riding high once again. However, the testimony of Oliver North and the success of 1981 indicate a limit to congressional imperialism. Presidents do not have to think of Congress as it is today as a given, an immovable object that has to be accommodated. Congressmen too are elected officials. Change simply requires enough citizens in enough districts and states to turn against those congressional incumbents who refuse to act as responsible lawmakers. It is not even necessary for all or most of the current congressional leadership to be defeated. If these leaders believe that the public will punish congressmen who abuse their power, they will behave. At that point Congress may once again act as the lawmaking body which the Constitution intended it to be.

Changing Public Opinion

For Congress to change, public opinion about Congress has to change. Today most Americans are not unhappy with their senators and congressmen. On the other hand, most Americans also know very little about what their representatives do in office. Congressmen generally like to keep it that way. In their newsletters they write about constituent services and federal projects brought to their districts. They may ask voters their opinions on divisive issues, but they are loath to spell out their own positions or votes. It is often hard to tell from their literature even whether they are Republicans or Democrats.

This means that congressmen fear exposure of their partisanship. Their high reelection rate depends on the public's impression of them as neutral providers of benefits to their individual districts, not partisan supporters or opponents of controversial government policies. That is why incumbents are not so heavily favored in Senate races, in which the political views of the candidates are better aired than in House races.

What are the sources of public opinion? People get their opinions in part from their upbringing. Parents, churches, and schools teach them what to cherish and what they should aspire to. They also teach people what to respect. Thus, people learn to defer, perhaps more than they ought, to clergy, professors and scientists, newsmen, lawyers, and others that make up America's elite. And of course people form many of their opinions quite spontaneously, on the basis of their own passions and reasonings.

Public opinion is a reflection on public character. A free people must be a people with spirit: not just public spirit, but the private spirit that resents every tyranny, however petty, and is ever ready to fight back, growling that truly American slogan: "Don't tread on me." Such a people will resist being treated as a mass. If they have the power to change it, such a people, in the long run, will not submit to a government that interferes constantly and unnecessarily in the details of their lives and yet seeks to avoid accountability for that interference.

When James Madison raised the question of what would prevent Congress from making laws favoring special interests or from which it exempts itself, he answered:

> the vigilant and manly spirit which actuates the people of America—a spirit which nourishes freedom, and in return is nourished by it.

But he went on to say:

> If this spirit shall ever be so far debased as to tolerate a law not obligatory on the legislature, as well as on the people, the people will be prepared to tolerate anything but liberty.[4]

Presidential Leadership

If the American people still have the mettle Madison attributed to them, they will turn against congressional imperialism once they are *enlightened* about what Congress is doing and *led* by those they respect.

However, little can be done by private means alone. Those in the best position to enlighten the people usually favor congressional dominance. Universities, mainstream religious leaders, the legal profession, and the media generally like the current system. There are exceptions, of course, and some voices can be raised, and are being raised, calling attention to the scandalous conduct of some congressional leaders. But no challenge to the Washington establishment is likely to be strongly supported from these quarters.

A president, however, can help to create a new respectability for private sources of opinion that believe in constitutional government. Presidential honor should be accorded to outstanding citizens who are worthy exemplars and role models, not to those whom the elites consider respectable but may not deserve the honor. The president should not seek prestige, he should bestow it.

The story of President Kennedy's troubles with the scientists in the man-on-the-moon project is instructive. Most scientists in prestige institutions said the project couldn't be done and that it was not worth trying. But a smaller number of less famous (but no less competent) scientists said they could do it. Kennedy told the establishment scientists of his day "that if they could not do the job, he would find others who would. And he did."[5] As everyone knows, the project succeeded, and the scientists who made it happen *became* the respectable scientists of the next generation. The president, not academic scientists became the source of respectability.

A president also can publicly recognize and promote those who challenge the media elite. Why should he allow Dan Rather and Tom Brokaw to interview him when he can bring in other journalists from outside Washington? He thereby enhances *their* reputations and gets *their* names before the public. *They* become respectable. Why, moreover, should he give top billing in news conferences to newsmen known to be partisans of the Washington establishment? And why should a president give journalists free office space and special access inside the White House? An effective as well as popular action by a president might be to send them home. They can find their own offices and come to the White House when invited, like ordinary citizens.

Still, one should not overestimate what can be accomplished along these lines. As long as real power resides in Congress, private sources of authority will only respond weakly to honors emanating from the president. In the end, the system will change when Congress itself changes, and only the voters can do that. But they need a reason, and only the president has the public visibility and prestige to articulate authoritatively the reasons for dismantling congressional imperialism. The president should address the opinion of the public directly, by his own words and deeds, not just indirectly through private authorities.

PRESIDENTIAL CHARACTER, SPEECH, AND ACTION

A president who would successfully lead the nation back to constitutional government must have the right *character*, be able to present the right *speeches*, and undertake the right *actions* to guide the people to elect a new kind of Congress.

Character

No ordinary man can do the job. Any concerted opposition to today's cozy arrangements will arouse intense opposition. There are multitudes who profit from the current system, and many others support it out of conviction—or ignorance. It will take a leader of courage to withstand the heat and overcome the opposition. In this regard, Alexander Hamilton once worried that "stern virtue is the growth of few soils," but he also noted a "constant probability" that the presidency would be "filled by characters pre-eminent for ability and virtue." And a man animated by a love of fame would willingly undertake "extensive and arduous enterprises for the public benefit."[6] Our history gives us splendid examples of such magnanimity in our best presidents.

But spirit alone is not enough. The president will also need an understanding of what is at stake, and of what will have to be done to restore responsible government. He must see clearly that the cause of the presidency against Congress *in today's setting* is the cause of free government. If he thinks he would only be advancing his own private interest, or if he does not see that liberty itself is at stake, he will not act strongly or fight the necessary battles.

Executive branch officials today are acutely aware of congressional dominance over the executive, but they tend to accept it as an inevitable fact of life rather than the distortion of the Constitution that it is. Consider, however, that America in

1965 was a "complex modern society," but it did not yet have and did not need a Congress administering the local affairs and foreign policy of the nation through its committees and subcommittees. Betraying similar ignorance of the depth of the problem, some candidates in the 1988 presidential campaign spoke of "working with Congress" as though the problem of presidential-congressional relations were one of "communication" and not who is going to run the country and on what principles.

Speech

If the next president has courage and understanding, he also will need to *explain* what is happening in government. The rhetorical heart of a Constitution-restoring presidency must be a reassertion of the principles of 1776 and 1787, the founding moral principles of constitutional government.

"All men are created equal," the president should explain, means equality under the law. The kind of government we have now is a government of inequality and special privileges. Today we do not have government of the people, by the people, and for the people, where all are treated equally, but government of the few, by the few, and for the few, where decisions are made behind closed doors by and for powerful special interests. Indeed, some congressmen are so cynical that they openly admit that the law serves the private advantage of themselves and their friends.[7] The system functions on the one hand by means of Congress's refusal to make hard decisions in the open, and on the other by congressmen's covert control of the administrative details of the executive branch. In this system the president— the only government official elected by the whole people, and therefore responsible to the whole people and not just part of the people—is increasingly excluded from his constitutional role as co-lawmaker and sole executive.

In his speeches the president must appeal to the people's spirit. Spirit hates despotism: "Don't tread on me." This appeal can be articulated in two ways. First, he should say, get the government off our backs. Stop it from attempting to control the details of our lives. Let it govern in the open, manfully, in broad, general terms, not creeping around in secret manipulating us by appealing to our private greed and special interests.

Second, he should say, let us return to the idea of a people self-governed not only politically but morally. Many policies of government today have the effect of making us slaves to government by making us slaves of our passions. Tocqueville warned of this in his chapter, "What Sort of Despotism Democracies Have to Fear."[8] Government promises to take care of our every need—perhaps even provide us with every pleasure—if only we resign control of our lives to it. The push for federally-funded day care is an example. It sounds attractive to working mothers, but it has the effect of subsidizing mothers who are not at home raising children and forcing the husbands of nonworking mothers to pay the government to provide for the children of working mothers. The strength of the family as an institution independent of government is thereby weakened still further.

If the people become angry at being tread upon, they will support both the institutions of free government—elected representatives who truly rule and take public responsibility for what they do—and the moral habits essential to the survival of free government.

Action

Supporting the president will be the Constitution itself. The powers of the presidency *are there*. A president with spirit will discover them, use them, and defend them. The Constitution assigns the president alone—not the Congress, not the bureaucracy—"the executive power" (Article II, Section 1). He alone is given the task of "tak[ing] care that the laws be faithfully executed" (Section 3). Any congressional encroachment on these powers (unless specifically provided for in the Constitution) or reduction of them or assignment of them to officials not responsible to the president is unconstitutional.

Congress is a *coequal* branch under the Constitution, not the supreme branch. Its only constitutional supremacy over the executive is the impeachment and lawmaking powers, the latter being confined to making laws, raising taxes, authorizing appropriations, and holding appropriate hearings. The executive is constitutionally *superior* to Congress in the exercise of such powers as execution of the law and acting as commander-in-chief of the armed forces. "It is one thing," said Alexander Hamilton,

> to be subordinate to the laws, and another to be dependent on the legislative body. The first comports with, the last violates, the fundamental principles of good government; and, whatever may be the forms of the Constitution, unites all power in the same hands.[9]

Therefore the *practical* heart of a Constitution-restoring presidency will require taking on the Congress. The president will have no quarrel with Congress as a lawmaking body, for that is its proper role. He will, however, do all he can to defeat congressional imperialism against the executive. He will seek or create opportunities to check and roll back the bad habit of congressmen trying to run the executive branch or evading the responsibility of lawmaking.

None of this will be easy. Suppose a president is elected on a platform of restoring government by rule of law, citing in his campaign the numerous abuses now being openly discussed in the media, along with others not yet exposed. Still, he will have to fight with Congress to recover his, and the people's, and the Constitution's, lost ground. Even if some congressmen are defeated as a consequence of his election campaign, the rest will fight back. They will bring to bear all their allies in the media, the courts, the bureaucracy, the universities, the clergy, and the legal profession against the president. Most of all they will use hard political power, and if possible the criminal law, against the president if they can.

But if it is not easy to change things, neither is it as difficult as it may seem today, when much has the appearance of being set in stone. An indication of congressmen's vulnerability is their fear of publicity. Congress rides high when it succeeds in presenting interbranch disputes over policy as executive branch violations of the criminal law. The executive recovers when he exposes these legal disputes as principled ones. Today, more than ever, the leaders of the imperial Congress are vulnerable to public rejection of their behavior and the beliefs upon which it is founded. The task is to raise the specter of illegitimacy by truthfully exposing the current state of affairs to the American people.

Oliver North put fear into congressional hearts when he revealed that a hearing that was supposedly about criminal violations was in fact about policy differences concerning communism in Central America. He and Admiral John Poindexter showed that Reagan's men were acting on behalf of the executive's express policy in Central America, and that Congress, in effect, was going after them for doing so. Democrat leaders in Congress were put on the defensive until they realized that Reagan was not going to take advantage of North's testimony in order to reassert executive authority in foreign policy. But the electrifying effect of North in the summer of 1987 is only a hint of what a courageous president could do by turning the tables on congressional inquisitors. His constant tactic would be to force the Congress into the light of day. Their apparently nonpartisan stands must be shown to be partisan, as indeed they are.

THE NEXT PRESIDENT'S AGENDA

There are many things that a president can do to challenge today's system. In general, he must reassert executive authority by carefully selecting confrontations with Congress over its habit of running the executive branch. What follows are some possibilities.

Take Charge of The Executive Branch

The president can constantly expose the behind-the-scenes administrative activity of committee chairmen. He could select the most egregious examples every day for public exposure. Example: "Yesterday, a staffer from Rep. Snort's office phoned an official in the Agriculture Department demanding that the regulations for administering farm subsidies be tailored to suit the needs of the farmers in his district. He threatened to review the Agriculture budget if the official did not comply. I directed the Secretary of Agriculture to inform Congressman Snort that this administration operates on the principle of equality under the law, as the Constitution requires, and that there will be no special consideration for any individuals, no matter how wealthy they are or how powerful their friends in Congress may be."

The president's appointed officials, in cases like this, would be more likely to resist Congress and support the president if they knew he would back them in such a conflict. Their loyalty would be stronger still if they feared removal from office for defying the president and deferring to Congress.

Challenge Congressional Ethics

As noted in Chapter 10, one of Congress's most effective techniques has been the use of the criminal law against executive branch officials. Some of these officials have been investigated and prosecuted for such actions as lobbying on behalf of friends; actions which are not only legal for congressmen but which they boast about in their election campaigns. What if the president refused to prosecute present and former officials accused of misconduct under various recent statutes unless Congress changed the law to include congressmen, their staffs, and ex-congressmen?

Congress' practice of exempting itself from the laws it passes, including civil rights and independent counsel statutes, has become a scandal widely discussed in the media. The president could announce that he will refuse to sign any law that contains such exemptions. He could also announce that he will submit legislation, to be drafted by his Justice Department, to repeal existing congressional exemptions, and that he will not sign the appropriations bill for congressional operation until this repeal was voted on by the Congress.

Refuse Continuing Resolutions

The president also could refuse to sign Continuing Resolutions. These massive end-of-the-year appropriations contain many thousands of pages, far more than any one individual can practically read. He should return these to Congress with the message, "an appropriation or a law, being general in its application, should be short enough to read. Any bill this long is going into administrative details properly executive in nature." Further, he could declare that the committee-prepared Conference Reports which accompany appropriations, which go into even greater detail than the appropriations themselves, *do not have the force of law*, since they have not been adopted by vote of Congress. James Miller, Reagan's OMB Director, made such a declaration in 1988, but he was forced to recant under congressional pressure.

Let the People Decide

How much a president can do will also depend in part on circumstances. These may occur independently of his own plans. A serious recession, for example, or an attack by an enemy on our citizens or armed forces, may offer unusual opportunities for action. Yet circumstances do not always catch statesmen by surprise. They can partly be changed or made by him.

No doubt Congress, or some members of it, might wish to impeach a president who attempts to restore constitutional government by challenging congressional usurpations. Anticipating this, perhaps even welcoming it, the president's job is to win enough popular support to defeat—or forestall—any impeachment move. This means he will have to act with the right combination of boldness and caution. But he must first reassert the presidency's historic constitutional powers and articulate the reasons for doing so. When the issue is framed properly, and the occasions for confrontation well chosen, the people will side with the president, and the rule of law—secured through the constitutional separation of powers—will prevail.

THE ROLE OF PARTISANSHIP IN THE REVIVAL OF SEPARATION OF POWERS

A president who would lead a renaissance of constitutional government will have to campaign on the issue, as Reagan did to some extent in 1980. He will have to undertake a partisan appeal and organize a group that can both carry the appeal to the people and become an effective force within the government. That group he must organize is a political party of constitutional government. Such a political party must be, at least at first, the anti-Congress party. *Limited government means a limited Congress*, a Congress that goes back to its main constitutional job, lawmaking, and ends its twenty-year foray into administration.

As things stand today, the Democratic Party, with its bastion in the House of Representatives, tends to be (but is not completely) the party of centralized administration. Democrats tend to favor a weak president and an assertive Congress. The party's main constituencies are government itself and groups dependent on government.[10]

The Republican Party, in contrast, has consistently won the presidency from 1968 to 1984. The only exception occurred when the Democratic candidate (Jimmy Carter) successfully portrayed himself as an outsider running against the Washington establishment. The Republicans tend to be (but are not completely), the party of decentralized *administration* but strong *government*. They tend to favor a strong presidency. They generally promote a vigorous anticommunist foreign policy but prefer local governments and individuals to govern the details of their lives and local affairs.

Yet neither party can be said today to be the party of the Constitution. The tendencies just named are real but partial. Many Republicans in Congress enjoy the current scheme almost as much as the Democrats. They are happy to enjoy the perks of the system, although not in the full measure of the majority Democrats. The ranking minority member of a subcommittee, with his additional paid staff, has some power, and he is not eager to challenge the system that gives him that power. During the Iran-Contra hearings, it was striking to observe how critical some Republicans were of the president, and how tepid was the support of many others.

Nor does a Democrat in the White House guarantee the cooperation of Congress. Jimmy Carter faced constant congressional recalcitrance during a presidency when the Democrats held big majorities in both houses. Evidently the institutional strife generated by congressional imperialism compelled even a Democrat president to defend himself, just as many Republicans in Congress are more loyal to their branch than their party leader.

Still, congressional Republicans (and many Democrats) will support a Republican president quickly enough if they believe that opposition incurs electoral risk. As noted above, Republican Party unity in Congress was never greater than in the key votes of 1981. In that year everyone believed Reagan was strong, and that opposing him might be enough to defeat congressional candidates.

A political party of constitutionalism would not have to be the majority party in Congress before it could be effective. One third of one house would be enough, acting with a vigorous president. This solid minority, supporting a consistent presidential veto, could bring business as usual in Congress to a stop and force the light of publicity on their doings.

The party of the Constitution could expose every known instance of private favoritism and insist on business in the open in which all are treated fairly. It would oppose legislation that refuses to be clear, or which attempts to micromanage the executive, or which further erodes the liberty and self-sufficiency of citizens. It would firmly support the president in his legitimate exercise of executive power. Its members would defend executive branch officials in hearings when they are badgered and insulted by congressmen. (Few Republicans or Democrats speak up on behalf of those officials today.) The party would challenge in speech and writing every action of the House and Senate leadership designed to lessen deliberation, undermine the president, conceal responsibility, or evade the law. Concerted challenges and actions of this sort, always accompanied by reasoned arguments explaining them to the public, could transform Washington.

There are already many men and women in Congress who would gladly do such things, *if* they were confident of support from the president. Others of like mind would run for office if they could see such a prospect for real change.

Many Americans worry that partisanship is something poisonous, a stance to be avoided by civilized men and women. It is perhaps regrettable that life involves conflict. "If men were angels, no government would be necessary."[11] Bad men and bad policies will prevail if good men fail to fight. The purpose of decent partisanship is not victory for its own sake but for the common good. When the Constitution is at risk, citizens must organize against those who are already organized to benefit at the expense of the liberty and property of the majority.

Americans must therefore overcome their reluctance to take sides. After Congress insured the collapse of Vietnam and Cambodia in 1975 by cutting off all military assistance to Southeast Asia, President Ford refused to blame Congress for this first American defeat in our history. Instead, he promised "no recriminations." This seemingly high-minded refusal to engage in partisan attacks on congressional leadership helped to solidify the control of Congress over the government. Since that time, has Congress shown self-restraint in *its* partisan attacks on the executive? While President Reagan instructed his lieutenants not to say anything harsh against the congressional leadership, congressmen were calling for the prosecution and jailing of executive branch officials whose actions were easily defensible within the president's constitutional prerogatives. This executive weakness entrenches the current system, no matter what "mandate" the electorate gives a president every four years.

INADEQUATE SOLUTIONS

We must put to rest a common misconception: that the courts, especially the Supreme Court, are the source of most of our difficulties with the federal government today, and that all can be changed by making the right judicial appointments. Conservative hopes invested in the Robert Bork appointment show how tempting this dream is.

Judicial Appointments

No "revolution" can be expected from judicial appointments for two reasons. First, "conservative" judges do not in practice behave much differently from "liberal" judges. Consider the track records of all the appointments of Nixon, Ford, and Reagan. Consider especially what happened to Justice Blackmun, who is only a more extreme example of what happens to all federal judges. Blackmun began as one of the most traditionalist justices, but soon won prestige and acceptance from the Washington elite by moving into the Court's "liberal" wing. The reason conservative justices do not behave much differently is that they are all educated in the same law schools and tend to defer to the university, journalism, and law school elites which are so influential in our public life. Lawyers are trained to respect that which is respectable. Hopefully, that is the law. But today it is the "law" in the Alice in Wonderland sense that it has come to be understood in the law schools and the courts, where "constitutional law" is typically studied with little reference to the Constitution.

Second, judicial appointments will not stop congressional imperialism because the great power of the federal judiciary comes from Congress itself. This becomes apparent every time Congress truly disagrees with the Court. The legislative veto was declared unconstitutional in *I.N.S. v. Chadha* (1983). Yet both the executive and legislative branches continue to respect numerous other laws with legislative veto provisions. Even more blatant was the response of Congress to the *Grove City* case. In that case the Court ruled that simply because one part of a private institution receives federal money (such as students in a private school who receive federally guaranteed loans), it does not mean that the entire institution must meet the panoply of federal affirmative action requirements. In 1988 an indignant Congress repealed that ruling in its "Civil Rights Restoration Act."

The problem of the courts will be solved when Congress is forced to rule through lawmaking. If Congress has had to pay a price for its administrative supremacy and guaranteed reelection, it has been to give the courts plenary power to decide the very policy questions that lawmaking properly requires. Congress has broad constitutional power over courts under Article III. Moreover, courts are dependent on a sense of legitimacy among the people and their leaders. Thus, if Congress changes, the Supreme Court, and the fashionable opinions currently embodied in its rulings, will shift to reflect the changes in its base of support.

Line Item Veto

Another much-discussed proposal is a constitutional amendment giving the president a line-item veto. No doubt such a provision would help, but it alone would not change the system. The problem is not just that Congress spends too much money on pet projects. It goes deeper: Congress not only wants to control the details of appropriations, but all other aspects of executive implementation as well. The line-item veto will not touch the full scope of congressional encroachment.

Parliamentary Government

Finally, the recent proposals of the Committee on the Constitutional System rightly recognize that today's antagonism between president and Congress is a problem. Their proposed solution, however, is a series of constitutional amendments that would move our system closer to a parliamentary government. It would allow members of Congress to serve in the executive branch, as in Britain, and it would change election dates to encourage simultaneous voting for presidential and congressional candidates.

These proposals, if implemented, would likely worsen our predicament. Under the proposals, the president would still be elected by the people, not by Congress. But Congress would have even greater executive power and yet still be without executive accountability. This would create an unworkable system half way between a true parliamentary government—in which the representative body is responsible to the people for electing the chief executive—and true separation of powers, in which the lawmaking body is deliberately kept out of the executive branch.

THE CONSTITUTIONAL SOLUTION

Much simpler and better than these several proposals would be to revive our Constitution from its present distortion by restoring the proper constitutional roles of the three branches of government. Let the primary work of Congress be to make laws and appropriations; of the executive, to administer them and to conduct the foreign policy of the nation; and of the judiciary, to judge the rights of individuals in cases at law.

Self-government and the preservation of individual rights are the twin offspring of our ancient principle that all men are created equal. Both are at risk in today's constitutional crisis. If the government, especially the president, acts as it should, the crisis will be resolved in favor of constitutionalism restored.

Notes

1. Quoted in John Wettergreen, "Constitutional Problems of American Bureaucracy in *I.N.S.* v. *Chadha*," 1987, mimeographed, p. 29. The reference to the 1972 CPSC legislation is on p. 25.

2. James Madison, *Federalist* nos. 48-51 (quoted phrases in no. 51).

3. Alexander Hamilton, *Federalist* no. 71.

4. *Federalist* no. 57.

5. Angelo Codevilla, response to critics, *Commentary*, vol. 85, January 1988, p. 7.

7. Codevilla's subject was the Strategic Defense Initiative, which prestige scientists today also generally oppose.

6. *Federalist* nos. 68 and 73.

7. See the remark of Rep. Whitten quoted in Chapter 5, above.

8. *Democracy in America* (Garden City: Doubleday Anchor, 1969), pp. 690-95.

9. *Federalist* no. 71.

10. John Wettergreen, "Demography of 1984's National Majorities," in *The 1984 Election and the Future of American Politics*, ed. Peter W. Schramm and Dennis J. Mahoney (Durham: Carolina Academic Press and The Claremont Institute, 1987). See also Wettergreen's essay above, Chapter 3.

11. *Federalist* no. 51.

14. Comes the Revolution

GABRIEL PROSSER

This chapter starts from the position that there is a dichotomy between the dominant culture that prevails in the nation and the culture that prevails among opinion elites. Some of the dividing issues have already been discussed in earlier chapters. Here the author argues that the president has to make the cultural differences explicit, through confrontation with Congress. Until these issues are settled, it is Congress that will be regarded as illegitimate.

Although sharply written, this is not a partisan chapter. The implication of the argument is that the importance of policy differences in American society must be understood and articulated. They are not simple differences over means, but fundamental differences over the ends of government and society. These differences have to be made explicit and presented to the people openly, so that they can be decided in accordance with democratic government.

To demonstrate the current imbalance of power between the president and the Congress, one need only recall President Reagan's last State of the Union address. It was memorable for its gimmicks, not for its content, and for good reason. The policy content of the annual presidential message has become relatively insignificant. What matters is the overall image of presidential leadership on the television screens of the nation. And so, Americans remember the way Mr. Reagan provoked cheers by hefting those massive legislative documents, implicitly mocking the Congress for doing business in such a shabby way, and threatening to veto any future continuing resolutions that thwarted his ability to control federal spending. The media loved it. The viewing audience enjoyed the good theater. The president appeared decisive and in charge. He clearly had the upper hand over Congress—for a few days. Then things settled back into their normal pattern, like a beach reforming its customary lines after a brief squall. Let the presidency have its hour in the sun, or klieg lights; the remainder of the day, and the year, belongs to the bosses of the imperial Congress.

Even the most dramatic State of the Union speech—or equivalent public relations ventures at other times during the year—produces only a momentary surge in presidential popularity, and even that is not translated into increased presidential power *vis-à-vis* Congress. And so a president who was reputed to be a strong leader and unusually persuasive in dealing with Capitol Hill was reduced, in his most important appearances before the Congress, to gimmicks, stunts, and gestures. He would arouse guaranteed ovations by talking about the accomplishments of real-life heroes and heroines invited to sit with the First Family in the balcony. Good theater, good TV shots, sometimes bringing tears to the eyes, sometimes bringing Congress to its feet, it enabled the president to bask in the reflected adulation of those "average Americans" he so much liked to salute.

Our purpose here is not to deprecate public relations gimmicks. They have their place. Indeed, the modern presidency is built upon them, given its limited base of constitutional power. The case can be made that the Reagan Administration should have used them more often, but more to the point of rallying the people against its congressional foes. Grandstanding is not bad, as long as it facilitates, rather than substitutes for, fundamental changes in the power equation between the White House and the Capitol.

A REVOLUTIONARY APPROACH

This is the first lesson to be learned by those who would reformulate that equation: There is no brass ring, no magic charm, no quick trick that will set things right. For the last eight years, conservatives in particular have sought the political equivalent of the philosopher's stone, some maneuver that would not only turn the tide but keep it forever at ebb: a presidential pledge to veto the continuing resolution that, by substituting for the various appropriations bills, rolls so much government spending into a single take-it-or-leave-it proposition; or letters to the president signed by at least one-third of the Senate or House to give him assurance that certain of his vetoes could not be overridden; or a dramatic presidential address to the nation to force members to support aid to the freedom fighters in Nicaragua. All these were important. They should have been used more often. But even all together, they could not begin to redress the imbalance of power between president and legislature.

That will not be done without a radically different approach to government, not just on the part of a handful of White House aides, but by their boss. Without total presidential commitment, it would be a waste of time. The next president must determine to change the way business is done in official Washington, not just to do it more successfully. The goal must be not to win more often within the current system, but to force the emergence of a better system through sustained conflict. The status quo is rigged against the presidency, as unfair as a sidewalk scam. It's simple: those who play by its rules will lose.

Needless to say, this is not what a new president usually is told. The men and women who cluster around a president-elect are typically caught up with the minutiae of how the system works at the time. It is not their mission to see beyond the limits of the way things have always been done. It will take an extraordinary president-elect to break out of that pattern. It will require someone immune to the petty rewards which the status quo offers to presidential collaborators. But it should not be beyond our faith in the American political system to generate, a chief executive sufficiently purposeful to apply to himself the advice of Faulkner:

> Refuse to bear it. Not for kudos and not for cash, your picture in the paper nor money in the bank. Just refuse to bear it.

STEP ONE: DENY LEGITIMACY

First, the new president must deny legitimacy to his congressional opponents and to the systems and structures which they control. That does not mean refusing to recognize the authority of a duly elected Congress, but taking great pains to send one consistent message to the American people concerning the president's adversaries. This will be beyond the comprehension of any executive or advisers who crave acceptance and legitimacy themselves. Only those who are personally sure of their place in history dare to challenge the places of others therein.

Every Decision Counts

Challenging the legitimacy of the imperial Congress involves excruciating detail. With whom will the new president meet, dine, be photographed? Each appointment is a signal. It affirms or repudiates the role of those with whom the president deals. If he meets with a leader of the congressional opposition, will he be televised laughing, trading jokes, engaging in all the staged interaction which is commonplace today? How, then, a few months later, will he convince the American people that his joshing buddy is betraying U.S. interests somewhere in the world? If, for the sake of a public relations gesture, he meets cordially with congressional leaders on the budget deficit and stands with them before the cameras in a display of unity, how will he rally the taxpayers the next week against the taxing exactions of those same leaders?

Such shortcomings must be avoided by any president who hopes to play a stronger hand against his congressional tormentors. It will be necessary, therefore, to pay close attention to seemingly trivial details: the order in which the new president meets with public officials, whether he visits certain congressional pressure groups, whether his meetings are televised and what reports are leaked to the press. All of this will send the most important signal of his administration: conciliation or confrontation.

Isolating the Opposition

Strong leadership is really at the heart of the matter. American politics has changed radically in the last quarter-century. The old truism no longer applies. Americans are not all united in wanting what's best for the country. We are not all in basic agreement about the value of liberty, the worth of the individual, the sanctity of the family, and the evils of Leninism (much less Marxism). Tragically, not all of us believe in the Constitution. A significant part of Congress scorns freedom as it has always been understood in this country and will do almost anything—steal an Indiana seat in the House of Representatives, trample the Constitution to make the District of Columbia a state, abet the gerrymander that deprives Californians of accurate representation in Congress—to bolster its power. A strong leader can use his office to rally his own congressional troops for the fights ahead. Others, unfocused or unwilling to use power for policy goals, pretend those fights can be settled amicably and thereby guarantee that they will lose.

STEP TWO: A MASTER IN HIS OWN HOUSE

Can a new president afford to take a conciliatory approach to adversaries? Only if the new administration is internally consistant and firmly in control of its key personnel. To effectively deny legitimacy to those who no longer deserve it, a president must control his own administration. This is the second step for a new chief executive who means to restore the presidency against the imperial Congress. It sounds so elementary that we probably take it for granted. As the last eight years have shown, that is a dangerous mistake. Before a president can alter the power equation with Congress, he must first be master of his own house. Otherwise, he will be caught between the pincers of the Hill on one hand and his own appointees on the other.

Personnel: Managers or Foot Soldiers?

Betrayal, discordance, and contravening purposes within any administration are self-inflicted wounds upon the presidency. The Reagan Administration's fixation upon management, rather than policy and ideas, had its natural consequences: most senior positions in government were filled with managers. But managers are not necessarily the best choice for shock troops. Under relentless attacks by segments of Congress, managers cooperate rather than defy. When they see their seniors—members of the Cabinet for example—trading with the opposition, they emulate them. They tend to respect a status quo, any status quo. And they assume the legitimacy of institutions and systems while keeping their distance from those who would topple or radically transform the apparatus. After all, that is what sound management is all about. But managing the status quo is not what a revolution is about. When congressional committees summoned before them the managerial class placed into high office by presidential personnel, most of the president's appointees behaved true to form. They were deferential to authority (even when it was an authority hostile to the presidency), subservient to bullies, and eager to please those who held the pursestrings.

If the next chief executive wants to avoid the same fate, he must staff his administration—and not just the White House, but the departments and agencies down to at least the Deputy Assistant Secretary level—with people who know how to stand up to Congress in policy, in speech, in correspondence, in testimony, at the polls, and, if necessary, in court.

Loyalty Is a Two-Way Street

It must be said that loyalty works both ways. If the front-line troops of an administration suspect that, once wounded, they will be thrown to the wolves, they will make sure they do not get bloodied in the first place. In the Reagan Administration, presidential loyalty has been personal, not political or ideological. The president has stood by certain old friends or retainers despite ample reason to walk away from them. On the other hand, employees or nominees not part of the president's personal circle have been on their own when attacked by Congress. As such, friend and foe alike learn the lesson. Over the long run, no president will have any greater loyalty from his subordinates than he has demonstrated to them—or to their common cause—in times of trouble.

To restate the proposition: It is imperative that a new president secure his base in the executive branch. Sound personnel choices are only the start of that procedure. All administrations start out somewhat centralized and degenerate toward government by Cabinet. (The Reagan Administration began by extolling Cabinet control and then carried it to extremes.) That is an inevitable tendency, but not an inexorable result. There should be a stick to every carrot, in this case, a well-exercised firing power which keeps the entire executive branch on guard, either eager to please the White House or fearful of angering it. Nothing takes the place of a few deserved dismissals for ensuring everything from Cabinet obedience to promptly returned phone calls from Assistant Secretaries, from supportive departmental testimony on the Hill to speedy bureau acquiescence in budget proposals.

In opposite circumstances, almost all of an administration's energy is consumed by internal strife, jurisdictional disputes, policy disagreements, and most of all, budget battles. The time, personnel, and resources that should be directed against Congress on budget issues are wasted in domestic disagreement. By the time an administration agrees upon its position, it stands fractured and anemic before its determined opponents.

STEP THREE: LEAD THE PARTY

The third measure necessary for reasserting executive authority is to solidify the president's base within his own party in Congress and beyond. That can mean taking formidable chances to secure party leadership on the Hill, that if not loyal, is at least in harmony with the president's program. It means leveraging the influence and prestige of the presidency to command more support from the key congressional institutions of the party. The president, for example, upon whose personal appearances and endorsements individual members and House and Senate campaign committees depend for much of their fund-raising, should make his participation in their survival dependent upon adherence to his agenda. He should absolutely cut off from any executive branch assistance the one or two members of his party who are most antagonistic toward his policies. Only then will other members take seriously his insistence upon conformity.

This all leads toward the creation of a *real* political party: an institution functioning to gain and wield power, with a common identity and mechanisms for enforcing its leader's policy on key issues. That is difficult to achieve, but not impossible. A few simple steps from a determined president would take his party a long way in the right direction. We have already mentioned the stigmatizing of the few most offensive congressional members of his party and the conditioning of presidential fund-raising and campaigning upon loyalty of the members involved. Beyond that, an essential is appointing as party chairman a loyal activist whose tenure depends upon all-out deployment of party resources and energizing the total party apparatus to support the president in major battles.

Discipline and Trust

As Franklin Roosevelt discovered in 1938 when he attempted to purge Senators Millard Tydings and Walter George, it isn't easy for even a dynamic chief executive to impose discipline upon his party in Congress. But even in losing, FDR strengthened his hand in party affairs over the long run. That is a lesson worth pondering by those who have rightly concluded that the presidency will remain weak until its occupant commands party loyalty on the Hill.

In this regard too, it must be noted that loyalty endures only when it is mutual. A president who cracks deals with leaders of the opposition party behind the backs or over the bodies of his own troops wins short-term victories at the price of long-term impotence. Examples can be found in the Reagan Administration's willingness to ally itself with congressional Democrats to secure tax increases (TEFRA in 1982 and DEFRA in 1983) or to increase foreign aid. After that, the president never regained what he had had with at least a part of his party in Congress: the trust, the sense of common purpose, and the surety that, overall, they were marching to the same drummer toward a shared goal. Mr. Reagan began his term with something rare for a new president, his own team in Congress, especially in the House, with a remarkable sense of loyalty to him. Within two years, that was shattered.

One might ask how it could have been otherwise. After all,

certain officials of the Reagan Administration demanded those higher taxes and expansions in budgets. The president was caught between them and his supporters on the Hill. What was he to do? To answer that, we need only emphasize that putting the executive branch in order must come before the search for congressional loyalty. Failure to do the former ensures failure in the latter. A president who is not master of his own house will never secure his base in the Congress and in the broader party structure. And a president without that congressional base will rather rapidly become marginal, or even irrelevant, in setting the direction of national policy.

STEP FOUR: ENERGIZE THE PUBLIC

A fourth ingredient in restoring the presidency and curbing the imperial Congress is the involvement of the American people. The tragic fact is that the American people generally do not care about the procedings on Capitol Hill, perhaps because they know so little about them. Ironically, they laugh at jokes about Congress, but reelect incumbents at a rate which virtually makes elections unnecessary. Every biennium, only a dozen seats in the House are seriously up for grabs; a change of six or eight Senate seats would be big news. One wonders what it would take to provoke the voters enough to effect significant changes in the status quo. Matters are surely not helped by a news media that reports only the most sensational events on Capitol Hill. (And some that should be sensational, like the extraordinary tax hike imposed against the elderly to finance the aptly named catastrophic health care bill, are not adequately explained until they become *faits accomplis*.)

Informing the People

It is simply impossible for the average citizen to be come informed about congressional proceedings from press and network television coverage that often is so distorted as to be laughable to the participants in the events reported. Hill staffers and members are accustomed to reading stories in major papers by famous journalists, which bear only the most fanciful resemblance to what actually transpired before their eyes on the House or Senate floor the previous day. It is interesting, though not productive, to speculate about the reasons for this pattern. Perhaps because the work of Congress lacks the glamor of the presidency, it generates dull or shoddy reportage. Perhaps it is just too easy for reporters settled in the press galleries to make the same old calls to the same old contacts, parroting a party line out of sloth rather than ideology. Whatever the reasons, a president cannot rely upon the regular news media to keep the public informed about his battles with the Congress.

He must do the informing, any way he can; and he must do it constantly, not merely in the few days before a crucial vote in Congress. A few speeches, no matter how stirring, are not enough. A president who wants to make headway against the establishment on Capitol Hill must convince a rather large portion of the American public that they have a long-term vital interest in the outcome of his battles with Congress. During the first six months of the Reagan Administration, the White House succeeded in doing that. Citizens who formerly had only the dimmest notion of the differences between legislators and executives were caught up in the dramatic events taking place in Washington. They got involved—if only to the extent of phoning their representatives with the message not to come home if they voted against the Reagan economic package—because someone made them believe they had a personal stake in what was transpiring.

Ordinary Citizens as Lobbyists

The liberal interest groups are almost always in a poised reaction mode. And that is the major reason their success is so disproportionate to their numbers. In normal times, members of Congress can expect to hear—or be visited by—superbly organized networks of advocates: grantsmen, program managers, state and local officials whose projects depend upon federal dollars, clergy avaricious to redistribute non-ecclesiastical wealth, "activists" whose grassroots crusades curiously depend upon largesse from the nation's capital. That is the routine state of affairs. What made the Reagan legislative victories of 1981 possible was the ability of the White House to drown out that routine with the larger and louder voice of taxpayers who for once believed their intervention could make a difference.

Unfortunately, the administration then went back to business as usual, failing to sustain public involvement in the battles that lay ahead. By the end of its first year, the Reagan presidency had learned to play the legislative game by its old rules, the ones rigged to assure victory for a liberal congressional majority. The president was never again able to rally the public.

Truth in Government

A future president—and by extension, all his appointees and the national party apparatus of which he is the head—must dailyhammer home to the public two simple messages: first, how they will benefit—how their values will be embodied in public policy—if the president wins his battles; and second, how they are already losing, and will bear even worse burdens, at the hands of the president's opponents.

That means getting much more specific than most presidents are willing to be. He has to do more than run against "the Congress," as a generic institution. He has to tell victims of muggings and rapes that Congressmen X, Y, and Z, who have bottled up anticrime bills in their subcommittee, are partially responsible for those assaults because they value the rights of criminals more than the rights of victims. He must tell outraged parents that Senator W, who thwarts all efforts to clean up federal family planning programs, is personally responsible for federal grantees' giving contraceptives to their children without their knowledge and consent. He must tell the embittered teachers, workers, and students who are denied equal opportunity by racist affirmative action schemes that these particular senators stole their job, their promotion, or their scholarship. And he must tell the families who stretch their budgets every month to make ends meet that these particular congressmen killed off a work requirement for welfare recipients. If Senator V has secured a public subsidy for the parking garage at Washington's opulent Kennedy Center for the Performing Arts, the taxpayers should know.

But this, of course, is petty politics. Official Washington will scoff and scorn. Presidents should concentrate on cosmic matters and transcendent issues. They do, and that's why they have so little power *vis-à-vis* the imperial Congress. If "Martin, Barton, and Fish" were proper targets for FDR, then Congressmen X, Y, and Z, and Senator V, should be fitting targets for the next president.

This is not demagoguery. It is truth in government. It is accountability. To use a much older phrase, it is bringing deeds of darkness into the light. On the rare occasions when that has been done in recent years—the Senate battle over ratification of the Panama Canal treaty is the best case in point; certain pay-raise votes are other instances—members of Congress have had to pay a significant price for transgressing their constituents' wishes. The Reagan Administration may have occasionally profited from such exposure, but it has not generated and directed it, much to its eventual debility.

Keeping the Public Interested

To break the Hill's liberal imperium, a president simply must have a vocal public on his side, not for a month or so, but throughout his term. But how can that level of interest be sustained? The public is easily bored by government, or, to be precise, by most of the people in government. Critical votes come rarely. The first 100 days are over in a flash. Excitement wanes. Washington's internecine snapping takes a back seat to summer vacations and whether the kids need braces. A president must therefore keep the pot boiling in order to keep his grassroots troops in the field. He must devise ways to expose legislative tricks (like the amazing parliamentary way, in April 1979, that Majority Leader Robert Byrd thwarted passage of legislation to restore school prayer by limiting the jurisdiction of the federal courts, a feat which the news media never really explained to the public). He must be ready to expose Hill scandals and make the most of them; and that definitely includes openly directing federal prosecutors to prosecuted crooked congressmen. (The Reagan Administration's only venture in this regard was its prosecution of Congressman George Hansen, an Idaho Republican, jailed for technical violations of federal election laws.)

This does not, of course, include trumped-up charges or harassment. When a president, personally or through others in his administration, sets out to rally the public against certain members of Congress, his accusations must be accurate, and his indictments must be justified, both for the sake of his credibility and for the more important sake of justice. Nor is this the burden of only the executive branch. Imagine what could have been if the Republican majority controlling the newly constituted 97th Congress in January, 1981 had known how to handle its new power. If its leadership had learned any lessons from the Democrats' dominance of Congress for three decades, it would have immediately taken an accusatory, investigatory stance.

Learning to Lead

Practically every Republican senator in 1981 was a chairman of at least one subcommittee. Yet none of them held hearings on the scandals of the Carter Administration. None of them, for example, rehashed the Bert Lance affair. None of them subpoenaed Dr. Peter Bourne to talk about his involvement with illegal drug abuse and to find out what Jimmy Carter, or others in his administration or on the Hill, knew about it. And no Republican senators called for criminal investigations of the Carter-era officials, at the State Department and in the White House, who may have abetted drug smuggling by Panamanian officials. Was there any Carter appointee who sat squirming under high-intensity television lights as a senatorial committee picked the bones of his past memos and left his reputation in shreds?

Of course not. Republicans do not behave that way. They also do not retain a majority for long. If Mr. Reagan's Senate allies had made the most of their opportunity in 1981, if they had thrown the entire liberal establishment on the defensive with exposés of misconduct, waste, and duplicity by the Carter crowd, they, their president, and his legislative agenda might have fared far better in the elections of 1982 and thereafter.

The Pentagon budget is another example. Its excesses, overruns, and occasional thefts were blamed on the Reagan Administration every time Secretary Weinberger announced a problem had been found and was being corrected. The scandals, in fact, had been discovered and exposed by the Republicans. Most of those scandals were the debris of the Carter years, and earlier, and should have forever been branded that way at the outset of 1981.

The uncaring or incompetent officials of previous administrations should have been summoned before Senate panels to be confronted, on national television, with evidence of their offenses. Witnesses representing taxpayer groups could then have demanded personal restitution from those who allowed the boondoggles to occur. Casper Weinberger himself could have pointed accusatory fingers at those who had preceded him and thereby directed national ire where it belonged. Instead, Republicans in the Senate and in the administration let bygones be bygones. There were no villains, no crooks in the past. So when the DOD ripoffs were discovered, the incumbents were to blame. And America's defense budget still has not recovered from the public relations black eye it received during those early Reagan years, from the calculated campaign by the liberals to blame others for what they themselves had wrought. The administration could have taken similar steps to arouse public interest in its agenda and to make the American people understand that siding with the president over the long haul is in their vital interest. The Education Department could have exposed the social engineering fostered through Carter's grants for the revision of textbooks. The Justice Department could have made public all its internal paperwork concerning the liberals' assault on religious freedom in the attempted exclusion of a federal judge from an ERA case on the grounds of his Mormon affiliation. Some administration office should have reported on the amount of tax dollars illegally used by the Carter Administration to lobby for the ERA. The FBI should have been turned loose against the looting of Legal Services Corporation funds by radical political organizations. All this is to propose nothing more than aggressive pursuit of possible misdeeds, along the lines of Senator Inouye's inquiry concerning Oliver North.

These exercises in exposure are not ends in themselves. They serve to keep the public involved in the struggle between the presidency and the imperial Congress. For decades, all the exposure has been one-way, and so the public interest has leaned that way: against the executive. This has been one of the most effective tactics of the imperial Congress, or rather of its liberal members. It can not be countered by protestations of innocence from the executive. It must be met, indeed preempted, by actions in kind.

Invoking Democracy

There is another instrumentality by which the president's grassroots allies can be provoked into action against his opponents in the Congress. Several states have laws that provide for the recall of U.S. senators. Those laws were enacted during the Progressive era and were hailed for decades thereafter as major liberal reforms. One hears little of them lately. The idea of allowing voters to end a member's term by special referendum smacks too much of direct democracy. Legally, it is a controversial matter; for the Constitution, mute on the subject, specifies six-year terms for senators and two-year terms for representatives. Whether the people of a state can cut those terms short, even by processes duly enacted in their legislature or through state constitutional amendment, is not clear. What is clear is official Washington's bipartisan aversion to the entire subject. During the Senate debate on the Panama Canal treaty in 1978, one of the television news networks reported that treaty opponents were researching various state recall laws in order to launch recall drives against certain pro-treaty senators. The reaction of the nominal leader of the anti-treaty forces in the Senate was to condemn the idea, as if no senator should be punished for transgressing the overwhelming opinion of the folks back home. As it turned out, several of them were punished, in the elections of 1978 and 1980, in which twenty pro-treaty senators lost their seats (seven more retired). That lesson should not be lost on any future president determined to break the imperial Congress. His legal staff should update available research on state recall laws, and he should be prepared to foster such legislation in states where it might become useful to his supporters in the future.

It is imperative that the president keep these kinds of issues before the American public. Otherwise, public interest in his success will fade; and when the people are not looking, Congress will return to what it does best.

STEP FIVE: MASTER THE CONGRESSIONAL PROCESS

This brings us to the fifth measure by which a future president might reformulate the power equation between his office and Congress. He must turn the established processes of the legislature against it, in the same way certain oriental martial arts turn the force of an attacker against him. He should begin with the confirmation process.

Turning the Confirmation Process on Its Head

In the current system, the executive branch tries at all costs to avoid confrontation and controversy in congressional scrutiny of its nominees. Most appointees practically beg for confirmation (though there have been notable exceptions, some of whom were subsequently confirmed). Nominees for anything from an assistant secretary to Justice of the Supreme Court are usually in an apologetic mode for virtually anything that displeases a senator on the committee with jurisdiction over the nomination. And so male nominees abruptly resign from men's clubs to which they have belonged, without guilt, for many years. Behind the scenes, nominees whose past partisanship may offend a senatorial inquisitor are instructed, by White House officials, how to trim their sails and appear apologetic. Of course, some nominees need no such tutoring. They appear before the confirming committee ready to disavow not only their own political records, but the policies of the president as well. There must be a dozen different ways in which a nominee can signal committee members or staff, in public or in private conversations, that he or she will not take too seriously this or that controversial policy of the chief executive. Sometimes the disavowal is as simple as a firm pledge to obey every word of the law and to heed the (nonbinding) directives which members (and more often, congressional staff) put in unread committee reports on various bills.

Sometimes this distancing from the presidency is more overt, as in the case of Cabinet members who do not equivocate about their intention to run their own departments. The first and last rule of the confirmation process for nominees is to not rock the boat. The less that happens, the easier things are not only for the nominee but for the administration officials responsible for his or her confirmation. This may be acceptable for an administration allied with the bosses of the imperial Congress, but it is shortsighted for any president at loggerheads with them. Each of his nominations should be seen as an opportunity for the administration to make a point with the people. Each nominee should be a banner-carrier, thrusting the president's policies in the face of an unresponsive—and by implication, malfeasant—Congress. Such an approach turns the current system on its head. Instead of avoiding controversy, nominees should welcome it. (Or, at least, the president should welcome it on their behalf.) While appointees should be respectful, they should also defy intimidation. Their mission is not to get confirmed and appointed to a nice job but to use the public forum of the confirmation process to rally popular support for the president and to focus popular ire against his congressional foes.

A more radical departure from current procedures and attitudes cannot be imagined. The same, however, should hold true of the congressional oversight process. Committees and subcommittees of the House and Senate incessantly hold hearings at which administration officials are supposed to present the views, and defend the stewardship, of the executive branch. Most administration officials view these occasions as something between a nuisance and a peril. A misstatement can ruin a career, a careless remark can touch off a media firestorm. And so administration witnesses tend to rely upon carefully prepared texts, as bland as they are wordy. Even that precaution does not protect a witness whom a committee member is determined to excoriate or otherwise torment. That process is a bully's delight. Most victims are unprepared to fight back or, even if they are so inclined, forbidden to do so by the rules of the hearing or by their superiors, who do not wish to antagonize members. The pattern is so entrenched that one easily recalls the rare exceptions: Robert Bork's unavailing attempt to salvage truth in the environs of the Senate Judiciary Committee; Bill Bennett's insistence upon common sense from members committed to the sad status quo in education; Gary Bauer's polite defiance of the House Education Committee, none of whose members, he pointed out, had ever been a teacher.

Their performances did not set the norm, which was much closer to the conduct of Bennett's predecessor, Terrell Bell, who had a remarkable ability to explain presidential policy in ways that suggested his own opposition to it. Few administration officials were as consistently unreliable as he, but equally few saw a request to testify before a congressional committee as a golden opportunity to hoist the president's flag, bait his opponents, and call upon the American people to teach these guys a lesson.

All of which brings us back to an earlier point: the kind of men and women proposed by the Office of Presidential Personnel for jobs in the administration. Bennetts and Bauers are not a dime a dozen, but neither are they so rare that an administration should have as few of them as the executive branch does now. The success of any of these strategies for turning the procedures of Congress toward presidential interests will depend upon the president's proper staffing of his administration.

The Legislative Game: Playing All Four Quarters

Another congressional procedure which could be made to strengthen the presidency rather than enervate it is the tiresome legislative process itself, from committee consideration to floor action, to enactment or veto. All of that is fine as long as the president's proposals are advancing steadily. That situation, however, is rare. More likely, every step of the way diffuses or contravenes the point of an administration proposal.

In almost all cases, a president sits helplessly by as the legislative machinery chews up his initial bill and turns it into something quite different. That is the prerogative of a legislature, but it does not mean a president must acquiesce in its results. He can of course veto the bill, but by then it is often too late to contravene the congressional consensus developed during the legislative process or the public misperception engineered by his opponents. Or more likely, he can claim a dubious victory, putting the best front on things. A classic example is the catastrophic health insurance bill of the 100th Congress, a presidential proposal made worse and worse at every legislative step but nonetheless signed by Mr. Reagan, who could not bring himself to repudiate his own progeny, no matter what Congress had made of it.

To effectively play the legislative game, a future president must understand that it is won or lost at every scrimmage line—subcommittee, committee, floor amendments—not just at the official goal line of final passage. It is folly to allow the opposition to charge along the field with relatively little opposition and then attempt to tackle them a few feet from the goal line. And they must face counterattack—not just defense—at every juncture. Though this sounds obvious, it is unusual for an administration to play the game that way. More frequently, the executive branch will hope its problems just go away. Perhaps things will stall in subcommittee. Perhaps the bill will be improved in full committee. Maybe a floor amendment or two will take care of defective legislation. Or the conference committee between Senate and House may iron out things to the president's liking. But such is a loser's philosophy. It puts the White House perpetually on the defensive, always trying to stop the inevitable at the last possible moment, when the president has only one tactic left: the veto, which by now is far less likely to be employed because so much of Congress, including members of the president's own party, will by then have committed against his position.

In fairness, let us state the opposing view, which would be advanced by many officials within the current and previous administrations. The White House cannot handle all legislation. Most of it must be delegated to the departments and agencies. Thus it is unrealistic to expect the president to take as much interest in, or say as much about, a subcommittee's handiwork as he does about final passage of a major piece of legislation. A president's legislative credibility moreover, cannot be stretched too thin. His veto threats must be reserved for the most important matters. And, he needs to retain flexibility and room for compromise on most matters. Otherwise, he will be in lone disagreement with most of what the Congress enacts. In short, the present system is the best the presidency can do.

Much of that is true, but it does not excuse a woeful lack of

White House involvement in and direction of administration activities at every level of legislative business. Perhaps the distinction can be clarified by an example: the Grove City fight of the last two congresses which culminated, early in 1988, with the overriding of the presidential veto of one of the most radical bills to come to a vote in decades. How, one needs to ask, could matters have gotten that far? Why wasn't a stake driven through the heart of this legislative monster earlier in its gestation? To give credit where due, the Reagan Administration consistently opposed it, year after year. Various departmental officials testified against it, wrote letters to members, and strategized. That helped members opposed to the bill to stave off its enactment for quite some time.

In the end, however, it all availed nothing. For as soon as the liberal establishment decided the time was ripe—that is, public support for Mr. Reagan had slipped and his administration was being pecked apart by scandal and dissension—it forced the bill to final passage and overrode his veto. Could things have been different? Probably, if for the last several years the administration had fought the Grove City battle publicly, not in the halls of Congress but in the churches, fraternity halls, and small businesses of America. If, that is to say, the president had excoriated the bill's sponsors at every step of its legislative advance; if he had let its Republican backers—and more important, their state party members—know of his anger at their defection; if administration officials had used the hearing process to create a ruckus that the public would notice, by making accusations, and hurling epithets if need be, to accurately convince the American people that their liberties were being imperiled by the legislation under review.

All of which is considered terribly bad form. But it's darn good politics, and it gives the president a fighting chance to impose his will upon a Congress in which he does not command an automatic majority. No wonder this approach by the executive is an anathema to liberal leaders on Capitol Hill.

Winning the Fourth Quarter

Nothing pertaining to Congress is quite as simple as described here. There will always be exceptions and complications. But they do not invalidate the general principle: The presidency must be more active, involved, combative, aggressive, accusatory, rambunctious, disruptive, and demanding at every step of the legislative process in order to get the public's attention and command the public's support well ahead of the ultimate showdowns with Congress on the floor of House and Senate upon final passage or veto votes.

Showmanship is essential to the success of this approach. Which of President Reagan's vetoes does the public remember? No one sees a veto and practically no one reads a veto message, which may be summarized in a single sentence by the news media. But for important bill signings, a savvy White House staff arranges elaborate displays for publicity, whether Rose Garden extravaganzas or Oval Office pomp. It provides a photo opportunity to let the public know something significant has happened, something that just might touch their lives or affect their interests. Why not the same, or even more intense, treatment of vetoes? We will never know if it would have made a difference if Reagan had signed the veto of the Grove City bill before a huge convention of religious groups, upon whose ecclesiastical affairs the bill encroaches. We will not know if Reagan's veto of the highway bill, the override of which was one of his worst defeats in the 100th Congress, would have been sustained if the veto had been signed and waved about for the cameras at a large gathering of taxpayer groups, who presumably would have then understood their vested interest in pressuring members to uphold the veto. These and similar events were unthinkable in the Reagan Administration, as if a veto were a private matter between president and Congress. Instead, a veto should be made the political equivalent of a soccer goal before a jammed stadium, something that sets popular pulses to thumping, instills fervor in the president's supporters, and rallies the energized public to support him in the congressional showdown.

There is little need for further examples of this broad approach. If a future president is serious about strengthening the presidency, he has no alternative but to find—and in some cases, invent—ways in which the public, or at least that portion which may see its interests dependent upon his success, is drawn into the legislative process from start to finish. If that breaks new ground, better to shatter precedent than to have yet another presidency submit to the modern-day imperialism of Congress.

STEP SIX: BEGIN ON DAY ONE

All of this leads us to a sixth and, for now, final step a president-elect should consider in deciding whether he wants to seriously undertake the restoration of a power balance between executive and legislature. That is to effect, in the first weeks of his administration, a radically different perception of the presidency. If he is to convince the public that there will be no more business as usual, then he must act accordingly. A future president will never have a better opportunity to challenge the imperial Congress than at his inaugural, standing as it were at the entrance to the congressional lair with the eyes of the world upon him. Then and there, not in later State of the Union addresses, he must marshal his forces and lay down the law.

This must be followed, within days, by a series of dramatic actions, declarations, or initiatives which make clear to the public that indeed a dramatic change has already occurred. They must understand that things are going to be different, and different in a way that advances their interests. For example, the White House could announce it no longer accepts the constitutionality of the curious procedure by which Congress limits presidential nomination of judges in the District of Columbia and thereby secures lenient judges who perpetuate the District's extraordinary rates of crime and drug abuse. The president might assert, as some students of the subject have recently claimed, that he already has the line-item veto authority which President Reagan had begged Congress to grant him. Far-reaching executive orders must give various constituencies throughout the country the immediate conviction that this president, for a change, looks out for them. The nation as a whole needs to be jarred by this newcomer's determination to protect the country's vital interests, perhaps by ordering, on national security grounds, the immediate expulsion of dangerous aliens; or perhaps by using the National Guard temporarily in certain areas controlled by drug terrorists.

There is no reason a new president cannot visit the scene of a brutal robbery, to demand the death penalty for vicious criminals; no reason why he cannot march with pro-lifers down Pennsylvania Avenue; no reason why he cannot lead students in "illegal" prayer in a public elementary school; no reason why he cannot reaffirm resistance to all racism by revoking the federal affirmative action programs that have become *de facto* quota systems. Mr. Reagan was superb at the positive side of public relations gimmicks, associating himself with happy occasions. He will surely be remembered in history as one of our most pleasant presidents. If his successor wishes more than that, he must be as adept in using the negative side of public occasions, to focus popular grievances against the Congress and to put himself forward as the solution Americans need.

In short, he must become the tribune of the people. This is the only role that will allow him to effectively counter the enormous institutional clout of Congress. It was the role Andrew Jackson, correctly or not, assumed for himself, thereby drawing such vilification and outrage as would frighten most modern presidents. He did survive it, however, and his place in the history of the presidency might tempt a future chief executive to be as daring.

That should not be too much to ask of anyone who aspires to the presidency. How long we will have to wait is an open question.

15. Recommendations

The authors of this volume paint a relatively gloomy picture of the current state of affairs. They uniformly identify the separation of powers as a critical element of the U.S. constitutional system, and emphasize the importance of reinvigorating it.

Most of them make recommendations, either implicitly or explicitly. Some of those recommendations are extracted here for convenient reference. As noted in the text, many of the recommendations relate to the executive branch, but there are nearly as many for Congress. Some are broadly philosophical; others are quite practical. Some are long-term; others can be accomplished at once. Some can be accomplished unilaterally; others will require cooperation between branches of government. Finally, we should note that some of the recommendations are contradictory. It is one measure of the health of our polity that observers differ on what needs to be done. Given the seriousness of the crisis in the separation of powers, we welcome the views of all those who understand the peril.

EXECUTIVE BRANCH RECOMMENDATIONS

The next president's first order of business is to recognize the philosophical case for the separation of powers, and his constitutional supremacy in the area of foreign policy. This philosophical position must pervade the entire executive branch so that it is sensitive to encroachments, and prepared to repel them. As Chapter 14 makes plain, the appointees of the next president have to understand that they are not being brought in to "manage" their departments. Though there is nothing wrong with managerial competence, Presidential appointees' primary task is to serve as foot soldiers in the battle to carry out the President's agenda.

Foreign Policy

While the erosion of the separation of powers has proceeded in both the foreign and domestic policy arenas, the need for redress in foreign policy appears to be the first priority, for two reasons: First, foreign policy has traditionally been regarded as an executive branch function; and second, the primary obligation of a sovereign state is to protect itself. While it has been asserted that Congress can conduct a foreign policy, there is no empirical evidence to support the assertion. Accordingly, the president must reassert his supremacy in this area. **The president has to resist encroachment by members of Congress on his defense and foreign policy responsibilities** (see Chapter 4). **Publicity is one way; action under the Logan Act is another.** More specifically, **the president should announce his intention to ignore the Byrd Amendment to the INF Treaty and go out of his way to find an occasion to challenge it.** At the same time, **the president should repudiate the "two-treaty" theory advanced by the Justice Department Office of Legal Counsel and the White House Counsel during the INF debate.**

The president should immediately seek repeal of the War Powers Act. In the meantime, it should be ignored as an unconstitutional infringement on executive authority.

Domestic Policy

In domestic policy, the primary requirement, emphasized by many of our authors, is the need to maintain control over the policy formulations of cabinet and subcabinet officers. **The president should impose discipline on his executive branch officers by firing them for insubordination.** But discipline is not obtained only by sticks. The president has a considerable number of carrots. **The president should use the rewards available within the executive departments to honor those members of the permanent bureaucracy who are diligent in following his program.**

Executive-Congressional Relations

A big part of the problem is the relative permanence of Congress as against the fleeting tenure of executive branch political appointees (see Chapter 5). The resulting temptation of executive branch officials to cater to members of Congress has to be fought. Here are two suggestions: **The president should publicize the efforts of members of Congress to influence executive branch decisions. He should also use the mechanism of his national party to influence Congress and impose some measure of discipline on the members of his own party** (see Chapter 14).

To help in the task of maintaining influence in Congress, **the vice-president should spend a great deal of time performing his constitutional function as President of the Senate. He should act as a forceful advocate for the president's program, not merely as a "liaison" to Congress.**

The president must be involved at every stage of the legislative process, either personally or through political appointees who share his program. He should not wait until the legislative pie is baked to ask for a change in flavor (see Chapter 14).

In defending his executive establishment against congressional encroachment, **the president should ignore, or challenge directly, some detail of micromanagement of an executive department** (see Chapters 4 and 5). There are sticks available for use against Congress, too. **The president should seek inclusion of members of Congress and their staffs under the Ethics in Government Act** (see Chapter 10).

Independent Agencies

As Nolan Clark demonstrates in Chapter 11, one important aspect of the erosion of executive power is the proliferation of "independent" agencies performing administrative functions but not accountable to the president. **The president should assert control over the independent agencies by firing all commissioners** (and reappointing them immediately to an "acting" capacity to maintain continuity). Alternatively, **he should provide explicit policy direction to selected commissions and fire commissioners who resist this policy direction.**

Structural Reforms

There are a number of structural problems that need to be addressed. Some deal with the concrete power and prestige of the executive office, some with the relationships between Congress and the executive. On the first of these fronts, **the president should seek repeal of the constitutional amendment limiting a president to two terms.** It violates the people's right to the president of their choice, and weakens the institution of the presidency.

On the second front, **the president should veto any continuing resolution that includes more than one appropriations bill,** and **if Congress does submit omnibus spending bills containing more than one appropriations bill, the president should assert his authority to veto individual titles of such a bill. Any provision of a bill which has been previously presented to the president and vetoed should be stripped from the bill and considered null and void.**

The Appointive Power

The presidency is on the verge of losing control over its own appointment process, in particular, the appointment of federal judges. Accordingly, **the next president should decline to submit names of potential judicial nominees to the American Bar Association, and should ignore any recommendations the ABA makes.** In an even more fundamental challenge to the organized bar, **the president should instruct the Secretary of Education to withdraw from the American Bar Association the right to accredit law schools.**

In the meantime, **the president should use his power to ap-**

point judges during congressional recesses and his power to make "temporary," acting appointments to force action by Congress on his judicial and executive branch nominees. In particular, the Senate Judiciary Committee's "screening committee" for judicial nominees should be publicly attacked until it is abandoned (see Chapter 12).

The Judiciary

It is important to note that the three branches of government are coequal. While deference is due to a coequal branch, submission to it is not (see Chapter 13, footnote 9). That is especially true with respect to the least democratic of American institutions, the federal court system. **The president should remember that he has just as sacred an obligation to uphold the Constitution as does the Supreme Court, and he should find many occasions to demonstrate, publicly, his disagreement with Court decisions in areas where judicial activism has distorted the meaning of the Constitution.**

The president should maintain the position (shared by every president who has considered the question) that the Independent Counsel Law is unconstitutional. He should refuse to cooperate with this gross deformation of our legal system. He should also be prepared to defend the doctrine of executive privilege against both court and Congress. **The president should reassert the doctrine of executive privilege, and defend it with all his powers, even against adverse court decisions.**

Public Relations and the "Bully Pulpit"

Particularly in this day and age, presidents have an unparalleled opportunity to take their policy case directly to the people. **The president should be ready to use the public relations resources and the power of administrative hearings to generate and consolidate public opinion behind his policy positions.**

The president should use the confirmation hearing process as a way of selling his program on Capitol Hill and to the public. Nominees should be instructed to follow the adminis-

tration's position, and not to yield to the confrontation they will receive from Congress. The president must be willing to stand behind his employees who demonstrate such loyalty, and be willing to fire those who do not.

The president and his top appointees should be active in selling their philosophical position both to the general public and to the opinion elites in academia, the media, and the professional organizations. Philosophical principles must be tied to concrete examples at every opportunity.

Finally, the president should help create and legitimize new centers of authority and information, using the powers of his office to bestow prestige upon experts who may disagree with the prevailing views of the Washington establishment (see Chapter 13).

LEGISLATIVE BRANCH RECOMMENDATIONS

Most of the recommendations for Congress involve internal reform of operating procedures. While it may be unrealistic to expect Congress to reform itself, the list of suggestions is impressive, and could be expanded substantially, just from criticisms levelled by the members themselves.

The Budget Process

Clearly the heart of the legislative process today is the development of the federal budget. We may argue about whether that is a healthy development or not, because it was not always so. As long as it is, however, there are steps Congress must take to assure that the budget *process* does not drive budget *policy*. Specifically, **Congress should refrain from omnibus continuing resolutions, and should enroll appropriations bills separately for presentation to the president for his signature or veto.** All this requires is self-discipline.

To enact other reforms changes in rules, laws, or even the Constitution will be required. For example, **the practice of waiving budget deadlines can be dealt with by requiring a su-**

permajority to accomplish it. That would help maintain the integrity of the budget process.

In addition, to ensure more permanent results, some of our authors maintain that **Congress should adopt a balanced budget amendment, and should give the president a line item veto** (see Chapter 6), though these proposals are not without their detractors, even among the conservative community (see Chapters 12 and 13).

Other recommendations for the budget process include the following:

• **Congress should adopt a "negative check-off" on rescissions recommended by the president. In other words, the rescissions of budget authority take effect unless Congress takes affirmative action to reject them** (see Chapter 6).

• **Budget resolutions adopted under the Budget Control Act should require the president's signature.**

• **Allocations of spending authority contained in the Budget resolutions should be binding on the appropriations process unless changed by a two-thirds vote.**

• **The "baseline," or "current services" budget concept should be abandoned** (see Chapters 4 and 6).

Another interesting possibility, not discussed by any of our authors, is to **tie spending programs to specific revenue sources,** so that trade-offs between taxes and programs would be made explicit.

The Committee System

There are reforms to the committee system needed to make Congress more accountable to the people, and to permit good administration of laws passed by Congress. On the first point, **proxy voting in committee should be done away with.** On the second, **Congress must reform its committee system so that executive branch agencies are responsible to fewer committees.** In addition, the people's business should be done by the people's representatives, not by outside interest groups. Accordingly, **lobbyists for outside groups should not be given the "privileges of the table" at committee hearings and mark-ups.**

Staff

It seems indisputable that, as demands on the members' time grows, staff become more powerful. Any talk of limiting the terms of members, often proposed as a remedy for the ills of Congress, is premature without assurances that the result would not be even more power flowing to a permanent, professional staff. Some recommendations touching on staff have already been made, but **staff should not be permitted to cast votes for members in committee mark-ups or conference committee meetings.** Furthermore, **staff should not be permitted to sit at mark-up tables and explain positions of their principals.** Moreover, **staff should not be allowed into the House and Senate chambers.** In general, **the size of professional staff should be reduced.** A strong case can be made that the need of staff to justify its own existence produces a drive for more legislation and increased meddling in the business of the other branches.

Politics

Americans have a right to expect that their representatives deal with difficult political, which is another way of saying policy, problems. Accordingly, **Congress should avoid resorting to outside commissions to solve its knotty political problems.** Further, while consultation and cooperation with the executive branch is desirable, **the negotiation of binding agreements on important matters ahead of time, for the purpose of avoiding public debate and record votes on crucial issues is subversive of responsible government.**

Leadership

Any organization requires leadership. However, it is not becoming to a democratic government to endow some members of the legislature with substantially more power than others. **The discretion of the leadership in the House to control size and composition of exclusive committees should be removed** (see Chapter 7). In an even more fundamental effort to reduce overweening leadership power, **the two houses of Congress should adopt rules providing for a limitation of terms in the leadership.**

The Minority

Where democracy is to flourish, minority viewpoints must be heard. **In the Senate, the trend towards elimination of minority protections must be reversed. In particular, erosion of the rights to extended debate has gone too far, and the right of the minority to offer non-germane amendments is in danger** (see Chapter 9). **The peculiar character of the Senate as the guarantor of minority rights must be maintained.** But procedural guarantees are not enough. The minorities themselves must have the courage and resolve to take advantage of their opportunities. **Minority members in both houses of Congress should assert their positions forthrightly.** Where their position is a minority in Congress, but not in the nation as a whole, **they should enlist the aid of the president in exercising their leverage on the majority.** With respect to the protection of minority rights in committee, **both houses of Congress should adopt rules providing for allocation of committee seats and committee staff on the basis of party strength in the respective bodies** (see Chapter 7).

The Rules

Representative government is impossible where politicians are able to hide substantive votes behind procedures. Obviously, votes on procedural matters are needed from time to time, but the increase in their use is troubling. **"Self-executing rules" should be done away with, and the trend toward closed and restrictive rules, which limit amendments in the House of Representatives, reversed.**

Some rules go beyond the mechanics of operating a legislative body, and now provide an arsenal which can be used to assure reelection (see Chapter 8). If the members are to remain accountable to their constituents, **Congress should reduce the perquisites available to incumbents. Areas marked for trim-**

ming should include the franking privilege, free publications for distribution to constituents, and subsidized public relations counseling and services. Finally, **Congress must not exempt itself from laws it passes** (see Chapters 10 and 13). Some areas of its activities will have to remain privileged, but in such areas as working conditions and wages, federal rules are no more inconvenient to Congress than they are to the rest of America. That is the point.

* * *

The American Experiment has endured for more than 200 years. To a large degree, its success stems from divided and separated powers. If our polity is to last, that critical mechanism must be revivified. It can be, through concerted action by men and women of foresight and courage. It is the contention of this volume that it can be done, and that the effort is worth it.

ABOUT THE AUTHORS

Gordon S. Jones, Editor, a veteran legislative analyst, has worked for Senator Jake Garn, Senator Paula Hawkins, the Senate Republican Policy Committee, the Department of Interior, and the Environmental Protection Agency. He also ran an editorial and political consulting firm during his 20-year career in the nation's capital. A native of Salt Lake City, Jones has degrees from Columbia College, Stanford University, and George Washington University. He served for five years as Vice President for Government Relations of The Heritage Foundation.

Dr. John A. Marini, Editor, is an Associate Professor of Political Science at the University of Nevada-Reno. He has served as Special Assistant to the Chairman of the United States Equal Employment Opportunity Commission in Washington, D.C., and on the faculties of the University of Dallas and Ohio University-Athens. He is the author of numerous articles on public administration, campaign finance, and bureaucratic politics. His most recent work (in progress) is *The Politics of Budget Control: President, Congress, and the Administrative Process.* Dr. Marini serves as an adjunct fellow of The Claremont Institute and holds a Ph.D. in government from the Claremont Graduate School.

Clifford Barnhart is the pseudonym of a veteran staff assistant to members of the House leadership.

John Hiram Caldwell is the pseudonym of a veteran legislative and executive branch official.

Nolan E. Clark is the director of Policy Development at the Federal Trade Commission. He also served as Associate Adminitrator for Policy and Resource Management of the U.S. Environmental Protection Agency at the beginning of the Reagan Administration.

Dr. Mark Crain, Professor of Economics at George Mason University and Research Fellow at the Center for Study of Public Choice, served as Special Assistant to the Director of the Office of Management and Budget. He holds a B.S. in economics from the University of Houston (Texas) and a Ph.D. from Texas A&M University.

Gordon Crovitz is Assistant Editor of the Editorial Page and member of the Editorial Board of the *Wall Street Journal.* He is the co-editor of *The Fettered Presidency: Legal Constraints on the Executive Branch,* (American Enterprise Institute, 1988). Mr. Crovitz, a Rhodes Scholar, holds an undergraduate degree from the University of Chicago, a law degree from Wadham College, Oxford University, and a J.D. from Yale Law School. He is a member of the New York State Bar Association, which honored him with a first-place prize for his 1987 editorials on legal issues relating to the Iran-Contra affair.

Dr. Margaret N. Davis serves as Legislative Assistant for budget, tax, energy, and environmental issues for Senator Phil Gramm. She has prepared several federal budgets, bills and amendments for Senator Gramm, including the Balanced Budget and Emergency Deficit Control Acts. Prior to joining Senator Gramm's staff in December of 1985, Dr. Davis served as an Energy Economist for the American Gas Association. She holds degrees from Emory University and Virginia Polytechnic Institute and State University, and a Ph.D. in Economics from George Mason University.

Michael E. Hammond is currently the general counsel to the Senate Steering Committee. He has served in the past as special assistant to Senator James L. Buckley, and as a law clerk in the U.S. Attorney's Office in the Eastern District of New York. Mr. Hammond received his B.A *magna cum laude* from Washington University in St. Louis and his J.D. from New York University School of Law. He is a member of the Supreme Court Bar, the New York Bar, and the District of Columbia Bar.

Douglas A. Jeffrey is Director of Scholarship at The Claremont Institute and Editor of *The Claremont Review of Books* and

The Proposition. He has written for numerous newspapers and journals. Jeffrey is currently completing his doctoral dissertation in politics at the University of Dallas.

Dr. Charles R. Kesler, a Claremont Institute adjunct fellow, is an assistant professor of government at Claremont McKenna College and the Claremont Graduate School. He is editor of *Saving the Revolution: The Federalist Papers and the American Founding,* and co-editor, with William F. Buckley, Jr., of an anthology entitled *Keeping the Tablets: Modern American Conservative Thought.* Kesler graduated *magna cum laude* from Harvard College with an A.B. in social studies, and holds an A.M. and a Ph.D. in political science from Harvard University.

Herman A. Mellor is the pseudonym of a Department of Defense official and former Capitol Hill aide.

Gabriel Prosser is the pseudonym of a long-time legislative and executive branch official.

Dr. Thomas G. West is Associate Professor of Politics at the University of Dallas and an adjunct fellow of The Claremont Institute. He has written articles for numerous newspapers, journals, and scholarly periodicals, and is editor and translator of *Four Texts on Socrates.* West holds a B.A. from Cornell University and a Ph.D. in government from the Claremont Graduate School. In July 1988, West joined The Heritage Foundation as a Bradley Resident Scholar.

Dr. John Adams Wettergreen, Professor of Political Science at San Jose University, is the author of a book entitled, *The Regulatory Revolution,* which describes the growth of regulatory powers in the federal government. He formerly served as a Bradley Resident Scholar at The Heritage Foundation. Wettergreen holds a M.A. and Ph.D. in government from Claremont Graduate School.

Peter M. Weyrich is a staff writer and research analyst on social policy at the Free Congress Center for Child and Family Policy. He is the author of the monograph: *The Human Costs of*

Divorce: Who is Paying? He has worked as a reporter for the *Initiative and Referendum Report*, published by the Free Congress Center for Law and Democracy.

ABOUT THE
HERITAGE FOUNDATION

The Heritage Foundation was established in 1973 as a nonpartisan, tax-exempt policy research institute dedicated to the principles of free competitive enterprise, limited government, individual liberty, and a strong national defense. The Foundation's research and study programs are designed to make the voices of responsible conservatism heard in Washington, D.C., throughout the United States, and in the capitals of the world.

Heritage publishes its research in a variety of formats for the benefit of policy-makers, the communications media, the academic, business and financial communities, and the public at large. Over the past five years alone, The Heritage Foundation has published some 1,000 books, monographs, and studies, ranging in size from the 564-page government blueprint, *Mandate for Leadership II: Continuing the Conservative Revolution*, to more frequent "Critical Issues" monographs and the topical "Backgrounders" and "Issue Bulletins" of a dozen pages. At the start of 1981, Heritage published the 1,093-page *Mandate for Leadership: Policy Management in a Conservative Administration*. Heritage's other regular publications include *National Security Record*, *Education Update*, and *Policy Review*, a quarterly journal of analysis and opinion.

In addition to the printed word, Heritage regularly brings together national and international opinion leaders and policy-makers to discuss issues and ideas in a continuing series of seminars, lectures, debates, and briefings.

Heritage is classified as a Section 501(c)(3) organization under the Internal Revenue Code, and is recognized as a publicly supported organization described in Sections 509(a)(1) and 170(b)(1)(A)(vi) of the Code. Individuals, corporations, companies, associations, and foundations are eligible to support the work of The Heritage Foundation through tax-deductible gifts.

ABOUT THE
CLAREMONT INSTITUTE

Established in 1978, the Claremont Institute promotes the principles of limited government, free enterprise, liberty, traditional morality, and individual responsibility. Claremont sponsors monthly and quarterly publications including *The Claremont Review of Books* and *The Proposition*, publishes books through its *Studies in Statesmanship* series, and conducts lectures and conferences on topics concerning American constitutionalism, political philosophy, Asian-American affairs, and state policy in California and Minnesota. By educating citizens and policymakers about the ideals upon which America was founded, the Claremont Institute seeks to ensure the application of sound principles to state and national level public policy decisions.

NOTE: Nothing written here is to be construed as necessarily reflecting the views of The Heritage Foundation or the Claremont Institute, or as an attempt to aid or hinder the passage of any bill before Congress.